DAVID WENTZ

Pastoring: The Nuts and Bolts

Options and Best Practices for Leading a Church

DOING CHRISTIANITY
Pastor David Wentz

First published by Doing Christianity 2019

Copyright © 2019 by David Wentz

First edition

ISBN: 978-1-7331285-1-3

This book was professionally typeset on Reedsy.
Find out more at reedsy.com

Dedicated to my wonderful wife Paula.
Your selfless love and dedication to God, our children and me
has been an inspiration throughout our marriage and ministry.

Contents

INTERNATIONAL ACCLAIM

"A superb book and educational aid for pastors and church leaders - a 'one stop shop' of what they need to know to lead and run a church. Easy to read – it flows naturally, is down to earth, and it's well and clearly organized. I really like the Points to Remember at the end of each section. They're a good recap and way to assure the reader understands the key take-aways."

Nancy Plaxico, Managing Director, Project Concern International

"What a beautiful book! Will be useful for every minister of the gospel, not only pastors. Highly recommended for Bible college and seminary."

Evangelist Isaac Olayinka Adeyemi
Nigeria National Director at Great Commission Coalition
Director of Studies, Nigeria at Trinity Evangelical Christian University

"I find myself not just reading it, but also studying it. It's an amazing work that is incredibly Scriptural. I've been in ministry for 15 years, and I'm learning a great deal. I'm currently training another guy to be a pastor. This will be a valuable asset. I don't say this about a lot of books, but this one impresses me. This is one book that I will highly recommend to all pastors."

Pastor Jesse Bingaman, Ebenezer Bible Church, Selinsgrove, Pennsylvania

"A wonderful book."

Pastor David Ssebowa, Arise and Shine Christian Ministry, Light Secondary School, Uganda

"There's plenty of wisdom within the minds and hearts of pastors who have been at it for a long time. David Wentz is one such pastor. *Pastoring: The*

iii

Nuts and Bolts is a pleasure to read, and covers the A to Z of pastoring well. The author intentionally writes in such a way that the content speaks to pastors in a variety of cultural contexts. That alone sets it apart and adds value. The scope of what he covers is vast and important. He sticks to the essentials, and includes wise cautions that new pastors probably would not be aware of. While many books specialize in one area of pastoral responsibility, this is a comprehensive introduction to most of what a pastor needs to have in view. May many young pastors read and humbly apply the wisdom of years captured in this book."

Pastor Ken Cavanagh, Fall Creek Community Church and yChurch, Fishers, Indiana

"The entire team is really thanking you because some phrases have become commonly used words on a daily basis."

Pastor Musinguzi Ibrahim, Uganda

"Very well done. Should prove to be very practical and useful to those in pastoral ministry around the world. Very easy to read, delightful even. I like your use of stories and illustrations from your vast experience – a nice balance with the biblical verses and context which anchor what you say in the eternal truth of God's Word. You use cultural sensitivity, balance, strength of thought and conviction without off-putting dogmatism. This will give the book appeal and usefulness across the many different faith expressions and church traditions. There is a need and great space for a book like yours, David."

John Fletcher, Senior Vice President of Global Missions, Pioneers

"A breath of fresh air and inspired by the Holy Spirit. The only recommended change is your title. The word pastor limits who might read it. Laity and clergy would benefit. Well written and informative."

Pastor Lois Cannon, Trinity United Methodist Church,
Huntington, Indiana

"A good introductory book on the 'Nuts and Bolts' of Pastoring. You can read it from cover to cover or read those pages that you need additional insight into. *"...carrying God's presence in love and power is not something only pastors do. It's the responsibility of every Christian."* This is a book that you will want to read and re-read many times."

Pastor Bob McIntyre, Metamora Church of Christ, Metamora, Indiana
Past President, Mid-North Church Council, Indianapolis, Indiana

"A very practical book. I wish I'd had it when I was starting out in ministry."

Pastor Allen Bates, West Eminence Christian Church, Eminence, Missouri

"In my work there was a problem with leadership among the pastors who joined me. They lacked a lot in knowledge and practice about leadership and pastoring. I have ever since been trying to mentor them. One day I came across Pastor David's work. The book has been really revolutionary. It has helped me improve a lot in all areas in ministry and as a result the church is growing. It has helped me become not only a better pastor but also a better person, more organized and focused. I have also noticed great change in my pastors, they are now more mature and responsible. I therefore recommend this book to every pastor."

Pastor Abraham Manya, Beth Adonai for All Nations Ministry and
Christ Fullness Biblical and Pastoral College, Kenya

"Very well written. I would highly recommend as a textbook or reference book, especially for new pastors. It also offers a great deal of practical information for those who have been in the ministry for a while."

Pastor Darrel Moen, Immanuel Lutheran Church, East Aurora, New York

"It was a pleasure reading this. Congratulations on a job very well done. I was encouraged, learned a lot, and garnered an increased appreciation for pastors!"

Erik Sellin, former Publisher, Classic CD Books

"Thanks for the privilege of reading your book. I found it to be practical, readable, Biblically supported, and helpfully outlined."

David Highfield, Baltimore-Washington Conference of the United Methodist Church

("now in my 51st year of ordained ministry and mostly retired")

"One of the best books I have read. Anyone who reads it, particularly church leaders, won't remain the same. I got at the right time when the church was crumbling. It saved a lot."

Pastor Otieno Steve Mito, Kenya

"Highly practical for pastors (and church leaders or missionaries) of all ages and stages of life. I've recommended the book wholeheartedly to others. I was impressed with Pastor David's easy-to-read writing style and the way he made pastoring so practical, largely by his real life story-telling from his own experience. I also like his rock-solid commitment to a biblical foundation in how to view the pastoral ministry with its many aspects. Being a missionary, I also see practical value to this book being in the hands of pastors around the world. I highly recommend this book and was personally challenged in my own walk with Christ by Pastor David's teaching again and again."

Amazon customer review

INTRODUCTION

Work hard so you can present yourself to God and receive his approval. Be a good worker, one who does not need to be ashamed and who correctly explains the word of truth. – 2 Timothy 2:15

In 2008 I had the privilege of speaking at a Christian conference in Turkey. The following year I was asked to lead a teaching session for pastors and church leaders in two of Turkey's great cities. This book started when some of those pastors asked me to write what I had taught them.

It expanded when I realized how many pastors in other countries, including America, wish they had more practical training in the art and science of pastoring. In fact, churchleadership.org says that over half of American pastors feel that their schooling did not adequately prepare them for the reality of leading a local church[i].

Eight years after that first conference in Turkey, I retired with thirty-four years of experience as a full-time pastor. In that time I served six very different churches, and I'm serving a seventh part-time in retirement. I attended three seminaries from different traditions, with fellow pastors from a variety of backgrounds. I read widely and try to think openly about the best ways of "doing church."

Pastor, church leader, or interested Christian, in these pages you will find basic principles and practical tips for organizing and leading a local congregation. My hope is that if you could have only one book other than the Bible, this one would be most helpful. I've tried to include everything you really need to know.

My intention is not to prescribe one particular way to do church.

Not all Spirit-led Bible-believing Christians do it the same way; in fact, practices differ widely. My goal is to present basic principles and ideas that will help pastors and church leaders from all cultures, especially those who have not had the chance to attend a Bible school or seminary. Read, pray, think, talk with others, and trust God to guide you in what is best for your particular situation.

We'll start with some background about God's purpose in inventing church. Then we'll focus on how to do the things that fulfill that purpose. I call it "doing church."

Some of it you will already know. Wonderful! But I bet you will also find a lot of new ideas and different perspectives. So go ahead and read it all, or at least skim it. The practical tips will work better if you take time to think about the options and put them in place before you find yourself in an urgent situation.

This book is meant to be used, not just read. Especially in Parts Two and Three, each chapter can be a stand-alone reference. Use the Table of Contents to find what you need, when you need it.

These ideas come from over thirty-five years of personal experience, much study of churches, many conversations with other pastors, and a lot of prayer and Bible study. **I tried my best to eliminate cultural and denominational assumptions and make these thoughts universal.** After all, people are people all over the world, and God's truth is true in every situation. Where different churches do things in different ways, I try to explain the differences and the reasons as best I understand them. There are many different ways of doing church. Learn as much as you can, and prayerfully decide what is best for your gifts and situation.

My prayer is that the Holy Spirit will use what follows to help you equip your people to effectively carry out God's three-fold purpose for the church.

Basic Presuppositions

Everybody starts with some foundational things they believe are true. In talking about church, here are my starting points. I won't take the time to try and prove them here, but I do want you to know where I base my thinking.

The Bible is the word of God

The Bible is God's written message to us. It gives us God's perspective and God's will. Its authors were inspired by the Holy Spirit and it is true in all it teaches. We must accept the Bible's authority and obey it as best we can.

That said, there are many Bible passages on which sincere Christians differ about meaning or application. **God is not upset about these differences.** He knew this would happen when he gave us the Bible. Let's rejoice in the freedom to use our God-given minds, and let's try to learn from each other.

Where the Bible is not specific, we are free to be creative

If the Bible is not specific about something, it doesn't mean it's not important. It is always important to learn how God wants you to do something. But if the Bible is not specific about how something is to be done, we can assume there are a variety of acceptable methods. God may want you to do it differently than someone else. In most pictures of the Christmas story, Joseph is walking to Bethlehem, while Mary rides a donkey. They traveled differently, but that doesn't mean one of them was wrong.

Of course, **the way God wants you to do something will never contradict the Bible.** But not everything is described in the Bible. The internet is not in the Bible, but that doesn't mean God doesn't want your church to have a Facebook page. As long as you're following Biblical principles, let the Holy Spirit bless your creativity.

God wants the church to be in order

God, the creator who made us in his image, likes to see our creativity and personality as we do his work. One look at Jesus' ministry shows he doesn't like rigidity or legalism. The pattern for a worship service described in 1 Corinthians 14 assumes much Spirit-led spontaneity. But it also sets some limits. In fact, later in the same chapter Paul writes, *Be sure that everything is done properly and in order* (1 Corinthians 14:40). **In creation God brought order out of chaos. I do not believe God wants his church to bring chaos back in!**

Cultural elements are spiritually neutral

England is often cold and rainy, so the English people developed a style of clothing that covered their bodies with warm layers. This functional style of clothing came to be seen as a sign of civilization. Wearing anything less came to be seen as uncivilized, and indeed as unchristian. In the 1800s English missionaries went to Africa to spread the gospel. Along with it they spread certain elements of English culture – including their idea of the kind of clothes that Christians should wear. The sad result was African Christians in the steaming jungle believing they could only be Christian if they were sweating in British style clothes. They, and the missionaries, were **confusing culture with Christianity.**

In today's mobile age, many church leaders are ministering in settings different from where they grew up. They have come to help the local church, and we thank God for them. But unless they have lived in the local culture for decades, they cannot understand it the way a native does. Without even realizing it, they import their own ideas about the proper way to express Christianity or do church. These fit their own background, but they may not be right for their new setting. If one of these well-meaning outsiders tells you to do something, and your heart says it may not be right for your people or your church, wait a bit. Pray sincerely about it. Maybe God does want you to try it. If God tells you that, go ahead. But if God does not tell you clearly, then listen to your heart. **Adopt, adapt or reject** the new idea, as you feel is right. I learned a long time ago that God wants me to be me, not a poor imitation of some famous Christian on television. And God wants your church to be itself, not a poor imitation of some other church.

Hearing God

God speaks to his people. His people need to learn how to hear, understand and obey what God says.

That starts with the Bible. **The Bible is our rule of faith and practice, but it's not a book of rules.** It's a book of stories and histories, laws and rituals, songs and poems, letters, dreams and visions, given by God to many different people in different cultures and time periods. The better we understand all these differences, the better we can properly discern how the things we read in the Bible apply to us in our own culture and time and situation.

Before God established the church, the Holy Spirit came only on certain people at certain times. When one of these people had a word from God, everyone else was required to accept it.

On the day of Pentecost God fulfilled his promise to pour out his Holy Spirit (Acts 2:17), and the church was born. Now, every Christian has the Holy Spirit all the time. Romans 8:14 says, *All who are led by the Spirit of God are children of God.* **Every Christian has the ability and the responsibility to learn how to recognize the leading of God's Holy Spirit.** Teaching this skill is one of our main jobs as pastors.

Differences of Opinion

So what happens if people disagree about what God is saying?

John Wesley founded the Methodist family of denominations in the 1700s. Among his many important contributions was a simple list of four steps for discerning God's truth about a question. This set of four guideposts has come to be known as the Wesleyan quadrilateral.

1. **The Bible** This is always our starting point. Prayerfully read. Consider textual, cultural and historical contexts. Compare Scripture with Scripture, studying other passages to be sure you are getting the whole Bible teaching on the subject. Recognize whether a passage is stating a universal principle, or whether it's an example of how a principle was applied in a certain situation – which allows you to apply the same principle in a way that fits your own situation. Most of the time this is all we need. If we still have questions, we go on to the other three points, giving more or less weight as they are more or less clear.

2. **Historic Christian understanding** – How have other Christians understood this question, across time and across the world? Respect the insights of the saints who have gone before us. Wesley called this "tradition."

3. **Prayerful discernment** – Do we sense a leading from God? Wesley called this "experience," because a leading from God should be something we experience, not just an academic exercise.

4. **Reason** – Using normal decision-making processes, what seems best?

Very often sincere, knowledgeable Christians go through all these steps, and still end up with different understandings. For example, the Bible does not clearly prescribe or describe any one form of church government. That is why there are so many different ways of organizing and administering churches among Bible-believing Christians. What then?

Saint Augustine, the great African theologian, said, "**In essentials, unity; in non-essentials, liberty; in all things, love.**" An "essential" is a belief or practice that the Bible clearly indicates is necessary for eternal life. On those there can be no compromise. But there are very few of those. For everything else, believe and do as you feel God leading you, allow others the same liberty, and look forward to full understanding when we all get to heaven.[ii]

God calls the church the body of Christ (1 Cor. 12:27), the bride of the Lamb (Rev. 19:7), the temple of the Holy Spirit (1 Cor. 3:16). Peter says, *You are a chosen race, a royal priesthood, a holy nation, a people for his own possession, that you may proclaim the excellencies of him who called you out of darkness into his marvelous light* (1 Peter 2:9 ESV). Taking leadership in something like that is an awesome responsibility. I pray God uses the ideas that follow to help you be a blessing to God, your people and the world.

Points to Remember

- There are many "right" ways of doing church. I pray this book will help you find the right one for you.
- Where the Bible is not specific, God encourages prayerful creativity.
- God wants the church to be free but not chaotic.
- Don't confuse culture with Christianity.

[i] Churchleadership.org, Statistics on Pastors, 2016 update.

[ii] Right here I may need to ask you to apply this principle of grace. In America I work with many talented female pastors. I know many Christians feel the Bible prohibits women from ministering in certain ways. I believe God calls, equips and uses women as well as men in all aspects of ministry, and I believe I can support that from the Bible. This book is not the place to argue that point. However, I have chosen to use grammar that includes the possibility of women being pastors, as well as men.

I

GOD'S THREE-FOLD PURPOSE FOR THE CHURCH

Before we get into how to do church, let's look at why. Why did God invent the church? Scholars have advanced various ideas. My own thinking goes back to the very beginning, and it builds on the way Jesus most often referred to God: as Father. Don't worry if you disagree with some of my ideas. The practical points in the rest of the book will help you anyway.

1

GOD IS A FATHER AND THE CHURCH IS HIS FAMILY

Beloved, we are God's children now; what we will be has not yet been revealed. What we do know is this: when he is revealed, we will be like him, for we will see him as he is. – 1 John 3:2

The Family of God

I have sometimes considered developing what I call a "theology of fun," based on the idea that God created the universe just for the fun of it. Certainly nobody could force God to create! But I think there must be more to it.

Let's start at the beginning. Not Genesis 1:1, *In the beginning when God created. . . .* I want to get behind that, to why God created. To do that we have to look at God himself.

How many ways can you think of that God is described in the Bible? God is great, God is just, God is holy, God is good, God is merciful. God is our refuge and strength and salvation. God is a spirit and a consuming fire. All these are descriptions of God. But one verse is not a description, it's an equation. 1 John 4:8 says, *God is love.* **Love is God's essence. It's who God**

is.

What is the greatest characteristic of love? Love wants to share. It's a relationship. **Love must be shared, or it isn't love.** That doesn't mean it has to be reciprocated, but there must be one who loves and one who is loved.

Since eternity, God has shared love in the Trinity. One of the most basic understandings of Christianity is that there is only one God, but this one God exists in three persons: God the Father, God the Son (who came to earth as Jesus), and God the Holy Spirit. Without this community of divine persons to share love, God could not be love.

God, who is love, has been sharing love since eternity. But God's love is not only eternal, it's infinite. It's overflowing. God's love wanted to overflow the Trinity.

What provides the greatest opportunity for an ongoing expression of love? A family - different personalities living together, adapting to each other, adjusting to each other, caring for each other, putting each other first. A family creates infinite possibilities for love. So God decided to create a family to share his love, with God and with each other.

God could have created us so that we had no choice but to love him, but that wouldn't be real love. God could force us to act like we love him, but that wouldn't be real love. **Love is only real if it is freely given.** God wanted to share real love. So God gave us free will.

Unfortunately, our free will doesn't just give us the opportunity to freely love God. It gives us the opportunity to cause a lot of trouble as well. We see this in the very first human beings God created.

Adam and Eve shared love with God for a time. Genesis 3 implies that God used to enjoy walking with them in the Garden of Eden. But one day they exercised their free will to disobey God, and that time of innocent family fellowship was broken.

> *They heard the sound of the LORD God walking in the garden at the time of the evening breeze, and the man and his wife hid themselves from the presence of the LORD God among the trees of the garden. But*

the LORD God called to the man, and said to him, "Where are you?" –
Genesis 3:8-9

**God experienced the heartbreak of a father whose children turn
against him and get lost in the world.** Adam and Eve's disobedience
broke up God's family. The whole rest of the Bible records God's plan
throughout history to bring his children back.

For a while God tried to relate to the whole growing human race, but
they turned from God and became so wicked that God had to destroy them
all in Noah's flood (Genesis 6-8). He tried again with Noah's descendants,
but instead of trusting God, they built a tower and put their trust in it.
They were unified, but not in God. To keep it from happening again, God
confused their language, and the human race scattered across the earth
(Genesis 11).

So God changed strategies. He decided to relate in a special way to
one group of people, who would get to know and love him. Then they
could invite the rest of the world into God's family. God chose the children
of Abraham, the nation-family known as the Hebrews, Israel, or the Jews.
King Solomon understood. He prayed at the dedication of the Temple in
Jerusalem, *"that all the peoples of the earth may know your name and fear you,
as do your people Israel"* (2 Chronicles 6:33 ESV).

God's Desire

God's desire has always been to live among his people. When Israel
wandered in the wilderness, God told Moses, *"Have the people of Israel build
me a holy sanctuary so I can live among them"* (Exodus 25:8).

When the Hebrews conquered the Promised Land and started living in
houses, God approved David's plan to build a house where God could live.
It was called the Temple, and God filled it with his presence (2 Chronicles
6:1). For the next thousand years, a series of temples in Jerusalem were the
focus of God living among his people.

Unfortunately, **somewhere between Solomon and Jesus the Hebrews**

lost their understanding of what it meant to be God's chosen people. They forgot God chose them as messengers to invite the whole world into his family. Instead, they began to believe God chose them to be the only members of his family. Instead of welcoming other nations, they scorned them.

So God started again, with Jesus. But this time membership in the family wasn't by genes but by choice. The Bible says, Abraham's physical descendants are not necessarily children of God. Only the children of the promise are considered to be Abraham's children (Romans 9:8). The "children of the promise" are the church.

The church – all people, of Jewish or non-Jewish descent, who put their faith in Jesus – is now the family of God. And our loving Father has commanded us to bring as many people into the family as will accept the invitation. When we do that, we become the fulfillment of God's desire to live among his people. *Don't you realize that all of you together are the temple of God and that the Spirit of God lives in you?* (1 Corinthians 3:16). *Where two or three gather together in my name, I am there among them* (Matthew 18:20).

God so longs to live among his people that when we die, God takes us to live with him until the end of time. And at the end of time, when everything is put the way God wants it, where will God live? With his people. *I heard a loud shout from the throne, saying, "Look, God's home is now among his people! He will live with them, and they will be his people. God himself will be with them* (Revelation 21:3).

God is not looking for a place to live in. He has that in heaven. **God is longing for a group of people to live with**. God's plan in creating human beings was that we would be his family. Fulfilling that plan is what the church is all about.

Three Purposes

Like any father, God desires a home where he can rest and be himself. Like any father, God desires to raise up children who will be like him. And because God is the ultimate and infinite Father, God desires for his children to bring other people to become part of God's family – ideally, every other person in the world!

These three desires of God show us the three purposes of the church.

First, the church exists to **create a loving family home** where God can rest and be himself. *Now arise, O Lord God, and enter your resting place* (2 Chronicles 6:41). The way we do this is traditionally called worship.

Second, the church exists to **raise God's children** to be like their heavenly father. *Imitate God, therefore, in everything you do, because you are his dear children* (Ephesians 5:1). The way we do this is traditionally called discipleship.

Third, the church exists to equip God's children to **bring other people** into God's family. *Go and make disciples of all the nations, baptizing them in the name of the Father and the Son and the Holy Spirit* (Matthew 28:19). The way we do this is traditionally called evangelism.

Everything we do as a local church – in fact, everything we do as Christians – should contribute to fulfilling one or more of these three purposes. How do your church's programs stack up? Anything that doesn't help advance one of these purposes is an unnecessary drain on the church's time, energy and resources that can hinder our ability to do things of eternal value.

The next three chapters will look at these purposes more closely.

Points to Remember

- God created people to share his love as a family.
- God's desire is to live with people as a father lives with his children.
- The church exists to create a loving family home where God can rest and be himself.
- The church exists to raise up God's children to be like their heavenly father.
- The church exists to equip God's children to bring other people into God's family.

2

THE CHURCH IS GOD'S FAMILY HOME

Don't you realize that all of you together are the temple of God and that the Spirit of God lives in you? – 1 Corinthians 3:16

In the Garden of Eden, God came to walk with his people in the cool of the evening (Genesis 3:8-9). In the desert of Exodus, God came to accompany his people in their wanderings (Exodus 29:45-46). In the Promised Land, God moved in with his people in glorious fire and smoke (2 Chronicles 7:1). When the people of Israel turned away from God, he pleaded with them to change their ways so he could again live with them (Jeremiah 7:3). Since the Holy Spirit came at Pentecost, God lives among and within his people (2 Corinthians 6:16). And at the end of the age, God will live with his redeemed and restored people forever (Revelation 21:3). From Genesis to Revelation, from the beginning of creation to the end of time, **God's desire is to live with his people** – his family.

We know that God is everywhere, all the time. Ephesians 1:23 says Jesus *fills all things everywhere with himself.* Yet somehow God wants to be with us, his children, in a special way.

Sometimes the presence of God is more than a theological concept.

Sometimes it's almost tangible. I bet you've said it yourself: "I could feel the touch of God." Or, "God really visited us today."

I don't know about you, but I don't want to settle for just a touch from God, or even a visit. I never want to treat God as some kind of cosmic mailman who stops by just long enough to deliver some gifts. Those experiences of God are better than nothing, but as far as I'm concerned, when God shows up, I don't want him to leave. I want him to move in to stay. I want my church to be the place where God decides to come and live, at least part of the time.[i]

So how do we get God to move in with us? What kind of place attracts him? What kind of people?

God Rests on Our Worship

Psalm 22:3 says of God, *You are holy, enthroned on the praises of Israel.* When God's people worship him, their praises form a spiritual throne. They provide a place for God to sit and rest.

In your church's times of worship, are you giving God a strong, thick, comfortable throne of praise? Or is your praise throne kind of thin and flimsy, maybe with holes in the cushion where some of your folks aren't joining in? Maybe they're afraid they don't sing well, or they're distracted or grumpy about something. Maybe they just don't understand the concept of praise.

Whatever the reason, if we don't give God a comfortable place to sit down, can we really blame him if he doesn't stick around?

Good, strong, God-honoring praise doesn't come automatically to most people. As church leaders, we need to train our people to give God the kind of worship that will make God say, "Now there's a throne fit for a king. I think I'll go rest there for a while. I might even move in with these folks!"

Did you ever have a new neighbor move in near you? Some neighbors move in very quietly and you may not even know they moved in. Others throw a big party and everyone knows they are there.

When God moved into the temple Solomon had built, he was more like the second kind of neighbor. Here's how the Bible describes it:

> *So Solomon finished all his work on the Temple of the LORD . . . the priests carried the Ark of the LORD's covenant into the inner sanctuary of the Temple . . . Then the priests left the Holy Place. All the priests who were present had purified themselves, whether or not they were on duty that day . . . The trumpeters and singers performed together in unison to praise and give thanks to the LORD. Accompanied by trumpets, cymbals, and other instruments, they raised their voices and praised the LORD with these words:*
>
> *"He is so good! His faithful love endures forever!" At that moment a cloud filled the Temple of the LORD. The priests could not continue their service because of the cloud, for the glorious presence of the LORD filled the Temple of God.*
>
> *Then Solomon prayed, "O LORD, you have said that you would live in a thick cloud of darkness. Now I have built a glorious Temple for you, a place where you can live forever! . . . And now, arise, O LORD God, and enter your resting place . . . "*
>
> *When Solomon finished praying, fire flashed down from heaven and burned up the burnt offerings and sacrifices, and the glorious presence of the LORD filled the Temple. The priests could not enter the Temple of the LORD because the glorious presence of the LORD filled it. When all the people of Israel saw the fire coming down and the glorious presence of the LORD filling the Temple, they fell face down on the ground and worshiped and praised the LORD, saying,*
>
> *"He is good! His faithful love endures forever!"* – 2 Chronicles 5:1,7,11,13,14; 6:1,2,41; 7:1-3

This was not your ordinary church service. God's presence was so overwhelming that the priests could not even enter the Temple. There was something there that all the people could see, and when they saw it they fell face down on the ground.

This kind of manifestation of the presence of God was not limited

10

to Bible times. In the mid-1800s in America, people riding in their buggies to hear evangelist Charles Finney fell under the power of the Holy Spirit as their buggies crossed into the county in which he was preaching. In the Welsh revival of 1904-1905, farmers in their fields fell to the ground under great conviction of sin without a preacher anywhere near.

In the late 1990s I often attended evening services at a church where God's presence was powerfully felt. I heard one of the pastors there tell of his brother-in-law, a skeptical unbeliever. One day this pastor picked up his brother-in-law at the airport. On the way home he stopped by the church for something. The brother-in-law decided to go in with him. As they went in the door, the brother-in-law suddenly fell to the ground, crying, "What is this?" The power of God had overcome him. The skeptic became a believer.

Obviously, this kind of thing doesn't happen very often, and we shouldn't expect it to. Most of the time, God moves in more quietly. But when God wants to make a commotion, who are we to try to stop him?

So what kind of worship invites God to sit down and stay a while?

God wants worship that is free

In America, and perhaps other places as well, many churches seem to give the impression they think maybe God has a headache, or maybe he's asleep, and they better be as quiet as they can so as not to bother him. Obviously there is a place for quiet reverence, and there is a place for silent waiting on the Lord. But when the Bible talks about praising God, it's usually describing something quite a bit noisier. Listen to Psalm 150, for instance.

Praise the LORD!
Praise God in his sanctuary;
praise him in his mighty heaven!
Praise him for his mighty works;
praise his unequaled greatness!
Praise him with a blast of the ram's horn;
praise him with the lyre and harp!

Praise him with the tambourine and dancing;
praise him with strings and flutes!
Praise him with a clash of cymbals;
praise him with loud clanging cymbals.
Let everything that breathes sing praises to the LORD! Praise the
LORD!

Trumpet blasts, loud clanging cymbals, strings and flutes and tambourines and dancing – sounds like a party going on!

Please understand that **this is not specifying a particular style or format of worship**. A traditional liturgy of written prayers and responses can be expressed with tremendous joy and enthusiasm. And dancing and weeping in worship can become a dry repetition of expected responses. The issue is not style, but passion.

Every time of praise doesn't have to be loud and exuberant, of course. Your praise and worship must be led by the Holy Spirit, and the Spirit will lead differently at different times. But you need to **train your church to feel free to cut loose now and then**. Teach them to give God the same kind of praise they give their favorite football team when they score a goal. Otherwise God may say to himself, "If I go visit them, I can't stay long. There's no place for me to sit down!"

God wants worship that is true

Jesus said,

> *The time is coming—indeed it's here now—when true worshipers will*
> *worship the Father in spirit and in truth. The Father is looking for*
> *those who will worship him that way. For God is Spirit, so those who*
> *worship him must worship in spirit and in truth.* – John 4:23-24

The kind of worship God is seeking combines true teaching with the freedom and power of the Holy Spirit. That's a delicate balance that

12

requires you as a leader to be constantly seeking the guidance of the Holy Spirit.

People may say, "But what if I don't feel like praising God? How can that be true worship? Won't I be a hypocrite if I sing words I'm not feeling?"

Obeying God when you don't feel like it isn't hypocrisy, it's faith. This is particularly true of praise.

Listen to Habbakuk, the Old Testament prophet:

> *Even though the fig trees have no blossoms, and there are no grapes on the vines;*
>> *even though the olive crop fails, and the fields lie empty and barren;*
>> *even though the flocks die in the fields, and the cattle barns are empty,*
>> *yet I will rejoice in the LORD!*
>> *I will be joyful in the God of my salvation.* – Habbakuk 3:17-18

When your body just wants to sit, and your mind just wants to sulk, your Christian spirit still wants to praise God. Choosing to follow your spirit in praise is a God-pleasing act of faith. It strengthens your whole person and puts it in proper order.

Just about every passage in the Bible that describes worship mentions music. Whether your music ministry is one person valiantly trying to get your people to sing, a choir accompanied by piano or accordion or guitar, or a whole band with the latest sound equipment, they must set the example in worship. **Your worship leaders should be your lead worshipers.** Musicians must know at least as much about worshiping God as they do about singing or playing. Musicians who are more concerned with showcasing their skills than with bringing people into God's presence are like sharp rocks in the middle of your church's cushion of praise. God isn't going to want to sit there very long!

Of course, as human beings, our motives are never 100% pure. Don't let a fear that you might have hidden ulterior motives stop you from serving God. And there's nothing wrong with a singer or musician feeling good about how they sound – or a preacher, for that matter. A solo can be as much an offering as a prayer. Don't stifle God's gifts. Let the praise flow!

God wants worship that is shared

In his first letter to the church in Corinth, Paul spends a lot of time talking about different aspects of public worship, starting in chapter 11 and going all the way through chapter 14. Near the end of that segment he summarizes what a worship service should look like.

> *Well, my brothers and sisters, let's summarize. When you meet together, one will sing, another will teach, another will tell some special revelation God has given, one will speak in tongues, and another will interpret what is said. But everything that is done must strengthen all of you.* – 1 Corinthians 14:26

Many Christians, and many Christian leaders, seem to have the impression that a worship service is a performance put on by the people up front, and the rest of the church is the audience. The fact is, **there is only one person in the audience of a worship service, and that is God.** All the people (the Greek word means "each" or "every") should be actively involved in expressing worship, in whatever way the Holy Spirit leads them. As pastor or leader, one part of your job is to train your people to recognize the Spirit's leading and respond properly.

It doesn't come automatically. Some people are hesitant to open their mouths in public, while others are only too happy to claim the center of attention for as long as anyone will let them. As Paul advised Timothy, *Patiently correct, rebuke, and encourage your people with good teaching* (2 Timothy 4:2).

Be sure the structure of your church service provides an opportunity for people to participate in these ways. And be sensitive to the flow of the Spirit so that as these things begin to happen, you can be sure that everything is done in a fitting and orderly way (1 Corinthians 14:40).

God Wants Us to Be Good Hosts and Hostesses

If we want more than just a brief touch from God we have to make ourselves ready. We need to be good hosts and hostesses to the presence of God.

Each week as you plan for church next Sunday, prepare yourself. **You are going to be leading a group of people who are inviting the God of the universe to come in and rest awhile**. As pastor or church leader, your job is to equip your people to do that. What does that look like?

I have had the honor of sharing meals in Turkish homes many times, and every time I am impressed with what gracious hosts and hostesses the Turkish people are. They always put my needs and desires ahead of their own. They are careful not to do anything that would make me feel uncomfortable or offended.

This kind of gracious hosting comes from an attitude of hospitality combined with a careful attention to the needs and desires of the guest. We need to cultivate this same attitude and attention in our churches for our Sunday morning visits from God.

But it's more than that. **We don't want God just to visit us now and then. We want God to dwell with us**, to live with us. It's like being a real estate agent for the divine: "Lord, you're going to love this place. The people are so nice and friendly, just your kind of people. You'll feel right at home."

How do we teach our members to be the kind of people God will want to live with?

Preach and teach divine hospitality

Talk to your folks about the honor and privilege of welcoming God among you. When the praise and worship seems especially welcoming to God, point it out. Let the people know when they are doing well. Gently correct them when they aren't. It may seem obvious to you, but they are just learning.

Celebrate signs of God's presence

Discerning the presence of God is another learned sensitivity.

Solid food is for the mature, for those who have their powers of discernment trained by constant practice to distinguish good from evil (Hebrews 5:14 ESV). It's by training and practice that we learn to discern in the spirit.

A few years ago I was on a retreat with about fifty Christian men. One evening the music team started off just having fun with the songs, and people were laughing and talking. Gradually, the music took on a more worshipful feel. Suddenly, the presence of God was there in as powerful a way as I have ever known. I almost expected people to start falling down under the weight of God's glory.

In the midst of the awesome silence that followed one song, I became aware of two voices. Two men were sitting in the back of the room, still talking and joking and laughing as they had been at the beginning. These were both good Christians, respected in the church. But they seemed to be completely oblivious to the change in the spiritual atmosphere. **They had no idea that God had come into the room in an unusual way.**

I wish someone had stood up and pointed out what was happening. I don't think these brothers were deliberately being crass. I think they had never experienced God's presence in this way, and they didn't know what it was. Probably many others in the group were equally ignorant. They didn't know God was answering the invitation of their praise and worship. They didn't know what to look for, and they didn't know how to act when it happened.

I was not leading this particular retreat, so I didn't feel it was my place to intervene. Perhaps I should have been bolder, pointing out what was happening and celebrating it, so people would learn how to recognize God's presence and how to encourage it. But no one said anything, the two kept on talking and laughing, and the presence of God soon lifted – not just from them, but from the whole group.

Let God do what God wants to do

1 Thessalonians 5:19 says, *"Do not quench the Spirit."* Yes, the Bible says to do all things decently and in order (1 Corinthians 14:40), but God's idea of that may not always be the same as ours. In the same chapter we find directions for multiple prophecies, speaking in tongues, and even how to interrupt the speaker! (See verses 26-30). God does strange things sometimes – just read Daniel or Revelation. If God seems to be doing something, and you can find a similar thing described in the Bible, go with it, even if it threatens to mess up your standard order of worship. If God gets the idea that he won't be allowed to speak or act, why should he show up?

Teach your people not to offend God

Do not grieve the Holy Spirit of God, by whom you were sealed for the day of redemption (Ephesians 4.30 ESV). Another translation puts it this way: *Do not bring sorrow to God's Holy Spirit by the way you live* (NLT).

What kind of living brings sorrow to God's Holy Spirit? Unholy living, of course.

> *When you follow the desires of your sinful nature, the results are very clear: sexual immorality, impurity, lustful pleasures, idolatry, sorcery, hostility, quarreling, jealousy, outbursts of anger, selfish ambition, dissension, division, envy, drunkenness, wild parties, and other sins like these. Let me tell you again, as I have before, that anyone living that sort of life will not inherit the Kingdom of God.* – Galatians 5:19-21
>
> *Let there be no sexual immorality, impurity, or greed among you. Such sins have no place among God's people. Obscene stories, foolish talk, and coarse jokes . . . Don't be fooled by those who try to excuse these sins.* – Ephesians 5:3, 4, 6

In 2 Corinthians 12:20 Paul describes what he does not want to find when he visits a church: *I am afraid that I will find quarreling, jealousy, anger, selfishness, slander, gossip, arrogance, and disorderly behavior.*

Be honest, now: do these things ever happen in your church? If Paul is offended by a church where these things occur, how much more will they offend God?

God will love us even when we do these things, and he will visit us to try to help us change. But God won't make his home and resting place in a church where people persist in doing things that make him uncomfortable. It's like trying to get somebody to buy a house that has a bad smell. When we do these things we just smell bad to God.

"Worship the Lord in the splendor of holiness" (1 Chronicles 16:29; Psalm 29:2; Psalm 96:9 ESV). Living holy lives is such an important part of our worship that the Bible repeats it three times. We need to teach our people that God won't even listen to our worship if we are not at least trying to live right.

Points to Remember

- God is always everywhere, but sometimes there's a special presence.
- God rests on worship that is free, true, and shared.
- Learn to discern God's presence, and celebrate it.
- If God does something unusual but something similar can be found in the Bible, go with it.
- If something offends God, get rid of it.

[i] Tommy Tenney has written about this in excellent detail in his book, The God Chasers. I am indebted to him for many of the ideas in this section.

18

3

THE CHURCH RAISES GOD'S CHILDREN

Imitate God, therefore, in everything you do, because you are his dear children. – Ephesians 5:1

Every Christian is a child of God, adopted into the family (John 1:12). As pastors and church leaders, the second part of our job is to help these children of God grow up to be like their Father.

As a little boy I imitated my father. On the playground I imitated sports heroes. In the high school band I imitated great saxophone players. As a young pastor I imitated famous preachers. They say imitation is the sincerest form of flattery. It's also the first and best way to learn anything that goes beyond mere head knowledge.

But we can't see God. Most of the things we think of God doing are things that we can't do, at least not on our own. So how are we supposed to imitate God?

Being Like God Means Being Like Jesus

The Bible says Jesus is a perfect picture of God (Colossians 1:15; Hebrews 1:3). Jesus himself said, *"Anyone who has seen me has seen the Father"* (John 14:9).

Paul wrote, *I imitate Christ* (1 Corinthians 11:1). We imitate the Father by imitating his son, Jesus. The word "Christian" means "little Christ."

Ephesians 4 gives a job description for pastors and other church leaders.

> *Their responsibility is to equip God's people to do his work and build up the church, the body of Christ. This will continue until we all come to such unity in our faith and knowledge of God's Son that we will be mature in the Lord, measuring up to the full and complete standard of Christ. . . . growing in every way more and more like Christ.*
> –Ephesians 4:12, 13, 15

In other words, **equip God's people to do God's work until they resemble God's Son.**

The more people become like Jesus, the more they become like the Father. The second purpose of the church is to help people do that. **The real measure of a church is not how big it is or how famous the pastor is, but how much the people are like Jesus.**

At this point somebody is thinking, "Wait a minute. How can I be like Jesus? Jesus is God. I'm just a human being. It's unreasonable to expect me to be like him."

In my opinion, this is one of the most important points we need to get across to our people. Yes, Jesus was and is God. Your people must clearly understand that. But it is not unreasonable of God to demand that we become like him – because when he came to earth, he became like us. So your people must also understand that Jesus did not do his miracles through his own divine power, but through the Holy Spirit. And every Christian has that same Holy Spirit.

Jesus did what he did through the power of the Holy Spirit

Jesus' miracles did not come about through any inherent power he brought with him from heaven. Philippians 2:5-7 says,

> *You must have the same attitude that Christ Jesus had. Though he was God, he did not think of equality with God as something to cling to. Instead, he gave up his divine privileges; he took the humble position of a slave and was born as a human being.*

When Jesus left his throne in heaven to begin his cosmic rescue mission, he left all his divine powers behind. The Bible says he emptied himself. He didn't bring anything extra with him from heaven. He became a human baby in a human womb, just like every other human being who has ever been born.

For the first thirty years of his life, that's how Jesus lived. The one difference is that Jesus never sinned. But God knew that wasn't going to be enough for what Jesus came to do. So Luke 3:21-22 tells us, *One day when the crowds were being baptized, Jesus himself was baptized. As he was praying, the heavens opened, and the Holy Spirit, in bodily form, descended on him like a dove. -*

Jesus was still fully human, but now he had something extra. He had the Holy Spirit.

This was not an unprecedented thing. The Holy Spirit had come on people throughout the Old Testament. In Psalm 51:11 David prayed, *Don't take your Holy Spirit from me.*

Acts 10:38 says, *God anointed Jesus of Nazareth with the Holy Spirit and with power. Then Jesus went around doing good and healing all who were oppressed by the devil, for God was with him.*

The source of Jesus' miraculous power was not his deity. It was the Holy Spirit. The Bible doesn't say Jesus did good and healed people because he was God (even though he was). It says he did good and healed people because God was with him in the power of the Holy Spirit.

There's a fascinating verse in Luke 5:17. *One day while Jesus was teaching, some Pharisees and teachers of religious law were sitting nearby. . . And the Lord's healing power was strongly with Jesus.*

Notice that last phrase. Doesn't that imply that sometimes the Lord's healing power was not strongly with Jesus? Jesus' healing power was not inherent in him as a person. Jesus' miracles were dependent on the power of God, which came through the Holy Spirit.

When it comes to imitating Jesus, the first thing you need to teach your people is that Jesus did what he did through the power of the Holy Spirit.

Every Christian has the same Holy Spirit Jesus had

The second thing your people need to know as they seek to become like Jesus is that the same Holy Spirit who empowered Jesus lives in their own reborn spirits.

Forty days after the Passover at which Jesus was crucified, he ascended into heaven. Ten days later, on the feast day of Pentecost, he sent the Holy Spirit on 120 of his followers, and the church was born.

> *Suddenly, there was a sound from heaven like the roaring of a mighty windstorm in the skies above them, and it filled the house where they were sitting. Then, what looked like flames or tongues of fire appeared and settled on each of them. And everyone present was filled with the Holy Spirit and began speaking in other languages, as the Holy Spirit gave them this ability.* – Acts 2:2-4

The sound and the flames attracted a big crowd. They thought the house was on fire. Peter calmed them down, and then took the opportunity to preach.

When he finished, the Bible tells us, Peter's words convicted them deeply, and they said to him and to the other apostles, *"Brothers, what should we do?"*

Peter replied, "Each of you must turn from your sins and turn to God,

and be baptized in the name of Jesus Christ for the forgiveness of your
sins. Then you will receive the gift of the Holy Spirit. This promise is
to you and to your children, and even to the Gentiles —all who have
been called by the Lord our God." - Acts 2:37-39

The promise is to all of us. Your people need to understand: if they have turned from their sins and turned to God and been baptized in the name of Jesus Christ, then **they have received the gift of the Holy Spirit**, because God always keeps his promises. Ephesians 1:13 says it very clearly: *When you believed in Christ, he identified you as his own by giving you the Holy Spirit.*[i]

Let me ask you a question. How many Holy Spirits are there? Only one – the third person of the Trinity. If Jesus had the Holy Spirit, and you have the Holy Spirit, and there's only one Holy Spirit, then guess what? You have the same Holy Spirit Jesus had. Your church members have the same Holy Spirit Jesus had. Every Christian has the same Holy Spirit Jesus had. Paul wrote, *The Spirit of God, who raised Jesus from the dead, lives in you* (Romans 8:11).

Jesus became just like us, except that he had the Holy Spirit. But since Pentecost, every Christian has the Holy Spirit, too. That means every Christian can be like Jesus. What an exciting promise! Through the power of the Holy Spirit who lives in you, you can become more and more like Jesus.

What Was Jesus Like?

So what was Jesus like? What are we supposed to be teaching our people to become?

When I think of Jesus, several things come to mind. Like most people, I think of his godly character, his wise teachings, and his miraculous actions. As a pastor with a passion for the church, I also think of something else. It's not quite as easy to describe, but I am struck by the way Jesus provided for the expansion of his kingdom by the growth of the church. And I'm struck by the fact that all four of these aspects of Jesus' ministry were empowered by the Holy Spirit.

Spirit-filled character

Jesus was always kind and loving and generous and patient. Sometimes it was "tough love" in hopes of opening some eyes, as when he talked to some Pharisees in Matthew 23, but it was always love. Jesus was the ultimate example of integrity and character.

Galatians 5:22-23 says this kind of character comes from the Holy Spirit. *The Holy Spirit produces this kind of fruit in our lives: love, joy, peace, patience, kindness, goodness, faithfulness, gentleness, and self-control.*

These are not just emotions that make us feel good. **These are ways we treat each other.** Every time I encounter another person I try to remember to start with this silent prayer: "Lord, please let me set the tone of this interaction with love, joy, peace…" and on through the nine fruits of the Holy Spirit. I don't always remember to start that way, but when I do, I can often tell the difference.

If the Holy Spirit could produce that kind of godly character in Jesus, he can do the same for us – if we will give him the same free reign in our lives that Jesus did. Teach your people to examine themselves for these signs of godly character.

Spirit-led wisdom

Jesus always knew just what to do or say. Maybe more importantly for some of us, he always knew what not to do or say. Jesus always made the right decision.

One of my favorite Bible stories is when Jesus got word that his friend Lazarus was dying (John 11). Everybody expected Jesus to drop everything and rush to Lazarus to heal him before he died. Instead, Jesus stayed where he was for two more days. The result was an even greater miracle. But how did Jesus know to do that?

This supernatural wisdom was not part of Jesus' genetic makeup. It came from the Holy Spirit. Hebrews 5:8 says, *Even though Jesus was God's Son, he learned obedience from the things he suffered.* Jesus had to learn to hear and recognize and obey the guidance of the Holy Spirit.

Every Christian is called to learn the same things. Romans 8:14 says it's a defining part of who we are: *All who are led by the Spirit of God are children of God.*

Spirit-powered actions

When John the Baptist sent some of his followers to ask Jesus if he was really the Messiah sent from God, Jesus pointed to his miracles and healings (Luke 7:22). Supernatural actions proved who he was.

As we've already seen, Jesus didn't do these miraculous works through his own power or authority as the Son of God. He emptied himself of that when he left his throne in heaven. Jesus healed and performed miracles by the power of the Holy Spirit.

Acts 1:8 says that same power is available to every Christian. *"You will receive power when the Holy Spirit comes upon you."* **Part of learning to be like Jesus is learning to allow the Holy Spirit to act through us in supernatural power.**

As a church leader, if you are not familiar with signs and wonders, make it a priority to find someone who is and learn from them. Invite your people to join you in studying and learning about these things.[ii]

Spirit-impassioned multiplication

Jesus didn't try to do everything himself. The second half of Acts 1:8 says, *"You will be my witnesses, telling people about me everywhere - in Jerusalem, throughout Judea, in Samaria, and to the ends of the earth."*

That's a big mission. Reinhold Niebuhr wrote, "Nothing worth doing is completed in our lifetime." Jesus knew that his mission would last beyond his lifetime, and the lifetimes of his followers. Two thousand years later, we still have not completed the task. So Jesus focused his three years of ministry on teaching and training. **Jesus was passionate about recruiting and equipping people to reproduce his life and work.**

At the end of his earthly ministry, Jesus gave his disciples the job of reproducing themselves in others.

> *Jesus came and told his disciples, "I have been given all authority in heaven and on earth. Therefore, go and make disciples of all the nations, baptizing them in the name of the Father and the Son and the Holy Spirit. Teach these new disciples to obey all the commands I have given you. And be sure of this: I am with you always, even to the end of the age."* – Matthew 28:18-20

We often act as if Jesus' whole point was to get people saved and baptized. But that was just the beginning. Jesus went on, basically saying, "After you get them saved and baptized, don't stop there. Teach them to do the things I taught you to do."

The disciples taught Paul. Paul taught Timothy. And in 2 Timothy 2:2, he tells Timothy, *Teach these truths to other trustworthy people who will be able to pass them on to others.*

We can think of this as multiplication, or teaching, or discipleship. The word I keep coming back to is "reproduction." It's how a species survives. In the physical, God gave us a passion for reproduction. It's been said that the church is always one generation away from extinction. We need to ask to Holy Spirit to give us a passion for spiritual reproduction as well.

God's fatherly desire is that every human being will be like our big brother Jesus: filled, led, empowered and motivated by the Holy Spirit.

The Church: Nanny and Tutor

How do newborn Christians learn all this? What is God's plan for helping them grow and develop in Spirit-filled character, Spirit-led decisions, Spirit-powered actions, and Spirit-impassioned reproduction? Who is the nanny for these baby Christians? Who is their tutor?

The church is their nanny and tutor. The older sisters and brothers take care of the younger ones. The more mature brothers and sisters teach the less mature. And God oversees it all through us pastors and the other church leaders.

> *Now these are the gifts Christ gave to the church: the apostles, the prophets, the evangelists, and the pastors and teachers. Their responsibility is to equip God's people to do his work and build up the church, the body of Christ. This will continue until we all come to such unity in our faith and knowledge of God's Son that we will be mature in the Lord, measuring up to the full and complete standard of Christ.* – Ephesians 4:11-13

You and I, the pastors, teachers and church leaders, are God's plan for raising his children. There is no Plan B.

It's a huge task. I believe three actions are at the core.

1. Teach your people to carry out Romans 12:1-2

> *Dear brothers and sisters, I plead with you to give your bodies to God because of all he has done for you. Let them be a living and holy sacrifice—the kind he will find acceptable. This is truly the way to worship him. Don't copy the behavior and customs of this world, but let God transform you into a new person by changing the way you think. Then you will learn to know God's will for you, which is good and pleasing and perfect.* - Romans 12:1-2

When we become Christians, God makes our spirits new, but we still have the same bodies. We need to present them to God for his purposes. And we still have the same minds. We need to renew them with God's word. The first part of raising God's children is teaching them to do this.

Your people need to know that their bodies are important to God. What we do with our physical bodies has tremendous spiritual significance.

27

The world presents two false ideas about our bodies. The first false idea is modern materialism. It says that only the physical realm is real. Since your body is physical, what it wants is all that counts. As the hippies used to say, "If it feels good, do it!"

The second false idea is dualism. This originated with the ancient Greeks, but it's still popular today. Dualism says the spiritual realm is much higher than the physical, and only the spiritual will last into eternity. Since your body is just a lowly physical thing, whatever you do with it really doesn't matter.

Both these ideas are wrong. And they both lead to the same place – dishonoring God by dishonoring our bodies.

Materialism is wrong because human beings are not just physical. We're a unique and complex blend of the physical, psychological and spiritual realms – a trinity, like God, in whose image we were created. **God did not design our bodies to decide what we do, but to do what we decide.**

Dualism is wrong because God loves our physical bodies. He created them. He heals them when they get sick. He will make them new at the resurrection. God thought so highly of the physical human body that he sent Jesus to live in one. And when Jesus was resurrected from the dead and ascended into heaven, he didn't do it as a ghost. He did it in a physical human body (Luke 24:39).

Jesus presented his body to God in the ultimate obedience (Philippians 2:8). What we do with our bodies matters to God. To become like Jesus, teach your people to present their bodies to God.

But there's another part of the human trinity that needs to be dealt with if we are to become like Jesus. **We need to change the way we think.** We need to renew our minds.

All of us have our minds shaped by the mish-mash of things we are exposed to by our families, our schools, our friends, our neighborhoods, the media, and everything else that makes up culture and society. A mind shaped by the world cannot understand the things of God's Spirit (1 Corinthians 2:14).

When we become Christians, the Holy Spirit comes to live in our newly reborn human spirits, but our minds still speak the language of the world.

Our minds have to be renewed. They have to learn a different perspective, a different value system, a different way of thinking.

This is not an automatic result of becoming a Christian. Our spirits are born again as a free gift of God, but we are the ones who have to present our bodies and renew our minds.

How do we renew our minds? We fill them with the word of God. We replace old thought patterns with Bible thought patterns. We replace old stories with Bible stories. We replace the world's values with God's values. We intentionally choose activities and entertainment that feeds and reinforces the things of God instead of the things of the world.

As your mind is renewed, it becomes more and more able to communicate with your spirit, more and more able to receive and understand the things of God. (See Paul's prayer in Ephesians 3:18-19 – a great prayer for you to pray for your people.) Your mind becomes more and more like the mind of Jesus. To become more like Jesus, teach your people to renew their minds.

2. Teach your people to act on God's word

It's not enough to have God's word - you can have medicine in your cabinet, but just having medicine won't cure you. It's not even enough to believe God's word - you can believe medicine will cure you, but that belief won't do anything if the medicine stays in its bottle. If you want anything to happen, you have to do something. If you want to be cured, you have to get the medicine out of the cabinet and swallow it. And if you want to grow in God, you have to get his word off the shelf and act on it. *Just as the body is dead without breath, so also faith is dead without good works* (James 2:26).

When God brings to your attention a certain commandment or promise in the Bible, act on it. Act in faith that the reason God drew you to it is because he wants to do something. **Very often God waits to do things, even things he wants to do, until someone prays or acts on God's word** (Ezekiel 22:30).

In the Bible, God has given us the operator's manual for human life. When your people need something, teach them to search the Bible for promises and principles that apply to that situation. Teach them to find the conditions, the "if" clauses that accompany almost all of God's promises.[iii] Then show them, by example, how to fulfill the conditions and claim the promises, and to persevere until the answer comes.

3. When necessary, apply 2 Timothy 4:2

Paul told Timothy, *Patiently correct, rebuke, and encourage your people with good teaching (2 Timothy 4:2).*

Teach your people. Create opportunities for them to practice what you taught them. If they don't get it right, gently correct them and encourage them to try again. **You're not just teaching concepts, you're training lives.**

Some people don't like to be corrected. If they start to develop an unteachable attitude, Paul says it's your responsibility to rebuke them. Pastors need to be willing to do it, and people need to be willing to accept it. Otherwise, they'll never grow up to be like their Father.

We're not going to become like Jesus all at once. It's a process. Some of us have been working on it for fifty years or more. But just because it might be slow doesn't mean it's hopeless.

Start with yourself. Ask God to show you one thing in your life that you could change this week to help you become more like Jesus. It might be something about how you live and relate to people: Spirit-filled character. It might relate to how you seek God in your decision-making: Spirit-led wisdom. It might be about trusting God to step out in something that seems impossible: Spirit-powered actions. Or it might have to do with how you pass all this on to somebody else: Spirit-impassioned reproduction. Make sure you yourself are practicing what you teach your people. You're the leader; you have to stay ahead of them.

Points to Remember

- God wants all his children to be like their big brother, Jesus.
- Jesus did what he did through the power of the Holy Spirit, and he gave the Spirit to us so we can do the same.
- The church is nanny and tutor for God's children.
- Train your people to be like Jesus in Spirit-filled character, Spirit-led wisdom, Spirit-powered actions, and Spirit-impassioned reproduction.
- Becoming like Jesus requires presenting our bodies and renewing our minds.
- As pastor, be willing to correct and discipline when necessary.

[i] Some branches of the church believe that there is a second blessing of the Holy Spirit, often called being baptized in or by the Holy Spirit; others believe the Holy Spirit comes only once, at salvation. That discussion is for a different place. For now, let's just leave it that every Christian has the Holy Spirit in at least some way.

[ii] Some churches teach that miracles, healings and other signs and wonders ended when the last of the twelve original apostles died, or when the New Testament was completed. I believe proper principles of Bible interpretation show otherwise. Besides, I've experienced many of these things myself! But if you feel differently, let's agree to disagree. Just follow 1 Thessalonians 5:21 and use the parts of this book you can agree with.

[iii] For instance, 2 Chronicles 7:14; Psalm 37:4; Matthew 6:33; Philippians 4:6-7. Sometimes the conditions are marked with the word "if;" sometimes they are more subtle.

4

THE CHURCH INVITES EVERYONE
INTO THE FAMILY

Therefore, go and make disciples of all the nations, baptizing
them in the name of the Father and the Son and the Holy Spirit.
– Matthew 28:19

Like everything else about God, God's love is infinite. It overflowed the
Trinity to Adam and Eve. It overflowed Israel to the Gentiles. And it
overflows his adopted family, the church. God's love invites every person
on earth to join his family. The third purpose of the church is to extend
that invitation.

What if your people learn to effectively invite their friends and neighbors
to join God's family, and the friends and neighbors respond? On Pentecost
morning there were 120 Christians in the world. Then the Holy Spirit fell,
and three thousand people joined the church in one day (Acts 2:41). What
if that happens to your church? Will your people know what to do? What if
the revival we all pray for starts tomorrow?

I think it's entirely possible that God will turn all the upheaval in the
Middle East and elsewhere to open people's hearts for a spiritual harvest
like the world has never seen. Praise the Lord for the harvest - but who is

going to care for all these new Christians?

The only ones who can care for new Christians are those who are Christians already. If real revival comes, there won't be enough pastors to personally disciple every new believer. You have to equip your people to do it (Ephesians 4:12). Motivate them. Give them confidence. Train them to carry God's presence in love and power to everyone they meet. Equip your people to be the church and have church any time, any place, with anybody. Then God can send revival, because he will know your people will be there for the new believers.

If you are a church leader, ask your pastor to equip you this way. Then step out in faith and try new things. From the very beginning, this is the main way the church has spread.

Acts 8 tells the story. I call it the four-stroke engine that powers kingdom growth. Let's take a look at it.

The Four-Stroke Engine that Powers Kingdom Growth

Stroke 1: Ordinary Christians spread the word of Jesus wherever they found themselves

> *A great wave of persecution began that day, sweeping over the church in Jerusalem; and all the believers except the apostles were scattered through the regions of Judea and Samaria . . . But the believers who were scattered preached the Good News about Jesus wherever they went.*
> – Acts 8:1, 4

Until the day this persecution began, almost every Christian in the world lived in Jerusalem. It was the nursery of the new-born church. But the time came when God decided his people had been watching the apostles long enough.

I remember the first time I noticed exactly who went out and started preaching the good news about Jesus. I had just assumed it was the apostles.

33

But look again at verse 1. The apostles stayed in Jerusalem. **It was all the ordinary Christians**, the same ones who ran from the persecution and scattered all over the countryside. They're the ones who told everybody about Jesus.

This wasn't a mission trip. They didn't start out to preach. I think it happened something like this: Imagine a Jewish believer named Jon hears that his friend Ike has been thrown in jail for being a Christian. Jon races home, grabs his wife and kids, and runs for the only place he can think of – Uncle Albert's house in Damascus. Jon and family show up at Uncle Albert's front door. Uncle Albert asks to what he owes the pleasure of this unexpected visit. Jon says he's being persecuted for following Jesus. Uncle Joshua says, "Who's Jesus?" And Jon and his family tell him the good news.

Ordinary Christians – not apostles, not prophets, not evangelists or pastors or teachers, just plain everyday believers – spread the word of Jesus wherever they found themselves. Do you have any ordinary Christians in your church? Train them to do the same.

Stroke 2: Ordinary Christians did the works of Jesus wherever they found themselves

> *Philip, for example, went to the city of Samaria and told the people there about the Messiah. Crowds listened intently to Philip because they were eager to hear his message and see the miraculous signs he did. Many evil spirits were cast out, screaming as they left their victims. And many who had been paralyzed or lame were healed. So there was great joy in that city.* – Acts 8:5-8

There's no indication that this Philip was anything other than an ordinary everyday Christian. There was a Philip among the seven chosen to run the food ministry in Acts 6, but even if it was the same person, that doesn't imply miraculous powers. We do know this is not Philip the apostle, because all the apostles stayed in Jerusalem. **So how did he do these miracles? The same way Jesus did: by the power of the Holy**

Spirit.

By the way, it's extremely unlikely that Philip went to Samaria all by himself. He certainly would have taken his family with him, and probably others came along as well. People fleeing persecution almost always go in groups. Philip was most notable, but we can be sure other ordinary Christians, so ordinary that their names are not even recorded, were doing the same kinds of things.

We've already seen that **Spirit-powered actions are a part of imitating Jesus.** Jesus himself promised it twice, before his death and after his resurrection. In John 14:12 he told his followers, *"I tell you the truth, anyone who believes in me will do the same works I have done, and even greater works, because I am going to be with the Father."* In Acts 1:8 he told them how it would happen: *"You will receive power when the Holy Spirit comes upon you."* A few years later Paul wrote about miracles as a normal part of church life (see 1 Corinthians 12:7-11).

Again, Philip and the other believers didn't set out to do miracles. They were running for their lives. But when people started asking why they had left Jerusalem, they told about Jesus. A big part of the story was how Jesus healed the sick, at first in person, and later through the apostles using Jesus's name. There are sick people everywhere, and I'm sure some of them said, "Can Jesus heal me, too?" So Philip, probably scared to death, remembered what he had seen the apostles do, and he did the same. And God responded with healings and miracles.

Ordinary Christians – not apostles, not prophets, not evangelists or pastors or teachers, just plain everyday believers – didn't stop with talking about Jesus. They did the works of Jesu,s wherever they found themselves. Train the ordinary Christians in your church to do the same.

Stroke 3: Ordinary Christians taught and cared for the resulting new believers

> *A man named Simon had been a sorcerer there for many years, amazing the people of Samaria and claiming to be someone great. . . . But now the people believed Philip's message of Good News concerning the Kingdom of God and the name of Jesus Christ. As a result, many men and women were baptized. Then Simon himself believed and was baptized. He began following Philip wherever he went.* – Acts 8:9, 12-13

Philip didn't leave Jerusalem with the goal of planting a church, but now here he was with a bunch of new believers on his hands asking, **"We believe in Jesus, now what do we do?"** Again, Philip did what he'd seen the apostles do in Jerusalem. First he baptized them. Then he started teaching them and helping them learn to imitate Jesus.

When my son John was in college he decided to visit Cambodia. He found a church in Cambodia, asked if they would be his local connection, bought a plane ticket, and took off. He thought he would just be kind of a Christian tourist, visiting churches and getting a taste of what it's like to follow Jesus in southeast Asia. They had a different idea. They thought he had come to teach them more about Jesus and the Christian life, and they wouldn't take no for an answer. So John reached back in his memory to what he had learned from sermons and Sunday School and watching his father the preacher, and he talked about those things. And God used him.

Philip and the other scattered believers did the same thing. They told people what they had learned from the apostles. When somebody showed special interest, like Simon the sorcerer, they taught them more. **When you suddenly find yourself taking care of a baby you do whatever you can, whether you feel qualified or not.** Spiritual babies should be no different.

Ordinary Christians talked about Jesus and did the works of Jesus. When people responded, ordinary Christians helped them start learning about

God and becoming like Jesus. The ordinary Christians in your church can do it, too. Encourage them and let them know you believe in them.

Stroke 4: The existing church guided and supported the new groups

> When the apostles in Jerusalem heard that the people of Samaria had accepted God's message, they sent Peter and John there. As soon as they arrived, they prayed for these new believers to receive the Holy Spirit. The Holy Spirit had not yet come upon any of them, for they had only been baptized in the name of the Lord Jesus. Then Peter and John laid their hands upon these believers, and they received the Holy Spirit. . . . After testifying and preaching the word of the Lord in Samaria, Peter and John returned to Jerusalem. And they stopped in many Samaritan villages along the way to preach the Good News. – Acts 8:14-17, 25

Ordinary Christians spread the word, did the works, and cared for those who responded. But the existing church didn't leave them on their own. As soon as they heard about a group of new Christians, **experienced church leaders stepped in to offer support and guidance.** They spent some time ministering, filling in what was missing and making sure the new church was well grounded. Then they went back home, and probably from there out to help and support other newly forming churches.

Notice the balance here. Philip and the other ordinary Christians told people about Jesus, ministered in various ways including healings and miracles, and taught and cared for the new believers. They didn't wait for the apostles and pastors and officially recognized church leaders to do those things. They recognized that **acting like Jesus in these ways is just part of what it means to be a Christian.** Peter and John encouraged this initiative and blessed it. But they balanced that encouragement with further instruction and oversight.

You need to maintain the same balance. Encourage your people to step out in faith to spread the word, do the works, and minister to the people who respond to them. But keep an eye on things. It's easy for eager lay people to make a variety of mistakes ranging from Bible interpretation to personal relationships - or they may just not know what to do. **As pastor you must always be ready to step in before ignorance or mistakes turn into problems.** That's why solid training in the Bible, theology and church history and in the practical matters of ministry is so important. By the same token, always be ready to receive guidance and correction yourself, whether it's through an official structure or an informal group of other pastors.

The engine in a car generates power by repeating the four strokes over and over: intake fuel and air, compress fuel and air, combust the explosive mixture, exhaust the fumes; intake-compress-combust-exhaust-intakecompresscombustexhaust-intakecompresscombustexhaust...

The kingdom of God grows the same way: tell the good news, do the works of Jesus, teach new believers, support the new group; tell-do-teach-support- telldoteachsupport-telldoteachsupport...

As an engine starts you can see the four steps. As it speeds up the details begin to blur. It's the same way with kingdom growth. We see the four steps clearly in the first half of Acts 8. It repeats in the second half of the chapter as Philip goes to Gaza. It repeats again in Acts 9:10-19 with Ananias in Damascus, and again in Acts 11:19-26 with unnamed believers in Phoenicia, Cyprus and Antioch. The details are not reported so clearly as the cycle repeats, but all the elements are there.

You can trace the cycle through history. In the 1500s the Reformation spread this way. In the 1800s the great expansion of the Methodist movement followed the steps. The recent expansion of the church in China and South America and Africa has followed the same cycle, as has the house church movement in the United States.

The Christian's Responsibility

Every Christian has a responsibility to carry God's presence in love and power to everyone they meet. Christians together have a further responsibility to be the church and be ready to have church any time, any place, with anybody. Pastors and other church leaders have a responsibility to equip, motivate and support their people to do these things.

Let's break that down a little.

Individual Christians have a responsibility

Every Christian should be a carrier of God's presence. What does that mean? When Peter and John were arrested for preaching Jesus, Acts 4:13 says,

> *The members of the council were amazed when they saw the boldness of Peter and John, for they could see that they were ordinary men with no special training in the Scriptures. They also recognized them as men who had been with Jesus.*

There was something about Peter and John that marked them as Christians. When the high priest came out of the holy of holies he had the smell of incense on him. People smelled it and knew he had been in the presence of God. 2 Corinthians 2:15 says, *Our lives are a Christ-like fragrance rising up to God.* Peter and John had something like a spiritual fragrance of Jesus about them. They carried God's presence. The spirits of the council members were able to detect it.

Jesus said, *"I am with you always"* (Matthew 28:20). God is always with us, but sometimes we're so much in the world that the signs of God's presence are covered up, like cigarette smoke covers up perfume. Teach your people what it means to *let your good deeds shine out for all to see, so that everyone will praise your heavenly Father* (Matthew 5:16). Teach them to carry the love and power of God's presence.

God is love (1 John 4:8). **To carry God's presence means to carry love.** Every interaction we have with other people, especially those who don't know Jesus, must demonstrate love – not judgment or criticism or fear or self-righteousness, but love. If people don't sense the love of God in you and from you, you aren't carrying God's presence.

But love that is powerless to help is empty sentiment. Jesus promised,

> *You will receive power when the Holy Spirit comes upon you. And you will be my witnesses, telling people about me everywhere—in Jerusalem, throughout Judea, in Samaria, and to the ends of the earth.* - Acts 1:8

To carry God's presence means to carry God's power. **The ministry of power is an essential part of carrying God's love to the world.**

What do I mean by the ministry of power? Doing the works of Jesus, as Philip did in Acts 8.

The night he was betrayed, Jesus told his disciples, *"I tell you the truth, anyone who believes in me will do the same works I have done, and even greater works, because I am going to the Father"* (John 14:12).

After his resurrection Jesus was more specific.

> *These miraculous signs will accompany those who believe: They will cast out demons in my name, and they will speak in new languages. They will be able to handle snakes with safety, and if they drink anything poisonous, it won't hurt them. They will be able to place their hands on the sick, and they will be healed.* – Mark 16:17-18

Paul wrote,

> *My speech and my message were not in plausible words of wisdom, but in demonstration of the Spirit and of power, so that your faith might not rest in the wisdom of men but in the power of God.* - 1 Corinthians 2:4-5 ESV

The Holy Spirit is a spirit of love (2 Timothy 1:7), so "demonstration of the Spirit and of power" means demonstrating God's love by using God's power. As your people carry God's presence in their everyday lives, God will lead them to opportunities to show God's love and power. It might be as simple as a smile. It might be listening to a problem, or offering to pray with someone. It might be helping in some other way. It might even be a miracle. The point is, **carrying God's presence in love and power is not something only pastors do. It's the responsibility of every Christian.**

Christians together have a responsibility

Individual Christians carry God's power, but when they are together that power is multiplied. Jesus promised, *"Where two or three gather together in my name, I am there among them"* (Matthew 18:20). Whenever any two or more of your people come together, whether it's in church or at home or if they just run into each other in the market, Jesus is there in a special way. Teach them to recognize and demonstrate that. Any two or more Christians should be ready to be the church and have church any time, any place, with anybody.

Let's unpack that last sentence.

People ask me, "Where is your church?" They want to know the address of the building. I'll often answer, "It's Tuesday morning, so most of them are at work." The church is not a building, it's people.

Then what do I mean when I say your people need to be the church? The same thing you mean when you tell someone, "Be yourself." It means, remember who you are, and act like it.

Whenever two or more Christians are together, no matter the place or circumstances, they need to remember that they are the church, and act like it.

What does that mean? For me, two things: loving each other, and being available for God to use.

Jesus said, *"Your love for one another will prove to the world that you are my disciples"* (John 13:35). Love shows itself in ways that can be seen: respect, caring, helping each other. When people see two Christians together, the first thing they should notice is the love.

The second part of being the church is being available to God.

In the physical realm, when your heads want to do something, what actually does it? Usually, your hands or feet or mouth. Your head decides and plans, but your body makes it happen. In the spiritual realm Jesus is the head and the church is his body (Colossians 1:18). If Jesus sees something that needs to be done, he very rarely just does it himself. Miracles happen, but they're not the way God usually works. Jesus the head decides how to demonstrate his love, but most of the time he makes it happen through us, his body.

Let's say two of your people are eating in a restaurant. One of them notices that the server is acting very worried. She asks what's wrong, and the server breaks down in tears. Jesus wants to comfort and encourage her. Luckily, two members of his body are there, to be his mouth and his hands – your church folks. They speak kind words, perhaps lay a comforting hand on her shoulder, and offer to pray for her. They are being the body of Christ, the church.

Any two or more Christians should be ready to be the church by loving each other and acting as the body of Christ.

Beyond being the church, Christians together should be ready to have church.

What if your people can't get to where your church meets? What if your building burns down, or there's a gasoline shortage, or terrorists start targeting church services? What if a great revival comes and the church buildings aren't big enough for all the people? Will your people know what to do? Do they have the confidence to invite their neighbors to join them in their house or in a lunchroom at work or under a tree, and have church?

Having church doesn't require a consecrated building, or a choir or band, or an ordained minister. These things can certainly make church better, but the first-century church didn't have any of them. Nor do many underground churches in places where Christianity is outlawed. Having church means two or more Christians spending time together in the name of Jesus. They can sing, they can pray, they can share what God is doing, they can read the Bible and talk about it. *One will sing, another will teach, another will tell some special revelation God has given, one will speak in tongues, and another will interpret what is said* (1 Corinthians 14:26). Whenever Christians worship God together they're having church.

Pastors and church leaders have a responsibility

Pastor, your job description is very simple: **equip God's people to do God's work until they resemble God's Son** (Ephesians 4:12-13). Equip them as individuals to carry God's presence in love and power to everyone they meet. Equip them as small groups to be the church and have church anytime, anywhere, with anyone they meet.

Teach them what they need to know. Demonstrate what they need to do. Provide resources. Make opportunities for them to practice small steps in non-threatening settings, so they gain confidence. Tell them why it's important. Watch what they're doing, and give feedback and support.

Look for opportunities to move people into ministry. You might start by simply asking them to tell a small group how they came to know Jesus. Depending on their talents, ask them to lead in prayer, or read Scripture, or lead a song. As they grow in the Lord, ask them to lead a group of some kind, or to become a shepherd for a small group of people, calling them if they miss church, caring for them and looking after them.

Always look for a chance to encourage your people and let them try bigger things.

Most important, soak your people in prayer, asking the Holy Spirit to work these things in and through them.

My greatest thrill as a pastor is seeing someone realize that God can use them, and step out in faith and begin to do things for God. If they start doing things I have been doing, it frees me up to do other things. If they start doing new things, that multiplies the ways God can work through my church. Either way it's a blessing.

Points to Remember

- Most church growth comes, not through pastors, but through ordinary Christians who have been trained by pastors.
- Individual Christians have a responsibility to carry God's presence in love and power.

- Christians together have a responsibility to be the church and have church any time, any place, with anybody.
- Pastors and church leaders have a responsibility to equip the people for this work.

II

BEING A PASTOR

The word "pastor" appears once, undefined, in the list of Christ's gifts to the church in Ephesians 4:11. The root meaning is "shepherd," possibly from John 21. It probably combines aspects of "elder" and "overseer" from the pastoral epistles. Beyond that, the lack of specifics allows much freedom for different gifts, personalities and cultural settings. So if your pastoral style is different from some other pastor, don't worry about it. Just trust God to guide and use you.

5

BECOMING A PASTOR

Then I heard the Lord asking, "Whom should I send as a messenger to this people? Who will go for us?" I said, "Here I am. Send me." – Isaiah 6:8

If you are already a pastor, please don't skip this chapter. Read it asking God to show you someone he might be calling.

You want to be a pastor, or you believe God is calling you to be a pastor, or someone has told you they think you could be really successful as a pastor. What does that mean?

Many pastors dream of having the largest church in town, or baptizing hundreds of new converts, or getting their own radio or television program. These can be great things, but they are only success if they are what God has called you to. Your success might look very different.

Jesus spent three years preaching, healing and doing miracles. After the greatest miracle of all, his resurrection from the dead, only five hundred people gathered (1 Corinthians 15:6).

Many of us would be happy to have a church of five hundred. But two years earlier, in John 6, five thousand people had come to hear him. In two years, Jesus lost 90% of his people!

Most pastors would not consider losing ninety percent of their church to be a sign of success. But Jesus didn't panic. Jesus did not come to build an institution; he came to build believers. Jesus measured his success, not by the number of his fans, but by the number of his followers. **For Jesus, success was people who were motivated and equipped to go out and continue his work.**

God's standard of success is not the same for every pastor. He may want you to build a large church or he may want you faithfully to care for a small church. He may want you to focus on teaching or preaching or healing or evangelism or social justice. He may want you to stay at one church for decades or serve many congregations. Ultimately the only true measure of success is whether you are faithful to God's call for you.

As the church of Jesus Christ, we have a three-fold purpose: to become a people among whom God obviously lives, to help each other become more and more like Jesus, and to carry God's presence in love and power in such a way that everyone we meet will want to join God's family through faith in Jesus Christ. No two pastors will do all that in the same way.

Still, there are some basics.

Basic Requirements for Being a Pastor

Not just anyone can be a pastor. Not just anyone should be a pastor. Here are basic requirements for anyone who would carry out this most demanding, and rewarding, ministry.

You have to love

The two greatest commandments of the Law are about love (Matthew 22:38-39). Jesus' new commandment is about love (John 13:34). Paul says the greatest spiritual attribute, even greater than faith and hope, is love (1 Corinthians 13:13). John tells us God himself is love (1 John 4:8). The most basic requirement for anyone who feels called to lead God's people is love.

You have to love God

You must love the LORD your God with all your heart, all your soul, all your mind, and all your strength. That's the greatest commandment (Mark 12:28-30), and it's a pastor's greatest need.

Some people become pastors because they think it's an easy way to achieve respect and a good living. They will soon find out differently. Anyone with the intelligence, drive and people skills to succeed as a pastor can certainly also succeed at other occupations that are easier and earn better respect and better pay. If money is what you love, being a pastor is the wrong place to look.

Others become pastors because they want to help people. That's a noble reason, but the pastorate is the wrong place to fulfill it. As a pastor you will help people, but it's a side effect of serving God. If helping people is your first love, consider being a doctor or teacher or social worker.

If you want to last as a pastor, your greatest passion must be to know and love and please God.

You have to love people

Jesus said that's the second great commandment (Mark 12:31). If you hope to spend all your time sitting alone with God and your books, you might be better off as a professor or a monk, because a pastor's job is people. You will listen to people, talk to people, counsel people, visit people and work with people in meetings. People will constantly be asking you for help. You'll be on call 24 hours a day. If you're not sure you like that idea, reconsider your career choice.

As a pastor you get to work with some wonderful people. Christian believers, especially mature ones, are the very best people there are on this planet. For me, spending time with people like that is one of the greatest rewards of the job. But people don't start off as mature Christian believers. People will come to the church in a wide variety of conditions and for a wide variety of reasons, most of them having to do with trying to get some need met. Much of your time will be spent with people like this. And sometimes their needs aren't pretty.

Jesus sought out people who were hurting. He sought out sinners and people who didn't have it all together. He explained it this way: *"Healthy people don't need a doctor - sick people do"* (Mark 2:17). A person who doesn't like to be around people who are sick shouldn't become a doctor. **A person who doesn't like to be around people who are not yet like Jesus shouldn't become a pastor.**

This is not to say you have to be an extrovert or a sentimentalist. God calls all kinds of people to be pastors. (I should know; I'm an introvert who started out as an engineer.) But your driving force for loving people has to be God's love. You won't last long in ministry if it isn't.

You have to be called by God

Pastors are on the front lines of the battle between good and evil. Just as snipers try to pick off enemy officers, the devil tries to pick off pastors. Being a pastor is the most rewarding thing I can imagine, but it is also full of extremely difficult situations. Surveys in the United States suggest that almost three-quarters of all pastors regularly consider leaving the ministry because of the stress.[i]

Becoming a pastor because somebody else thinks it's a good idea for you or because you think it might be a good career move is a recipe for a short and unhappy experience. **If you don't have a strong sense that God has called you to this and that God will support you and see you through, you are almost certain to burn out or break down.**

Every Christian has a calling. Being a pastor is just one way of serving God. If these warnings have made you feel discouraged about your calling, don't despair. God needs Christians in every walk of life. Civil servants, business people, tradesmen, retail workers, farmers, homemakers and people in every other kind of job can bless folks a pastor may never meet. If you are not called to be a pastor, that doesn't mean you don't have a calling from God; it means you have a calling to serve in some other way. But if God is calling you to be a pastor you will never find peace until you answer the call.

Pastors, always encourage your people to seek out what God is calling them to be and do. Teach them to consider their callings just as important and God-honoring as yours. And always look for those whom God may be calling to be a pastor.

God can call you directly

One day as these men were worshiping the Lord and fasting, the Holy Spirit said, "Dedicate Barnabas and Saul for the special work to which I have called them" (Acts 13:2).

The church leaders were doing their primary job and ours, which is serving the Lord. (The word translated "serving" could refer to worship or to other religious service.) They were focused on God, so when he spoke they heard his voice clearly. God directly and specifically called two people by name for a particular work.

This is the clearest kind of call. It is also the rarest. It seems that God reserves such clear calls or directions for those who will have difficult tasks ahead of them. If God calls you in this way, remember it well. Then when the tough times come, you can look back and reassure yourself that this was not a mistake. God called you to it and God will see you through it.

God can call you through church leaders

In Acts 16:3 Paul asked Timothy to accompany him on his evangelizing journeys. Apparently Paul saw potential in Timothy, and he took him on as a kind of protégé. Later, when Timothy had become a pastor, Paul wrote two letters to him which include some of the clearest Biblical instructions on how to lead a church.

If your pastor or another church leader asks you to help in some pastoral duty, or suggests you take some kind of pastoral training, take this as a sign that God may be calling you to pastoral service. Pray about it and discuss it with mature Christians you trust. It may not just be a request for help. It may be your call from God.

A sense of calling can grow gradually

A tent-maker named Aquila and his wife Priscilla appear three times in Acts 18. At the beginning they were nothing more than Christian believers who happened to have the same trade as Paul, and this coincidence brought them together. As they shared the same house with Paul, they naturally began to pick up some of what he was saying and doing. By the end of the chapter they had so grown in their ministry that they felt competent to correct the teaching of Apollos, one of the early church's most eloquent preachers.

It may be that you can't pinpoint a specific time or place when God called you to ministry, either directly or through someone else. Yet somehow you find that people are asking your advice, seeking your counsel, looking to you for leadership in church matters. If this is the case, pray seriously about whether this may be a sign that God is preparing you to be a pastor.

It's never too late to respond to God's call

Maybe you ran from God the first time you sensed God calling you. Maybe you weren't sure, or you were afraid, or you felt you couldn't leave your other responsibilities. Now you may be afraid you missed your chance. You may fear God will always be disappointed in you.

Please don't feel that way. Many successful pastors ran from God's call at first. Our God is the God of new beginnings. Jonah ran the first time God called him, yet God used him to save an entire city. I don't know if it is possible to reject God so strongly and consistently that he finally stops calling, but if you are taking the time to read this book, you have certainly not reached that point.

You have to prepare

Saul, who became the Apostle Paul, was already a highly trained expert in the Old Testament Scriptures when Jesus appeared to him on the road to Damascus. He immediately started witnessing to his conversion and new faith. Yet he was not given a leadership position in the church, and apparently he didn't seek one. Instead, he went into the Arabian desert for an intense time of prayer and study that may have lasted as long as three years. Then he went back home to Tarsus and made tents for a while. After that he spent several more years serving as assistant to Pastor Barnabas in the Antioch church. Scholars calculate that between Paul's calling and his first ministry assignment he spent as much as sixteen years in training and preparation. Being called is not the same thing as being prepared.

You may be naturally gifted in art or music, but until you train and develop your gifts, you can't be called an artist or a musician. In the same way, a person may be a gifted speaker and leader and truly be called from God, but until you acquire appropriate education and training you are not ready to be the lead pastor of a church. I say "lead pastor" because serving as an assistant pastor under a more experienced leader can be a very effective way to learn, as Paul learned from Barnabas in Antioch. During that time people may call you "pastor," but you will know you are still in training.

Most Christian groups have minimum requirements of education and competence before they will certify or ordain a person to be a pastor. There's a good reason for this. As a pastor, people will come to you with the most serious questions, questions affecting their eternal salvation. You are responsible before God to lead them right.

People will expect you to care for them in times of great personal need. They will expect you to guide them in relational problems and ethical and moral dilemmas. They will look to you for accurate information about the Bible and Christianity. And they will expect you to effectively administer the affairs of the church. While there is an element of natural skill in each of these areas, a good bit of education and training is also necessary. **Part of the calling to be a pastor is a calling to undergo necessary**

preparations and meet the requirements set by existing church leaders.

That said, I know there are groups of Christians who live far from an established church. It is best if they can develop a good relationship with an existing church, even at a distance, so they can receive some kind of pastoral care. I also know that sometimes this is not practical. If this is your situation, one of the group will have to take leadership. Praise God for the one willing to do it. Maybe that person is you. If so, make every effort to gain some training as soon as you can.

What kind of training does a pastor need?

You need training in practical matters

If you are going to be a pastor, you need to know how to do the things a pastor needs to do. Some parts may come naturally to you, but others may not. That training is the purpose of this book, but this book by itself is not enough.

Learn methods and techniques well enough to adapt them. Just because the Americans or the Germans or the Kazakhs do something a certain way, that doesn't mean the Turks or the Kenyans should. Just because another church in your city does it one way, that doesn't mean you should do it the same way. Find the underlying principles and prayerfully experiment with applying them in the way that best fits your situation.

As you study and observe how other pastors do things, remember 1 Thessalonians 5:21, *Test everything; hold fast what is good* (ESV). Or as I heard one pastor put it, "Be as smart as an old cow: swallow the grass and spit out the sticks."

What practical things do you need to learn?

You need to learn the Bible

Paul advised his protégé Timothy, *Work hard so you can present yourself to God and receive his approval. Be a good worker, one who does not need to be ashamed and who correctly explains the word of truth* (2 Timothy 2:15). Anyone

54

can read the Bible and be greatly blessed, but there is much to learn that helps bring out deeper levels of understanding. Knowing about the history and cultures of the Bible, shades of meaning in translations, or recognizing figures of speech, for example, can open up new depths of revelation.

You need to learn teaching and preaching

Crafting sermons and Bible lessons is a skill. I'm still learning how to convey God's message in a way that people will understand, remember, and apply to their lives. And that way is not always the same for every group of listeners.

You need to learn to recognize and follow the leading of the Holy Spirit

As a pastor, people expect you to be an expert in spiritual ministry. You lead worship, you minister to the sick and disturbed, you pray for the needs of the church, you deal with opposition in the physical and spiritual realms. Paul tells us, *All who are led by the Spirit of God are children of God* (Romans 8:14). Recognizing and following this leading is a learned skill.

You need to learn pastoral duties

You will be expected to baptize, marry and bury people, visit the sick, and celebrate the Lord's Supper. There are certain ways you will be expected to do these things, usually depending on the denomination or tradition to which your church belongs.

You need to learn church organization and administration

How do you choose leaders? Who makes which decisions? How do you deal with money and the building? How do you deal with the local government and community leaders? You may never think about such things until you find yourself in charge of a church, but they can literally make or break your ministry. These are the focus of Part Three of this book.

You need training in theology and church history

Somebody may say, "Isn't that pretty academic for a local church pastor? I know a lot of good pastors who don't know a lot about that stuff." When I first started into ministry, I felt the same way. I wondered why my seminary had spent so much time teaching me all that academic book-learning. What I wanted was practical ideas for how to grow a church! But the longer I have been in ministry, the more I appreciate the history and theology I was forced to learn.

Theology and church history can help a pastor recognize an error in doctrine or practice before it becomes a problem. They can also be very helpful in explaining the faith to those who have questions.

Nobody ever set out to invent a heresy. The great false teachings of Christian history were not developed to mislead folks. They came about as a result of honest, sincere people trying to understand and apply the Bible. When their ideas went astray, they didn't have the knowledge to recognize it.

For instance, let's say you didn't know the history of the hundreds of years of theological struggle to understand the fact that Jesus is both fully God and fully human. In trying to figure this out, you could conclude that when Jesus came from heaven to earth he didn't actually become human but just disguised himself as a human. Or you could decide that Jesus was just a man who somehow became God through spiritual exercises. Both of these are heresies that have plagued the church for centuries. This is not the place to go into the spiritual and practical problems that can arise from those wrong ideas, but rest assured they are many and serious. It is important for a pastor to be aware of these things. There are many similar examples.

I do want to add one note of caution. **There are many theological issues on which good, Bible-believing, educated Christians differ.** These are not matters of heresy versus orthodoxy. They are differences of interpretation within Christian thought. For instance, some churches baptize babies, while others believe only adults and older children should be baptized. Some denominations emphasize predestination, others emphasize free will. Beware of any teaching that does not acknowledge these and similar differences as legitimate theological viewpoints. Look for a school, teacher or book that clearly says, "On this issue some Christians believe A for these reasons, others believe B for those reasons." They may spend the rest of their time saying, "Here's why I believe A is better," but at least they have acknowledged the other opinion. This approach allows you to make your own choices, and to engage in intelligent conversation with someone who believes the other way. I even use this approach in my local church sermons and Bible studies.

Some ideas and interpretations fit within the spectrum of acceptable Christian understanding. Others do not. A pastor must be educated enough to know the difference and respond accordingly.

You need to keep learning and developing your skills

Initial preparation is necessary, but it is not enough. A person with a true pastoral calling will be self-motivated to continue reading and learning about God, the Bible, and new and better ways to help people and administer the church. Churches need to make sure their pastor takes advantage of new resources and continuing education.

I don't mean to imply that you can't be a good pastor without formal seminary training. If formal training is not available, there are many other ways to learn. I also don't intend to imply that you should refuse to provide leadership to a group of Christians, or even start a church if that is what God is calling you to do, until you have some kind of diploma. My point is that **there are important things to learn that will make you a better, more effective pastor, and you should take every opportunity to learn them.**

If seminary education is not available where you are, one option might be to attend seminary somewhere else. Of course, this is very expensive, and the typical seminary course requires a university degree and then takes three years of full-time study. If you feel that God may be calling you to this, be very careful and prayerful about the seminary you choose. Not all seminaries teach the same thing. And be sure where God is calling you before you go. I have been told that very often people who go to graduate schools in other countries wind up deciding to settle in that country rather than returning to their native land.

Thanks to the blessings of technology, many seminaries and Bible colleges now offer courses online. Nothing can take the place of live discussion in classrooms and coffee shops, but physically attending a school is often difficult or impossible. Online education is often your best choice if you have another job or live a distance from a school's physical location. Again, these classes vary widely in cost, quality, and theological perspective. Do your homework on them before you make a commitment.

Ordination

Once or twice someone has visited my church and introduced themselves like this: "Greetings in the name of the Lord! I am the Apostle So-and-So." When that happens, my first thought is, "Look out! This could be trouble." My experiences with such folks have not always been good. I have learned to beware of self-proclaimed pastors (or bishops or prophets or whatever title they claim) with no accountability structure. Don't become one of them.

The people of a local church entrust their pastor with their eternal destiny, not to mention an important part of their daily lives. What guarantee do they have that this pastor is qualified to lead them? The historical answer is ordination. **If you have the character and maturity to be a faithful pastor, you will be happy to submit your calling and preparation to a group of mature, experienced Christians.** They can help you and your church discern whether you are ready to take on the responsibility, and they can help you and support you down the road.

Paul advises, *Never be in a hurry about appointing a church leader* (1 Timothy 5:22). At ordination, a group of people goes on record that they know you, they have investigated you, and they are willing to state publicly that you are called, qualified and equipped to be a pastor. They are taking on a heavy responsibility.

For some kinds of churches, the ordaining group is the local congregation itself. In many denominations, only a body of those who are already successfully serving in ministry is authorized to ordain new pastors. These denominations usually have specific standards of training and experience that are required before you can become a candidate for ordination. I personally believe this approach provides a greater degree of protection for the people of the church, because those making the decision have been through it themselves.

Of course, no method can guarantee that every ordained person will turn out to be a good pastor. For that reason, another important element of ordination is accountability. Pastors are human, and unfortunately some may succumb to human temptations. Some become misguided and are in danger of leading their people into false paths. Some even seek to prey upon local churches for financial gain.

If this happens, **the same group that ordains a pastor should be able to provide oversight.** A body that grants pastoral credentials should be able to revoke them where necessary. This can often be done more objectively and effectively when the ordaining body is made up of other experienced pastors rather than the local congregation. The ordaining body should then work to rehabilitate the pastor, if possible.

In some countries religious leaders are accorded certain legal privileges. If this is the case, the government needs a way to tell the difference between those who are actually pastors and those who are just trying to get the benefits. It is helpful if the churches can show through their ordination process that they are self-policing in this area, so the government doesn't have to try to define who is a pastor. No matter what country you live in, you want the government involved in church business as little as possible.

Becoming a Pastor

A pastor without a church is like a driver without a car. How do you get connected with a church to serve? There are basically three ways.

You can plant a church

Many pastors become pastors by the simple means of starting a church. If God has called you to do this, it can be very satisfying and fulfilling. However, it is a lot of hard work, and the failure rate is high. If the church thrives and grows, the founding pastor can gain a lot of authority and influence. This can be a real blessing to God's work. However, accountability can become an issue.

You can be hired by a church

In some traditions, when a local church finds itself without a pastor for whatever reason, the congregation or its group of leaders is responsible for selecting and hiring a new pastor. This also implies that if the congregation is unhappy, they can fire the pastor, and if the pastor is unhappy or gets a better offer, the pastor can leave. This kind of organization can give a local church great independence. However, as pastor it can tempt you to preach what the people want to hear, or what might make you more attractive to a bigger congregation, rather than what God is telling you to say.

You can be assigned to a church

Some church groups have bishops or other authority figures who are responsible for assigning pastors to churches. While consultation is normally a part of this process, it is understood that the pastor will go to the assigned church, and the church will accept the assigned pastor. This requires a degree of trust in God's use of the denominational structure. However, it also frees pastors to preach and act as they feel led, without the fear of possibly losing their job if they displease influential church members.

Points to Remember

- If you want to be a pastor, you have to love God and people.
- If God isn't calling you to be a pastor, don't try it.
- Your gifts and calling need to be trained and developed.
- Ordination and a continuing relationship with the ordaining body or similar group provide safety and accountability.

[i] "Nearly 3 in 4 Pastors Regularly Consider Leaving Due to Stress, Study Finds." The Christian Post, June 21, 2014.

6

YOUR RESPONSIBILITY

Now these are the gifts Christ gave to the church: the apostles, the prophets, the evangelists, and the pastors and teachers. Their responsibility is to equip God's people to do his work and build up the church, the body of Christ. This will continue until we all come to such unity in our faith and knowledge of God's Son that we will be mature in the Lord, measuring up to the full and complete standard of Christ. – Ephesians 4:11-13

As a pastor, it's easy to think of your job as preaching, or taking care of people, or running a church. These are important tasks, but they are means to an end. Constantly remind yourself of the real goal. **A pastor's job is to equip God's people to do God's work until they resemble God's son.**

In Part 1, we looked at God's work in terms of the purpose of the church, and we examined what it means to become like Jesus. In this chapter we'll focus on how pastors can equip their people for those things. We'll start by looking at the ministry of Jesus, the author and finisher of our faith.

"The Spirit of the Lord is upon me, because he has anointed me to bring good news to the poor. He has sent me to proclaim release to the captives and recovery of sight to the blind, to let the oppressed go free, to proclaim the year of the Lord's favor." Jesus read this passage from Isaiah 61 in one of the first public

appearances of his ministry, and he said, *"Today as you listen, this scripture has been fulfilled"* (Luke 4:18-21).

If you look at the Isaiah passage, you will see that Jesus stopped reading right in the middle of a sentence. The next line, the one he did not read, refers to *the day of vengeance of our God* (Isaiah 61:2). Jesus was interested in good news and freedom. He left judgment and vengeance for God to take care of at the end of time.

At the same time, Jesus never compromised truth in order to please people or keep them coming to him. At the beginning of John 6, five thousand people were following Jesus. Many pastors would have said "Hallelujah!" and started a building campaign. Not Jesus. He told them the difficult truths that God wanted them to hear, and he kept on until by the end of the chapter almost all had deserted him. In John 8:30 many believed in Jesus because of what he said, including some of the Jewish leaders. Most pastors would have praised God and started a baptism party. But Jesus kept talking, and by the end of the chapter these same leaders were looking for stones to kill him.

This is not to say that a faithful preacher cannot also have a large church. The point is that as a pastor, **your first concern must be to proclaim God's word, not to make yourself popular.**

Jesus took the long view. It was fine with him if a lot of folks wanted to follow him around, but his focus was on preparing people who would carry on the work when he was gone. Jesus spent a little time with the crowds, more time with the disciples who followed him from place to place, and the most time with the twelve apostles, especially Peter, James and John. He carefully trained and equipped his followers. He taught them the truths, showed them how to apply them, and then sent them out two by two to practice. His last words recorded by Matthew are instructions to **follow the same pattern** in training and equipping others from every nation (Matthew 28:18-20).

Jesus is not the only biblical example of an effective godly church leader. Study the accounts in Acts of Christian leaders in action. Read Paul's letters to Timothy and Titus, chief pastors in Ephesus and Crete. These short letters are commonly called the "pastoral epistles" because of their practical advice for leading a church. Find lessons in the other epistles and Jesus' letters to the seven churches in Revelation 2 and 3. And don't neglect leadership principles that can be gleaned from the Old Testament, history and even the secular world – always filtering out the parts that are not in keeping with the message and ways of Jesus.

Your Responsibility

As pastor, some things are your responsibility, and some are not. Many church people will be happy to tell you exactly what they think your job is. **Make sure you get your job description from God.** He is the one you work for, not the church folks, even if God uses them to pay your salary.

Here are some responsibilities I believe are essential in every pastor's job description.

Minister to God in praise and worship

I read of a man in England who stopped one evening at a small country church just in time for the daily evening service. He was the only one there, so he was surprised that the pastor went through the entire service with grace and dignity. After it was over he asked the pastor what he would have done if he had not happened to be driving past and come in. The pastor said he would have conducted the service just the same.

"With no one here?" asked the man.

The pastor replied, "God is here."

1 Peter 2:9 and Revelation 1:6 tell us that we are all called to be priests. The function of a priest is to minister to God. The presence of other people is nice, but not necessary. In fact, in the Old Testament, the most important function of the High Priest's ministry was conducted in the Holy of Holies, where no other human being was allowed to come.

There are many ways to minister to God. Rituals, prayers, journaling, silence, even serving other people can be ways of ministering to God. The point is not how you do it, but why.

A good pastor has to be people-oriented. But never forget that **your first duty and responsibility is to minister to God.**

Hear from God

Perhaps the most important skill you can develop as a pastor is the ability to hear from God. I pray often, "Lord, help me know your will and your way with clarity, accuracy, confidence and timely obedience." It's not your church, and it's not the people's church. It's God's church. What does God want you tell them today? Where does God want you to take them this week?

After ministering to God, receiving God's guidance for his church is the most important thing you do. In fact, God's guidance will often come as you are ministering to God (Acts 13:2). That's why the devil tries so hard to distract you from it.

Don't let that happen. Devote whatever time it takes until you know God's direction. Then do it again tomorrow, and the next day, and every day, because God usually only guides us one day at a time.

The pastor is not the only person who can discern God's direction for a church. Often this kind of guidance happens best through a group of leaders. Sometimes there are people in the congregation who are especially gifted at hearing from God. As pastor, develop as many of these avenues of communication from God as you can.

Bring God's message and love to the church

As you spend time with God, God will show you different things. He may bring to mind certain Bible truths that the church needs to be taught for a certain time or situation. He may make you aware of areas that need to be addressed in sermons. He may show you a vision of where he wants you to lead his people in some new ministry or outreach.

All these things reveal God's love. Part of your job as pastor is to pass them on to the people as effectively as possible, in whatever ways are appropriate for the specific message and situation.

Bring the needs of the church to God

Your people expect you to be praying for them. As pastor, you may be the only one who knows all the different needs of the church and how they interact. Prayer is the most important thing you can do to get these needs met.

In my opinion, **one of the most important and most neglected truths in the church as a whole is the power of prayer.** I'm convinced that when we get to heaven we will be astonished at the things God wanted to do that didn't get done because we didn't pray (see Ezekiel 22:30-31). Spend much time in prayer yourself, and make prayer a priority in your church. Older people in particular may feel that they have little they can contribute. Yet they often have the experience and maturity, and the time, to become some of your most effective prayer warriors. Encourage them in this.

While you're at it, teach your people to pray for you. Some pastors develop an intercessory team whose main focus is to pray for the pastor. They call this a "prayer shield." It can make a huge difference in your ministry.

Lead the church to follow God

It's not enough to tell the church where God wants them to go and what God wants them to do. Somebody has to get out in front and lead the way. This is also your job. That doesn't always mean you have to literally be the first person in a certain ministry, although it might. Or it could mean you draw up a plan, or identify participants, or gather resources, to help others get something started.

There are many different leadership styles. Sometimes you need to be directive, sometimes you need to work with a team, sometimes you just need to get the right people together and let them go at it. Use whatever leadership style works best for you to see that your church follows where

God is calling.

Introduce people to Jesus

So far we've been talking about the church as an institution and the people who are part of it. What about people who are not part of the church and don't know Jesus? Paul wrote Timothy, *Do the work of an evangelist* (2 Timothy 4:5).

As your church grows and takes up more and more of your attention, you can find yourself spending all your time with church folks. This is natural. They are your friends, you share common values and beliefs and activities, you like being with them. Even if you don't like being with them sometimes (let's be realistic here), it's your job. And when you aren't spending time with church folks, you are spending time with God, or preparing sermons, or being with your family, or unclogging the church toilets, or any of the thousand other things that need doing. But **how can you do the work of an evangelist if you never spend time with anyone who doesn't know Jesus?**

It can be especially easy to fill your time with all those other activities if you are not one for whom personal evangelism comes naturally. Some pastors know all about the doctrine of salvation, but they find it very difficult to help people personally apply it to get saved. If this is you, it's important not only to make time to interact with those who need Jesus, but also to learn and practice some basic personal evangelism skills. Find someone good at it and ask them to give you some pointers. Go with them as they share the gospel. Don't be afraid to admit that there are things you still need to learn or improve.

Counsel

Things don't always go smoothly in life, even for Christians. People have trouble with their marriages or children. They face disappointments, temptations and addictions. They get bad news about their jobs or their health. Some of these people will come to you for help.

Psychology and psychiatry, like other fields of medicine, are wonderful gifts from God that can bring great healing. But they focus on the mind and emotions. They rarely deal with the spirit, if they even recognize its reality. That's where you come in.

1. **Start with prayer**. Invite the Holy Spirit to guide you and bring wisdom and healing, and continue to listen for his guidance.

2. **Listen.** If the person wants to talk, don't interrupt, except for clarification.

3. **Ask open-ended questions** if they haven't said enough.

4. **Look beyond the presenting problem.** Usually the first concern people talk about is not the underlying issue.

5. **Seek spiritual gifts** (1 Corinthians 12:8, 10, 31). Ask God for special gifts of knowledge, wisdom and discernment of spirits. Don't discount the possibility of the demonic, especially if there is a history of occult or pagan involvement. If you believe that is the issue, get help from a mature Christian experienced in this area.

6. **Share Biblical principles.** Read relevant Bible passages aloud and teach how to apply them. Many problems can be traced to believing the devil's lies instead of Bible truth. Write out scripture references so the person can go back to them.

7. **Give practical exercises** to reinforce and apply the Biblical principles. These might include Bible readings, verses to memorize, prayer suggestions, affirmations to repeat, books to read, and support groups.

8. **Refer** the person to professionals if you believe they need medical or psychological help.

9. **End with prayer.**

Providing Biblical counsel can be very rewarding, but it can also offer some snares. Beware of feeling like you have to solve all the person's problems. Don't let the person begin to intrude on your personal time or family life. And guard against inappropriate attachments.

Visit the sick, imprisoned and grieving

When people are suffering, the family of God should be there for them. Often, the pastor represents that family.

When I first started in ministry, my big question in these situations was, "What should I say? What should I do?" Often, saying and doing is not as important as just being there, sharing a "ministry of presence."

That said, there are some basic rules that apply to all these situations.

1. **Prepare yourself** with prayer, and open yourself for God's guidance.

2. If they are in a hospital, prison or other institution, follow the rules and **cooperate** with the staff.

3. **Don't say you know how they feel.** Unless you have been in the same situation, you don't, and they know it.

4. Avoid the temptation to explain why bad things happen to good people. It's an interesting intellectual exercise, but this is not the time for it. **Suffering people don't need explanations, they need comfort.**

5. **Read Scripture**. Ask God to show you what the person needs to hear.

6. **Pray** with them. Silently ask God to show you what to pray, then pray it aloud with faith.

7. After you leave, **take care of yourself.** Wash your hands. Recognize if it has been hard on you emotionally, and take time to recover. I make a practice of saying a cleansing prayer, using the authority of Genesis 1:28 and Mark 16:17 to command pathogens and spirits of disease or decay to leave my body, and inviting the Holy Spirit to fill me with life (Romans 8:11).

Help people learn to hear from Jesus for themselves

In the 1990s American church leaders started talking about how pastors should cast a vision for their churches, an idea of how God wants the church to look in the future. I asked God to give me a vision for the church I was serving at the time. I expected a picture of overflowing services, new ministries, perhaps a larger building. The only thing that came to me was an image of a person walking. I figured that couldn't be right, so I asked God again. Again all that came was the idea of a person walking. So I started prayerfully thinking about it.

I realized that when I walk, my brain doesn't consciously tell each part of my body how to move. "Shift weight to right foot. Pick up left foot. Swing left foot forward. Set left foot down. Shift weight to left foot…" If that's what it took, I'd never get anywhere, or at least I'd look like a rusty robot.

When you walk, each part of your body knows what it is supposed to do, and it does it. The movements all fit together smoothly because each part is connected with your head in subconscious coordination. Your conscious mind isn't even aware of most of the muscle movements involved.

I think God was showing me that this is how he wants his church to operate. The Bible calls the church the body of Christ (1 Corinthians 12:27). Jesus is the head (Colossians 1:18). Every member of the church, every Christian, should be directly communicating with Jesus, just as every part of your body directly communicates with your brain. A church where nobody does anything until the pastor tells them to will be as uncoordinated as a body where each motion has to come from a conscious thought.

Unfortunately, since the fall of Adam and Eve, human beings have not had a good connection with Jesus the head. That's what died when they ate the forbidden fruit. When we are born again, that connection is restored. But just as a person recovering from a stroke may need much physical therapy before the body learns to hear from the brain again, **Christians need spiritual training before they learn to recognize and obey the voice of their head, Jesus.** As a pastor, that training is one of your most important jobs.

Be sure you **teach your people that they will not all hear the same thing from God.** Think about your normal walking motion. What are your hands doing? They swing. Do they swing together, in unison? No, one hand swings forward, and at the same time, the other hand moves backward. Your hands are going opposite directions from each other. Does this mean one hand is right and the other is wrong? Of course not. It's necessary for them to go in different directions.

In the same way, God will not direct all your people to do the same thing at the same time. If they all try to do just what you are doing, or just what some respected elder in the church is doing, then a lot of other necessary things won't get done, and the church will have a tough time moving. So teach your people not to judge each other if they don't all do exactly the same thing. In musical terms, the goal is a symphony of harmonies, not a unison chorus.

Help people do what Jesus is leading them to do

What is involved in equipping people to do God's work? Recruiting, planning, teaching, training, demonstrating, resourcing, motivating, overseeing, correcting and evaluating are all important elements. **You need a plan and a process for each one of those elements, for every kind of ministry.**

Take time periodically, and especially when you are starting a new ministry or program, to think about each of those elements of equipping people. For each element, ask yourself, what is my plan? How well is it working? How much are other people involved? How much do they understand the process, and their part in it? The good news is, you don't have to invent all those plans and processes yourself. You can often borrow them from other pastors or learn them from books or conferences. As pastor, it is your responsibility to see that your people are able and ready to do what God is calling your church to do.

Then set them free to do it. If your church only does what you as the pastor tell them to do, you are limiting your church to your own ideas and imagination, or at the most, to your own ability to hear from God. Usually this also means that you will be expected to personally oversee the activity, so it often means than you are also limiting your church to the amount of activities you have time to attend.

On the other hand, if you teach your people to hear from God, you will find that they begin coming to you with ideas. Your job then will be to encourage them, perhaps connect them with others in the church who might work on the same project, provide them with any training or resources they need, and give them moral support. They will be motivated and excited. If they truly heard from God, they will most likely be successful. **And you can relax and watch your church move forward.**

Correct as necessary

What if somebody thinks God is telling them to do something that is clearly wrong? Then it is your job as pastor to correct them. And it is their job as a member of the church to accept that correction.

I remember the first time I did a study of how the Bible describes the pastoral role. I was amazed at how many times Paul told Pastors Timothy and Titus to correct, instruct, reprove and even rebuke their church members.

Correction is not an enjoyable part of the job. Some pastors even avoid such confrontations, for the sake of keeping peace. This rarely works. If someone thinks God is guiding them in ways that are contrary to Scripture or sound Christian practice, it will eventually lead to trouble, not only for them, but also for the church and for you. And **the longer you let it go, the worse the trouble will be.**

If you believe someone is in sin or error requiring a correction or rebuke, first make sure you are right. Verify the facts about what the other person is saying or doing. Then make sure it is indeed against Scripture or against God's clear direction for your church, and not just against your own opinion. When you speak, remember to speak the truth in love (Ephesians 4:15), with the emphasis on love. Think in terms of showing a child how to do something the proper way. And be sure to encourage them to try again. If they accept your correction, praise the Lord! If they don't, Jesus clearly laid out the steps to follow in Matthew 18:15-17. (I discuss this more in Chapter 17.)

Not Your Responsibility

As important as it is to know what your job is, it may be even more important to know what your job is not.

It's not your job to make everybody happy

Good pastors like people. When you like people, you want them to be happy. But you can't make everybody happy all the time. There are many issues in a church where Brother A likes things one way, and Sister B likes things another way. If you make Brother A happy, you make Sister B unhappy. **Not even Jesus made everybody happy all the time.** So don't worry about it. In fact, if some people discover that you are really concerned about keeping them happy, they will try to use that to control you and the church. Some of the biggest problems I have encountered in my ministry came when leaders in a church tried too hard to appease complainers.

People are usually happiest when they are comfortable, which usually means when they are doing the same things they have always done. But if we always do the same thing, we'll never grow, as a Christian or as a person. Somebody said, "If you always do what you've always done, you'll always get what you've always got."

Romans 12:2 says we are to be transformed. Transformation is change. Change makes many people unhappy. So sometimes your job as a pastor requires you to say and do things that will make some people unhappy. To be a faithful pastor, you have to say or do them anyway. **If you use wisdom and make sure the people know you love them, you will usually be alright.**

It's not your job to tell people what to do

In the late 1970s a movement called "shepherding" arose in many American churches. The basic idea was good: it was a time of revival in America and many new people were coming to Christ, including many young people without much experience in the world. Some pastors began to see it as their responsibility to help these new Christians make godly decisions, especially about important matters such as marriage, jobs, and buying a house. Unfortunately, what started as advice gradually became control. Church members were expected to come to their pastors or "shepherds" for guidance on every aspect of their lives, and follow their directions without question. This included such personal issues as what car to buy and even who to marry. Some pastors began to abuse this power. Many people left those churches or stopped going to church altogether.

There are no New Testament examples of authority figures in the church requiring obedience to their dictums, even in church business, much less in personal lives. Instead, the Bible says *Now our knowledge is partial and incomplete, and even the gift of prophecy reveals only part of the whole picture!* (1 Corinthians 13:9). When one person gives a word they believe to be from the Lord, others should weigh or judge it (1 Corinthians 14:29-31).

In the church age, no one person speaks infallibly for God – not even the pastor. God can use any Christian to speak God's word into a situation. Then God expects the hearers to weigh the word and compare it to the teaching of the Bible. Even the Apostle Paul accepted the freedom of other Christians to sharply disagree with him, except in matters of clear violation of Scripture (see Acts 15:37-39).

This means we should be careful about using Old Testament figures such as Moses and David as leadership examples for today. We can certainly learn from their methods of organization and dealing with people. But we can't follow them in demanding unquestioning obedience.

As a pastor, your goal is to help your people grow spiritually until they are like Jesus (Ephesians 4:11-13). One of Jesus' prime characteristics was his ability to hear from God. How can our people learn to do that if we are always telling them every detail of what to do?

As pastor, it is your responsibility to hear from God on behalf of the church you serve. It's not your job to take the place of the Holy Spirit for the individuals in your church.

74

It's not your job to do everything

Some pastors seem to feel that it is up to them to do everything around the church. Sometimes this is because they are not good delegators. Sometimes it's because they are perfectionists and feel that only they can do things right. Sometimes it's because they feel like they have to be constantly working.

The apostles served as pastors of the early Jerusalem church. When an issue arose around the food ministry, they didn't step in and take care of everything. Their response was, *"We apostles should spend our time teaching the word of God, not running a food program"* (Acts 6:1). Then they basically said, "Get a group together and deal with it yourselves."

If you are the founding pastor of a church of new converts, then for a time you may indeed be the only person who knows how to do the things that need to be done. But if you are a good pastor, you will be training and equipping your people for the work of ministry. Part of that training is to gradually give them responsibility for part of the work. **As your people mature and your church grows, you should be doing less and less of the routine work.** In fact, you should work toward the place where the only things you do are the things that only you can do. Your people should take care of the rest.

It's not your job to be served

I wish I didn't have to write this, but it's a sad fact that some pastors seem to feel they deserve all sorts of special honors and privileges, just because they are pastors. 1 Timothy 5:17 does say that preachers and teachers are to be held in special honor. However, this is to come from the people. **The Bible never says pastors (or anyone else) should demand to be honored.** In fact, just the opposite is true. We are to follow the example of Jesus, who washed his disciples' feet, and said, "The Son of Man came not to be served but to serve" (Matthew 20:28).

Points to Remember

- Your job is to equip God's people to do God's work until they resemble God's Son.
- Being faithful is more important than being popular.
- Minister to God, hear from God, and speak for God.
- Pray for the church, equip the church, and lead the church.
- Know what is not part of your job.

7

YOUR AUTHORITY AND ACCOUNTABILITY

You must teach these things and encourage the believers to do them. You have the authority to correct them when necessary, so don't let anyone disregard what you say. – Titus 2:15

Your Authority

Leadership experts talk about two kinds of authority: "positional authority," and "personal authority," sometimes called "moral authority."

Positional authority is the authority you have to make decisions or demand obedience because of the position you hold. In other words, people do what you say because you're the pastor. Different systems of church government give pastors different amounts of positional authority.

In some systems, if you are the pastor, you have the final say on every decision, without consulting anyone except God. In other systems you work together with a designated body of church leaders to discern God's direction. In some systems the pastor is given authority over a specific area such as worship or preaching, and a body of church leaders decides everything else. And in some systems the pastor is little more than an employee who is expected to submit to the direction of the church leaders in all points. In a later section we will look at different ways decisions are made in different church systems. For now, **it is important that you and your people are agreed about the amount of positional authority the pastor carries.**

Regardless of how your church is organized, **your real authority to influence and direct people comes from their perception of you as a person.** This is true to some extent in any organization, but especially so in voluntary organizations like a church, where if people don't respect you, they are free to leave.

Notice that I said "respect," not "like." People will grant you authority in their lives based on how they perceive your character, your relationship with God, your relationship with them and their friends, and your knowledge and ability. The more respect you earn, the more influence and authority you will have.

Making changes

Your influence and authority will be put to the test when you feel God leading you to change something. Some people see the smallest change as a major issue.

One woman came up to me after a worship service and said, "Pastor, you've changed everything!"

"I have?" I asked. "How?"

"The offering used to be after the sermon, and today it was before!"

Change makes most people uncomfortable. If you feel God is leading your church in a new direction, there are several things you can do to make it easier on everyone.

1. First and foremost, **cover the whole process in prayer.**

2. **Informally discuss** the idea with someone who shares your vision for the congregation, and let them begin planting seeds in conversation with others.

3. Use sermons to **lay the groundwork** for change. Usually this does

not mean proclaiming, "God told me he wants us to do this," although if God leads you to do it that way, go for it! More often it is better to use your sermons to show that your new direction is Biblical and timely. (If you can't support your idea from the Bible, you should re-examine whether it really came from God.)

4. At the right time, **present your idea** as an action proposal. The ideal is if your preaching leads others to suggest the same idea God gave you, but be ready to suggest it yourself if you need to. If possible, present it as something you're going to try for a while to see if it works, rather than as a permanent change.

5. **Expect resistance** to anything that is "not the way we've always done it," especially if you are not the founding pastor of the congregation.

6. **Know the stages of acceptance**. With every change, some people will be excited from the beginning, most will gradually come on board, and some will hold out until success is proven. Some may never accept it, and some may even leave the church. Prepare yourself and your leaders for that eventuality.

7. Finally, **remember that you can't force the church** to accept a change, even if it is from God. There are many sad examples of congregations using their God-given free will to refuse to accept God's new idea. That refusal often marked the beginning of decline for the church. If that happens to you, don't feel like a failure; even Jesus couldn't get most of the Pharisees to change their ways.

Sharing leadership

Sharing responsibilities in a leadership team is a good thing. Everyone has different strengths and passions. What may be drudgery for one person is a pleasure for someone else. This kind of shared leadership is valuable and important. I'll talk more about how to make it work in Part 3.

Some churches attempt to carry this idea to what I consider an unworkable extreme: two or more pastors with equal authority, with all decisions made by consensus. This sounds good in theory, but I've never seen it work well in practice. Inevitably something comes up where, for whatever reason, the leaders can't agree. What then? Sometimes "wait" or "do nothing" are not viable options.

Some people are just better leaders than others. No matter what the ideal says, the church folks are going to tend to follow one of the "equal leaders" more than the others. Or half the congregation will look to one pastor for leadership, and the other half to the other pastor. When a no-consensus situation arises, this divided loyalty can split the church.

The Bible has no example of successful shared leadership. When Paul and Barnabas tried it, they wound up splitting and going separate ways (Acts 15:36-40). Even the twelve apostles didn't share leadership equally. When a tough decision had to be made they looked to James (see Acts 15:6-21). There was always one person clearly in charge.

I'm not saying a church can't have more than one pastor. But **when you are one of several pastors or leaders, the different areas of responsibility must be carefully spelled out, preferably in writing.** You all must avoid trespassing on each other's roles, and there must be a clear, agreed-upon method for settling disagreements.

Your Accountability

Ultimately, as with all Christians, pastors are accountable to God. But **you'll avoid a lot of problems if you also have some clear line of accountability to people.** Some pastors claim that they are responsible only to God, and that they are the only ones who can properly hear from God. That is a recipe for trouble.

No one in the New Testament church claimed to hear infallibly from God. Rather, Paul tells us *we know in part, and we prophesy in part* (1 Corinthians 13:9 ESV). **Those who believe they are hearing from God should submit what they are hearing to others for verification** (1 Corinthians 14:29). Pastors are not exempt from this requirement.

Perhaps the biggest question that faced the New Testament church was the question of whether pagans were required to follow the Jewish law in order to become Christians. Acts 15 describes how it was settled. Peter, Paul, James and several other apostles and elders were there, including several whom God used to write the Bible. Yet none of them stood up and said, "You have to do it this way because I'm an apostle and I say so." No one said, "You have to do it this way because God told me." Instead, they talked, prayed and reasoned together, and together they reached a decision.

This doesn't mean you put all your decisions to a majority vote. You may decide God wants you to go ahead with something despite counsel to the contrary, as Paul did in Acts 21:10-14. But it does mean you should give serious prayerful consideration if Christians you respect believe you are hearing God wrong.

A clear line of accountability protects you as well as the church. In some churches, if you are the pastor, that means you handle the church's money. Or if you are counseling a young woman, you may be the first man to ever treat her with gentleness and compassion, and this may lead her to develop romantic feelings toward you. Pastors are human beings, and these temptations can be very strong. Knowing that someone will be holding you accountable, checking the financial records or asking about your relationships, can be a powerful help in resisting temptation.

Suppose you have done nothing wrong, but some suspicious or ill-intentioned person says you did. Later on we'll look at some practical ways to minimize the risk of such temptations and accusations. Even with the best systems in place, though, you can still be accused. An accountability system should have a clearly delineated process for dealing with such accusations, to protect you and to protect the church. This should include some way for knowledgeable, objective outsiders to investigate the allegations with such obvious integrity that reasonable people will accept their findings.

If there was actual wrongdoing, it is important that the church have a means of dealing with it. The church needs to be protected and healed, and the pastor needs to be disciplined and, if possible, rehabilitated (2 Corinthians 2:5-8). If the church does not fulfill its responsibilities in this area, often the only recourse is to the legal system of the nation. This invites the state to get involved in the internal affairs of the church. In my opinion this is never a good thing. It is much preferable if the church has an accountability system which can deal effectively with the situation (1 Corinthians 6:1-7).

What does that earthly accountability look like for you, the pastor? It depends on the system of church government your church follows. If you are in a system where the congregation chose or hired you, you are accountable to the congregation or its leadership body. If there is a bishop or presbytery or similar person or group in authority, you are accountable to them.

Every pastor needs someone who can hold them accountable beyond the people of their own congregation, even if there is not an official accountability channel. In certain cultures, or if you are the founding pastor of a church, positional authority can be very strong. The members may not feel they are able to confront you with unpleasant truths, even if you need to hear them. For your own spiritual protection, find or form a group of pastors who can hold each other accountable.

Points to Remember

- Being pastor gives you some authority, but being respected as a person gives you much more.
- Use your authority wisely, especially when you are changing things.
- Where there is shared authority, be sure everyone is clear about how that works.
- Clear lines of accountability protect you as well as the church.
- It is good to have someone beyond your own congregation who can hold you accountable.

8

YOUR PERSONAL LIFE

So whether you eat or drink, or whatever you do, do it all for the glory of God. – 1 Corinthians 10:31

Much to the surprise of some church folks, pastors are people, too. We have personal lives that are not necessarily all bound up in the church. You have personal time, personal money, a home, your health and your spirit to take care of. If you don't, you and your church will both suffer.

Your Time

Your time belongs to God. That doesn't necessarily mean it belongs to the church. Being a workaholic is no more laudable for a pastor than for any other profession.

In my experience, there is always more work than time. One of the most important things you can learn is how to prioritize your time. It's not enough just to cut out the bad things you shouldn't do, or even the useless things that just waste your time. **The problem is all the good things you feel you should be doing** – or the people in your church feel you should be doing.

The ideal schedule

I was told in seminary that to truly write a good sermon, you should spend one hour in preparation for every minute the sermon will last. If you preach one thirty-minute sermon every week, that's thirty hours a week in sermon preparation.

Everyone knows the ideal pastor spends at least two hours a day in prayer, and two hours a day reading the Bible, and two hours a day reading theology and history and current events.

Since one of your main jobs is helping your people grow like Jesus, every pastor should meet with at least three people every day for an hour each. And of course, you should lead at least two or three Bible studies and classes each week – counting preparation time, that's another two hours a day.

But how can your church grow if you aren't out meeting and talking with people who don't know Jesus? Certainly you should spend at least an hour every morning and afternoon on the streets talking to people as they go and come from work, as well as lunchtimes, and all day Saturday.

Then there are all the administrative details of running a church. To do that properly requires at least two or three hours a day.

Of course, one of the main duties of a pastor is to visit the sick, and those in prison, and those who are grieving. Add three hours a day for this, at least.

We haven't even mentioned meetings, with your leaders, other pastors, community leaders or government officials, and so on. Let's say three meetings a week, two hours each when you include preparation.

Add all that up and it comes to a minimum of 168 hours a week that you, as a good pastor, should be spending on your job. And there are 168 hours in a week. Perfect!

Of course, that leaves exactly zero hours for your family, for recreation, and for minor details like eating and sleeping. But who needs all that stuff? You're Super-pastor!

The reality

If you try to keep that schedule you might last about three days before you completely fall apart. **It's impossible for any human being to do all the things many people believe a good pastor should do. And God doesn't expect you to.**

That means two things. First, learn to hear God's priorities. If you are hearing God right, he won't tell you to do more than he designed a normal human being to be able to do. Second, don't allow yourself to feel guilty over the things you don't get done. If you listen to God and obey his guidance, you'll do the things God wants you to do, and that's all that counts.

I love the story in John 11 of Jesus raising Lazarus from the dead, but probably not for the reason most people do. I love the first part.

Lazarus, good friend and financial supporter of Jesus, is deathly ill. His sisters send a messenger to Jesus. "Lazarus is dying, come quickly!"

As a good pastor, what is your immediate response? Drop everything, of course, and rush to his bedside. That's what everyone expects you to do. You need to be there to pray. You need to be there to comfort the family. You need to be there to make sure Lazarus is ready to pass into eternity. How could a good pastor do anything else?

But what did Jesus do? He stayed where he was for two more days. Then he spent at least a couple more days on the road. By the time he finally got to Bethany, Lazarus had been dead and in the tomb four days.

Of course, we all know how the story ends. Jesus raises Lazarus from the dead. But what I find so freeing about it is that **Jesus didn't do what everyone expected him to do.** Instead, he prayed and found out what God wanted him to do. Then he did that.

Please don't misunderstand. This is an extreme example. The lesson is not to ignore your people's needs. If you have an emergency in your church, your place is with your people unless God specifically tells you otherwise. What I do want you to learn is to stop and give God a chance to specifically tell you. Ask God what he wants you to do. **Let God dictate your schedule,** not the expectations of people, including yourself.

Time management

God won't give you more than you can handle, but God does want you to handle things effectively. One important way of doing that is learning to properly manage your time. There are many systems, and many books that explain them, and different ones work best for different people. After more than thirty years in ministry, I'm still refining my time management and trying new things. It's not important which system you use, as long as it works for you. What is important is that you **develop a systematic way of keeping track of what you need to do**, so you can efficiently and effectively get it done.

I have a tendency to underestimate how long it will take me to do things. That means it's easy for me to over-commit myself. Before I realized this, it seemed I was always rushing, and always stressed out over things I hadn't completed.

One day when I was feeling this the most, the Lord led me to a verse that at first seemed completely unrelated. In Ezekiel 44, God describes what the priests are to wear when they are ministering in the temple. Verse 18 says, they shall not bind themselves with anything that causes sweat.

What did a Hebrew priest's wardrobe have to do with me? But as I prayed, I began to see something. God was saying he doesn't want me to bind myself, to commit or obligate myself, to the point that I'm sweating over whether I can get everything done. In the Old Testament **God didn't want his priests coming into his presence all hot and sweaty.** He doesn't want it in the church either.[i]

Pray through the day

One last word on the subject of your time. Martin Luther, father of the Protestant Reformation, reportedly said of his schedule one day, "I have so much to do that I shall spend the first three hours in prayer."

The busier you are, the more important is your prayer time. You can't use prayer as an excuse for not doing other things, but you need to use it as a preparation for them. Make a habit of mentally walking through each appointment and task of the day, holding it up before God for favor and blessing, asking for wisdom about priorities and preparation. You'll be amazed how much more smoothly your day will go. Time is like anything else: give the first fruits to God, and he will multiply it back to you.

Your day job

Not every church can afford to pay a pastor a full-time living wage. If you have an outside job, you owe your employer an honest day's work. You may be the only Christian your co-workers know. Your example will either draw people toward Jesus or push them away. Remember, you're not in the pulpit here. Your actions will speak louder than your words.

Your Home

You may own your own home. You may rent a house or apartment. You may live in a place the church owns or rents. You might even live in the church building. Wherever you live, **you need a place where you are not on the job.** "Pastor" is what you do, not who you are. You need a place where you can be who you are.

Policies and boundaries

When your church is your landlord, things can get complicated. When you are your church's landlord, things can get complicated. When the church has any involvement in your living situation, things can get complicated.

You can prevent a lot of complications if you **have clear policies, written down and agreed to ahead of time** by everyone involved. Who is responsible for getting the furnace repaired? Who has to buy a new oven if the old one breaks? Who picks it out? Who pays for it? Who decides when the walls need painted? Who decides what color? Who pays? If you have a clear policy about how to handle these things before something happens, it will make things much smoother when a situation arises.

You also need to **establish some boundaries between your work and your private life.** Especially if you are married, there are certain things you need to decide about your home. How will you balance hospitality against your family's need for privacy? How will you decide which people you will invite to your home for church business and which ones you will ask to meet you somewhere else? How much warning will you give your spouse before you bring someone home for dinner?

Is your home also your office, or do you have a separate place for church work? If you have a separate place, what do you do in each location? Which resources and books and records do you keep where? You might decide to use your home for work that requires quiet and concentration, such as prayer and study and writing, and use the office for meeting with people and doing administrative work. You might decide to do everything except church services at home. Or you might decide you want to do all your church work at the office, and keep your home as a sanctuary for you and your family.

The right answers to these questions will be different for everyone. They depend on your family, your home and church facilities, how long it takes you to get from one to the other, and your own personality. **Prayerfully consider these questions,** talk them over with your spouse and children if you are so blessed, and make some clear decisions. If you don't, you may find yourself falling by accident into practices that add unneeded stress.

Spiritual cleansing

About thirty years ago the church I was serving was going through some difficult times. New people with new ideas were coming into the church. Long-time members were happy to have the new people, but not their new ideas. Church meetings became stressful, and sometimes angry. I tried to play peacemaker in the meetings, but when I went home I often found that I was carrying the negative atmosphere with me. The result was that if one of the children started crying or my wife Paula needed some help, I would snap back in anger or stomp out of the house. One time I even punched a hole in a bedroom door with my fist!

As Paula and I talked and prayed about it one evening, we began to wonder if something spiritual was going on. We know that the devil tempts people into all kinds of evil desires and attitudes. We also know that the devil is a finite being. He has to delegate most of his dirty work to evil spirits or demons. 2 Timothy 1:7 mentions a spirit of fear. Could it be that I was being influenced by a spirit of anger? I knew I wasn't demon possessed. But **what if angry words at a meeting created a spiritual opening for angry spirits? And what if one of them attached itself to me?**

When I was a child I watched Popeye cartoons on television. When Popeye was trying to decide what to do, a little cartoon angel would appear on one shoulder, whispering in his ear, "Do the right thing." Then a little devil figure would jump on his other shoulder, whispering, "No! Do this wrong thing!" That's kind of how I pictured spirits of anger, or worry, or whatever.

If that was really what was happening, then according to Mark 16:17 I had the authority, in the name of Jesus Christ, to command that evil spirit to go away and leave us alone. Paula and I prayed, and decided to try it.

First we offered our house to God as a place set apart, a sanctuary where only things of God would be welcome. Then, with our children, we went through every room of the house, commanding all spiritual influences not of God to be gone in the name of Jesus, and inviting God's Holy Spirit to come fill the space (Luke 11:24-26). In the bedroom we prayed for a spirit of peace and rest, in the kitchen we prayed for health, in the living room for good fellowship and hospitality, and so on. We placed a dab of oil on the doorways to symbolize the presence of the Holy Spirit.

When we finished, we could already feel a difference. The house felt somehow brighter and more peaceful.

Having cleared ungodly spirits out of the house, now we needed to make sure we didn't accidentally allow any back in. We started doing what we called "cleansing." It's a **spiritual equivalent of washing your hands after visiting a sick person.**

Basically, whenever one of us returned home from being out, we stopped on the doorstep and said something like this: "In the name of Jesus Christ, anything not of God must be gone and may not come in here. Holy Spirit, please fill me with your grace and be with us. Hallelujah!"

Decades later we still follow this practice. It has made a huge difference in making our home a sanctuary of peace and rest in the Lord. When traveling, we spiritually cleanse hotel rooms in the same way. Of course, on occasion I still forget. I'm not home long before Paula senses that something is wrong. She'll ask me, "Did you remember to cleanse?" The difference is that real.

Whenever someone visits, after they leave we say a quick "cleansing" along the same lines, just in case something hitch-hiked into our house on them and stayed. (We never let our guests know we are going to do this.) Just to be on the safe side and so as not to be biased, we do that after anyone has visited, no matter who they are. We have even found it to be useful after a stressful telephone conversation, or after talking between ourselves about a difficult or painful situation in the church, or if we have watched something on television that introduces a negative atmosphere. Of course, we don't purposely watch bad things, but sometimes just watching the news can do it.

Do we believe ungodly spirits jump on our shoulders every time we go out? No. But I'm not very good at recognizing when one has, just as I'm not good at knowing when I get something dirty on the bottom of my shoe. Spiritual cleansing is an easy thing to do, so we do it every time, just in case.

Some may say it's all psychological. If you prefer to look at it that way, I don't mind. However you understand it, **we have found these steps to be of great value in making our home a sanctuary from the stress and negativity of the world.** I encourage you to find a way to do the same.

Your Health

In casual conversation we often use the same language to refer to spiritual and psychological issues. In this section I need to be a little more precise.

In 1 Thessalonians 5:23, Paul prays, *May your whole spirit and soul and body be kept blameless until our Lord Jesus Christ comes again.* You know what your body is: the physical part of you that interacts with the physical world, through your muscles and your five senses. Your spirit interacts with God and the spiritual realm, through prayer and spiritual discernment. What Paul calls your soul is the Greek word *psyche*, root of "psychology." It includes your emotions, intellect, memory, imagination and so on. It's how you interact with the realm of ideas and feelings.

The spirit, soul and body are three distinct parts of every human being, and we need to keep them all healthy.

When your body has a cold, your mind may have a hard time thinking. When your emotions are sad, your spirit may not feel like praying. Every part affects every other part.

I once heard a pastor talk about an experience he had just been through with his health. He mentioned how cars have gauges on their dashboard to report how they are doing: a fuel gauge, an oil pressure gauge, an engine temperature gauge, and so on. If all the gauges read within the acceptable range, then the car is in good shape.

This pastor said he had always believed that human beings have two gauges, a spiritual gauge that measures spiritual health, and a physical gauge that measures physical health. He worked hard at his relationship with God, and he worked hard at eating right and exercising, so he figured he was alright.

Then suddenly one day he had a total breakdown. After a long and slow recovery, he realized that there was a third gauge that he had overlooked: the emotional gauge. He learned that if we let our emotional reserves get too low, we lose our ability to deal with everyday situations. And he learned that replenishing your emotional reserves is like charging the battery in a car. If things are working right, the alternator in a car constantly recharges the battery as the car is driven. If the battery is allowed to drain, it can only be recharged slowly, using a "trickle charger" that trickles the electricity in a little at a time. In the same way, if you allow your emotional reserves to drain, they can only safely be charged slowly over time. He believes that the search for a quick jolt may explain why some pastors succumb to emotionally charged temptations.

91

As a pastor, you know about keeping up your spiritual life. There is plenty of advice available about how to stay physically healthy (although personally I must confess that I know it better than I do it). I would like to mention three quick things that I have found helpful with regard to keeping your emotional tank full.

First, **recognize what fills you and what drains you.** Some people and activities fill you with energy. You feel better when you are finished than when you started. Others drain energy from you. You have to work yourself up to face them, and recover when they are over. There is nothing wrong with this; it happens to everyone. A big step toward staying healthy is to recognize these differences and account for them. Make a list of the energizers and drainers, both people and activities. Arrange them in your schedule so you don't have too many drainers back to back. Schedule some energizers in between, or at least time for rest and recovery.

Second, **get enough rest**. Contrary to what our workaholic culture would have us believe, resting is not an unspiritual waste of time. American theologian Richard Foster said, "Sometimes the most spiritual thing I can do is take a nap." God made resting one of the Ten Commandments. After six days of creating the universe God himself rested (Exodus 20:8-11). So don't feel guilty about resting. Make time for it. It can be a pretty spiritual thing to do.

Third, **make yourself happy.** Some years ago my wife Paula was feeling kind of down about some things that had happened. She didn't want to keep feeling that way, and she didn't want to go to an expensive counselor or therapist. So she invented something she calls "Happy Therapy." "Happy Therapy" goes like this:

Step 1: Find something that makes you happy.

Step 2: Do it!

(I asked Paula to review my manuscript for this book. At this point, she wrote in the margin, "It worked!")

Depression can be a sign of a physical problem that needs medical treatment. But often it's just a matter of needing an emotional recharge. Never feel guilty about taking time to make yourself happy. Happiness is just a sign that you are emotionally healthy enough to do good ministry.

You can't effectively serve God, your church or your people if you are not healthy – physically, emotionally, spiritually, and in your relationships. Learn to rejoice in taking time for your health.

Your Money

John Wesley, founder of Methodism, said, "Earn all you can, save all you can, give all you can." At one time he was one of the best-selling authors in England, and consequently had one of the highest incomes, yet he died with little more than the clothes on his back – by his own choice. He consistently gave the rest away to those in need. He didn't leave much behind, but imagine his treasures in heaven!

Tithing

In 1976 I graduated from the University of Virginia with a degree in Systems Engineering. Two years later I left a good job with a good salary and moved two thousand miles to go to seminary so I could become a pastor. I had a wife and a baby. I went from a situation where I was able to live comfortably and save some money, to a situation where I had to truly learn how to depend on God.

As is common in America, most of the young mothers in our community and in our church worked at jobs outside the home. Early on, Paula and I prayerfully decided on another course. For our family, what Paula could give to our children by staying home full time with them was more important than whatever we could have bought for them if she took a job. We have never regretted that decision. It may not be right for everyone, but it was right for us.[ii]

Nonetheless, money was tight. Have you ever had to buy food for four teenage boys and a girl?

From the time we first got married we tithed our income. **We believed that if the Old Covenant required 10%, we who are in the New**

Covenant could not do less. Our understanding of Malachi 3:10 was that the tithe is the threshold, the minimum requirement that opens the windows of blessing.

We faithfully tithed through two years as an engineer at Ford Motor Company and three years in seminary. Then I became a pastor.

By this time we had two children. My income as a pastor was less than the official government poverty level. There reached a point when Paula and I started wondering whether we could afford to continue to tithe.

We recalled the old saying, "Time is money." I was putting all my time into the church and the ministry. Certainly that was worth something, we told each other. God knew our situation. Certainly he would accept my time in place of my money, wouldn't he?

We conveniently forgot that "time is money" is a quote, not from the Bible, but from Benjamin Franklin, the same person who said "God helps those who help themselves." God is not obligated to follow Ben Franklin's philosophies.

Anyway, we decided that instead of giving ten percent of my income to the church, the biblical tithe, we could cut it back to five percent.

We had thought we were in financial trouble before. Now the bottom completely dropped out. **It was only a few weeks before we decided we couldn't afford NOT to tithe.** So we started giving God his ten percent off the top once again, and somehow God rescued our finances. I didn't get a raise, we didn't receive some big gift, but somehow things got better.

That was over thirty years ago. We have never stopped tithing, and God has never stopped providing.

Actually, there was one other time when our personal finances got in very bad shape. We knew from experience that reducing our giving was not the answer. We decided to see what would happen if we increased our giving to God. After all, I had preached many times that you can't out-give God. So we increased our giving, and sure enough, it happened again: somehow, without any clear change that we could see, our financial situation cleared up. It's just like farming: **if you want a bigger harvest, you have to plant more seed.**

I'm sure you have heard many testimonies of God's faithfulness to those who tithe. I just want you to know that what I write here is not theory, but proven by personal experience. My financial security is not in a job or a bank account or a government program. My security is in the fact that I have put my faith in God, I have obeyed his commands, and I know he is faithful to fulfill his promises.

The question of **tithing to your local church can become confusing if you are the pastor**, especially if there is not a clear separation between your own money and the church's funds. What if you are the pastor of a brand-new church? Maybe it's not even really a church yet, just a group of Christian believers meeting together for fellowship and support and learning. You may be serving your church right now as a volunteer. You may even be paying the costs of the church out of your own pocket. How do you figure a tithe then?

You might be tempted to say, "I'm the pastor, any pay I get for pastoring comes from tithes and offerings, so if I tithe, am I not just tithing back to myself?" It may sound logical, but beware. It's just a short step to rationalizing accepting tithes from others, but not paying them yourself.

I don't want to be legalistic, and there are no hard and fast rules and definitions. But **for me personally, it's not really an offering to God if I retain control of it.** I believe it is very important, both for my personal spiritual health and for my pastoral example for my church, that there be no hint of a financial conflict of interest.

What I mean is this: it can be very tempting to find a way you can use your money for yourself but still call it a tithe. Make sure you give your tithe in a way that avoids this temptation. **No one should be able to accuse you of using God's money to benefit yourself.** If you control the church's money (which I do not recommend – see Chapter 17), give your tithe to a different ministry. If you have a group of leaders who oversee the money for your church, then you should tithe to the church. Be sure everyone understands that there are no strings attached. Your tithe should go into the same pot as all the other tithes and offerings, and be managed the same way.

It always amazes me how many people think pastors get rich from the offerings of their people, or from some kind of outside support. They may even think the pastor personally owns the church's property. There have always been people who sought worldly gain from religion, and the devil makes sure those are the stories the public hears. That's why your finances must be clear and above-board. I don't mean outsiders should have access to your personal financial records, but you should be able to answer legitimate questions and defend yourself against false accusations, should it ever become necessary.

Your people will watch to see what you do with your money. We are not to parade our giving before people to show off how spiritual we are. But as pastors it is important that our people know we don't just talk about God's faithfulness, we stake our lives on it. A leader is one who goes first and shows the way. Your people pray because you pray, and showed them the way. They read the Bible because you read the Bible, and showed them the way. And many will only give to the church if you give to the church, and show them the way.

Tithing is a difficult concept for many people, but the basic question is very simple. Am I going to obey God and trust him to fulfill his promises, or not? **If I only do the things that make sense to my human intellect, where is faith?** Tithing as a means of getting out of financial trouble doesn't make sense to my brain. But it's what the Bible says, so I do it. I've never known anyone who tried tithing in faith who was not blessed by the experience.

Pastor, you cannot afford not to tithe. You can't afford it financially, you can't afford it professionally, and you certainly can't afford it spiritually. Exactly how you calculate your tithe is something you need to prayerfully take up with God. But as a pastor, you must demonstrate the power of faith. Tithe!

Saving

Some people feel that saving money, especially saving to provide for the needs of old age, shows a lack of faith in God to provide. But Proverbs 6:6-8 tells us to learn from the ants. They store up food in summer to tide them over in winter. Many other Bible passages recommend wisdom and prudence.

God is the source of our security, but he uses earthly means, including savings, as the channel to provide for us. Emergencies can happen to anyone, and old age happens to almost everyone. Unless God clearly instructs you otherwise, always save a portion of your income to provide for yourself and your family in an emergency, or after you are unable to continue working.

Spending

In some traditions pastors take a vow of poverty. In others, pastors feel they should follow extravagant habits to demonstrate the abundance of God's provision. Most are somewhere in between. It seems to me you raise the fewest questions when your standard of living is about the same as that of most of the people in your church, or perhaps a bit more conservative.

When it comes to specific spending, I have always tried to follow a very simple rule: **ask God what he wants me to do.** If I prayerfully believe God wants me to buy something, I buy it. If I don't believe he wants me to buy it, I don't. Being married, of course, I always seek my wife's confirmation on these decisions, especially if it's a decision on which my natural desires might bias my ability to hear clearly from God. Matthew 6:33 promises that if we always seek to please God, he will always take care of us.

Protecting your money

It's important to **have clear boundaries between your personal money and church finances.** This can be very difficult if you are starting a church out of your home. Even if your church has a building or other property, many people will assume it belongs to you as pastor. If someone suffers some form of injury or loss related to the church, they may use legal means to try to force you personally to make reparations.

There are two ways to protect yourself from this kind of liability. The first is to make sure the church has appropriate insurance. If coverage designed for churches is not available in your situation, something similar to what is used by other kinds of religious or non-profit organizations, such as schools, may work.

The second way to protect your personal finances from liability is to establish the church as a separate legal entity. In America this is done by a process called incorporation – the same process used to protect the owners of small businesses. If a corporation, including a church, is sued, normally only the assets of the corporation are liable for judgment. The personal money and property of the pastor and other church leaders is protected. Look for something similar for your situation.

Your Sabbath

In American churches, people often joke that the pastor only works one hour a week – the length of many Sunday morning services. The reality, of course, is that one of the biggest problems for pastors is that they never stop working. We addressed this a little bit in the section on managing your time, but I'd like to look at it again from another perspective.

Jesus said, *The Sabbath was made to meet the needs of people* (Mark 2:27). In context, his point was that we are not to be legalistic about keeping the Sabbath. If you are like me, that's not the main problem. Right now, what I want you to see from these words is that God gave us the Sabbath for our benefit. If we don't keep a regular Sabbath time, we hurt ourselves, physically and emotionally as well as spiritually.

Technically, the Sabbath is from sundown Friday to sundown Saturday. That's the Jewish definition, and the Sabbath is a Jewish institution. In the early church, Christians started meeting on the first day of the week, which we call Sunday. They chose that day because it was the day of Jesus' resurrection. Most of the early Christians were Jews, and they continued to honor the Sabbath on Saturday. Then they met together on Sunday to celebrate "the Lord's Day." For most, this meeting was after work, since Sunday was just another working day in the early centuries of the church.

Many Christians of today think Sunday is the Sabbath, and if they try to follow the Sabbath rules at all, they apply them to Sunday. There is nothing wrong with resting and focusing on God on Sunday. It probably works very well for many people. But **for most pastors, Sunday is not a Sabbath of rest, it's a work day.**

Many pastors and church people haven't thought this through. If you consider Sunday your day of rest, that means you consider the other six days work days. If Sunday is actually a work day also, that means you don't have a day of rest. You are breaking the Fourth Commandment.

As New Testament Christians, we are no longer subject to the Old Testament law. That means we are not responsible for legalistically following Sabbath rules (Romans 14:5). But we still follow the Ten Commandments as basic principles, and Sabbath is one of the Ten Commandments. To my way of thinking, that means it is very important to God that you **regularly set aside one day every week for rest and reflection and special time with God.** Note that "rest and reflection" doesn't mean "catching up on all the other things you didn't get to through the week."

God's whole creation operates on rhythms. There's a warm season and cold season, rainy season and dry season, day and night. Light and other forms of energy vibrate in a rhythm we call "frequencies." Even the rocks are made up of atoms whose parts oscillate and vibrate in rhythms.

You are no different. You require a rhythm of work and rest. You can't rest all the time, but neither can you work all the time. You need both.

In the modern world, work is not necessarily physical activity. Many people work hard with their minds while barely moving their bodies. In the same way, rest is not necessarily lack of movement.

You rest your body every night by sleeping, but you also need a day every week to **rest your body by doing something different with it.** If your job requires a lot of physical work, rest may be sitting in a chair. But if your job requires hours of sitting in a chair, rest may mean doing something physical.

For me, Fridays are my "day off." That's when I spend time with my family, do things around the house, and so on. Years ago, after I learned that Sunday doesn't work as a Sabbath for a pastor, I considered Friday my Sabbath as well as my day off. But I found that Fridays quickly became filled up with family activities or chores around the house. These things are important, and you have to schedule time for them, but they are not Sabbath activities. So now I try to take Wednesday as my Sabbath day every week. For my church people, just to avoid confusion, I call it a retreat day or a prayer and study day. I try not to schedule any meetings on Wednesdays. If an obligation arises that I can't avoid, such as a funeral, I try to make up for it by taking Tuesday or Thursday for a Sabbath. I stay away from the office, and often I find it helpful to get away from home as well. A change of scenery can be very refreshing.

There is no one right way to take a Sabbath. **Find the way that works best for you.** Just be sure that one way or another, you take a day every week for rest and reflection and special time with God.

Be sure you take a full day. I have known some pastors who tried to take an hour this day to rest, and an hour another day to read, and half an hour on a third day to play a game, and tried to add all that up and call it a Sabbath. I don't believe that is what God has in mind. It doesn't provide the rest you need for your body or your soul. You need a full, continuous day.

You might object, "But what if someone needs me that day? What if a non-believer comes by the church to talk about Jesus, and I'm not there? I don't want anyone to go to hell because I wasn't on the job!"

Part of that objection is valid. If possible, try to be available when people are most likely to need you, and take your Sabbath when they are least likely – for instance, when most people are at work. Of course, if you also work a regular job with normal hours, this may be difficult, but pray about it and God will guide you.

The other part of that objection is exactly the reason God instituted the Sabbath in the way he did: it requires you to trust God for something that doesn't make sense to our human way of thinking. One of the most visible ways Israel was set apart from the surrounding nations was that they refused to work on Saturdays, even if the olives needed picking, or the grapes needed to be pressed, or the hay was going to get rained on. They trusted that if they obeyed God about the Sabbath, God would take care of them and their families – even when they felt that, as good farmers, they really should be out in the fields. In the same way, as pastors we need to trust that **if we obey God about keeping a Sabbath, God will take care of our churches** and potential new believers, even when we feel that, as good pastors, we really should be in our office or by our phone. Of course, if an emergency comes up, you respond (Matthew 12:11-12). But everything related to the church is not an emergency.

One more quick note: in addition to a weekly rest day, it is important to take regular vacations or holidays as well. In the Old Testament, God commanded his people to take several weeks every year for celebrations or "feasts." They were to do no work, but relax and enjoy themselves.

An occupational hazard of pastors is that we often come to feel that we are indispensable. Psychologists say it takes two weeks away to fully achieve the necessary mental and emotional benefits of a vacation. Many pastors fear that the church will fall apart if they go away for two weeks. Actually, the opposite is true. **One of the best ways for your people to learn and grow is to be left on their own for a short time.**

Once I was away from my church for three months. I arranged with nearby pastors to be available in case of an emergency, such as the need to conduct a funeral. Otherwise, the members of the church were responsible for everything, including conducting church services. They were very nervous when I announced the plan, but when I came back, several of them remarked, "The greatest thing that ever happened for my spiritual growth was when the pastor went away."

Take your Sabbaths. Your church will survive.

Your Spirit

It's not unusual for pastors to spend so much time caring for other people's spirits that they neglect their own. You pray for other people; be sure to pray for yourself. You listen to church members; be sure to listen to God. You read the Bible to prepare your sermons; be sure to read the Bible to feed your spirit. You challenge those who think they know all about God; be sure you keep seeking to know more of God. You urge others to regularly examine their hearts and lives; be sure you regularly examine your own.

Ministry is hard. It's so easy to make excuses. "I can't take time to pray and read the Bible right now. The people need me!" We can even feel noble about the sacrifices we are making for the sake of our church. But God said obedience is better than sacrifice (1 Samuel 15:22). That includes obeying God commands to wait on the Lord and be filled with God's Spirit (Psalm 27:14; Ephesians 5:18).

One of the Bible promises few people want to claim is John 16:33, In the world you will have tribulation. Sometimes this seems doubly true for pastors. We'll talk about dealing with problem people and situations in Chapter 19. The point for now is to not let them get you down.

We already looked at the importance of keeping yourself healthy and strong spiritually, physically and emotionally. When you are right in these areas, you have a head start on dealing with discouragement.

Getting discouraged is not a failure. Staying discouraged is. So how do you deal with discouragement?

If you are a pastor, I can promise that hard and unfair things will happen to you. You may feel that you have a right to be discouraged. But before you indulge in a pity party, consider David. One day, before he became king, he and his men returned from patrol to find their houses burned and their wives and families taken captive. Everyone was devastated. The men were so upset they were ready to stone David. But 1 Samuel 30:6 says, David strengthened himself in the Lord his God.

The Bible doesn't tell us exactly how David strengthened himself. But Paul, who knew a bit about discouragement himself, gives us an outline in

Philippians 4:4-8.

Always be full of joy in the Lord. I say it again—rejoice! Let everyone
see that you are considerate in all you do. Remember, the Lord is coming
soon. Don't worry about anything; instead, pray about everything. Tell
God what you need, and thank him for all he has done. Then you will
experience God's peace, which exceeds anything we can understand.
His peace will guard your hearts and minds as you live in Christ Jesus.
And now, dear brothers and sisters, one final thing. Fix your thoughts
on what is true, and honorable, and right, and pure, and lovely, and
admirable. Think about things that are excellent and worthy of praise.

Here are the steps I see in these verses:

Verse 4: Rejoice in the Lord. If you can't rejoice about your situation,
rejoice about something else: past blessings, or Bible promises, or the love
of your family, or the beauty of a flower. Listen to some uplifting music,
or even better, sing. Find something that points you to the goodness and
faithfulness of God, and focus on that. And act like you're rejoicing, even if
you don't feel like it. Do you think Paul and Silas felt like singing hymns,
shackled in that dank Philippian jail with their backs bleeding from the
whip? (Acts 16:25) Of course they didn't. But they determined that they
were going to rejoice in God in spite of the circumstances, and God gave
them a miraculous deliverance. *The joy of the Lord is your strength* (Nehemiah
8:10).

Verse 5a: Be gentle. Discouragement can make you want to lash out at
people or do rash things. Don't give in to those urges. Gentleness is strength
under control. As you remain gentle, the strength that discouragement saps
will begin to return. And often we become discouraged because we feel we
have failed somehow, so don't forget to be gentle with yourself.

Verse 5b: Remember that the Lord is near. God hasn't abandoned
you, even though it may feel that way. Remind yourself that God loves you,
God is with you, and God will care for you.

Verse 6: Turn your worries into prayers. Worry says, "Oh, what if this and this and that?" Prayer says, "Dear God, please handle this and this and that." Tell God your problems and thank him that he's going to take care of you.

Verse 7: Continue until the peace comes. A hundred years ago, American Christians used to talk about "praying through." Pray through the doubt, pray through the discouragement, pray through the darkness until the peace, the light or the answer comes. When you compare the size of your problems to the size of your God, you can't help but find peace.

Verse 8: Protect against future discouragement. Encourage yourself by focusing your thoughts on good things, positive things, things of God. Habits of thought are just like any other habits; they can be formed and broken. Develop the habit of refusing to allow yourself to entertain negative or discouraging thoughts. You can't keep the thoughts from coming, but you don't have to entertain them – or as somebody put it, "You can't stop the birds from flying over your head, but you don't have to let them build a nest in your hair." As soon as you notice a worry or a negative thought, tell it to go away in the name of Jesus. Then consciously start thinking about something positive and godly. Learn to renew your mind in the Lord and it will transform your life (Romans 12:2).

The devil wants you to stay discouraged, because when you are discouraged you aren't ministering as effectively as you can. So the devil will tell you you're a failure, or everybody hates you, or you're the only one who has ever felt this way. Most of all, he'll tell you that you can't let anybody else know how you feel. Don't listen to those lies. **One of the most helpful things you can do is find someone you can trust,** perhaps another pastor who will understand your situation, and share your story and your prayers with them.

Many places in the Bible give helpful examples. For instance, many psalms start with complaints but end with faith. I encourage you to do your own study of how people in the Bible strengthened themselves. Preach a sermon on those principles, because pastors aren't the only ones who face discouragement. Then practice what you preach.

Points to Remember

- Your time belongs to God; let him direct how you spend it.
- Your home is your own private space, even if the church provides it to you.
- You can serve God best if you are healthy spiritually, mentally, emotionally and physically.
- Trust God to guide your finances; he's better at it than you are.
- Take one day out of seven to rest from your work.
- Care for your spirit.

[i] This is not intended as an example of proper Biblical exegesis. Clearly, my stress level is not what Ezekiel had in mind when he wrote those words. But it is an example of how God can find ways to speak to those who are sincerely seeking to hear from him.

[ii] In some situations it may be better for the wife to work and the husband to stay home with the children. Often it is necessary for both husband and wife to work. The point of this section is not about who works and who doesn't, but about God's faithfulness in providing for our financial needs.

9

YOUR FAMILY

Do not provoke your children to anger by the way you treat them. Rather, bring them up with the discipline and instruction that comes from the Lord. – Ephesians 6:4

God does not require pastors to be married, though most are. If you don't have a family of your own, I hope this chapter will help you understand and support those who do.

Your Spouse

When I talked about managing your time I added up 168 hours per week of potential church work, leaving no time for family or anything else. You might have laughed when you read it, but I bet your spouse and children wouldn't. It's not good when your family feels like they have to compete with the church for your time and attention. Your priorities are God first, then your spouse, then your children, then your church. **Some pastors make the mistake of confusing the church with God. That's called idolatry.**

Some pastor's spouses see their position in the church as a ministry to which they feel a strong call. They may even serve as co-pastors. Other spouses, especially if they have their own career, see the church as strictly the pastor's job. Some knew they were marrying a pastor from the beginning. Others, like my wife, had to adjust to a call in mid-life that suddenly thrust them into something they never expected. Some have young children at home who require all their time and attention. Others have older children, or none. These differences can lead to large variations in how much the pastor's spouse is involved in the church.

Contrary to what some churches seem to think, when someone marries a pastor they don't miraculously learn to play the piano and lead a ministry. Never let your spouse feel obligated to meet the expectations of the church people. **No one should be made to feel that they have to do something they're not comfortable with, or act in a way that seems unnatural to them, just because they happened to be married to a pastor.** The lesson about Jesus and Lazarus applies to your spouse as much as you. One of the best things pastors can do for their spouses is to let them know that they will support their priorities and protect them from unrealistic expectations.

Your Children

In America, pastors' children have a bad reputation. The stereotype of a pastor's child is a rebellious troublemaker. When they grow up, many pastor's kids won't have anything to do with the ministry, or even the church. How does this sad situation happen?

Some pastors too often allow church business to take them away from doing things with and for their children. Some pastors too often tell their children they have to behave in certain ways or participate in certain events "because you're the pastor's child." Either of these can cause a child to resent the church – and by extension, resent God. Acting rebellious is a natural reaction.

God does not condone child sacrifice. That includes sacrificing your children on the altar of your church work.

My wife Paula and I have been blessed with five children. They are all grown now, and they are all strong and active Christian believers. Besides God's grace and our constant prayers, I'm convinced that one of the main reasons none of them rebelled against the church is that I always put my family first, and they knew it. Any of them will tell you I spent plenty of time on church work. They will also tell you that I made a point to give each child plenty of one-on-one attention. And I never told them they had to do a certain thing or act a certain way because of my job. I just tried to be as much like Jesus as I could, and they saw that.

Does that mean some church things didn't get done? Certainly. Did that hinder the advancement of God's kingdom? Perhaps a little. But in the long run, **I'm convinced the kingdom of God will advance much more through the ministries of my children than it would have if I had worked so hard and long in the church that it drove my children away.**

Your Example

Your family knows you better than anyone else. If they hear you preach about love and forgiveness, but at home you are harsh and demanding, or too exhausted from church work to give them the attention they need, what are they going to think about this God you serve? **Your Christian example starts at home.**

There's also a ministry side to how you treat your family. The people in your church are going to be watching you carefully to see what a Christian family should look like. Jesus said people will know we are Christians by how we love one another (John 13:5). What better place to demonstrate that than in your family?

Love shows itself in affection, protection, provision and respect. Let your people see (in an appropriate way, of course) that you are affectionate toward your wife and children. Let them see that you will protect your family from harm and intrusion, including the intrusion of too much church work. Let them see that you recognize the importance of providing for your family's needs. And let them see that you respect your wife and your children.

Notice I said, "let them see," not, "let them hear in your sermons." **Never use members of your family as sermon illustrations unless you get their permission first.** You don't want your family reluctant to come to church for fear you might embarrass them.

A Letter from My Wife

A young pastor's wife, who had moved with her husband to another city, wrote a letter to my wife asking some advice. With their permission, I'm including an edited version of that exchange.

> Dear Mrs. Wentz,
>
> How are you? I was just thinking about you this week and wishing we got to see you more. I am always telling people how lucky and thankful I am to know you.
>
> We've been having a lot of drama here lately. Actually, I'm sure there's always been drama, it's just that when you are the pastors you hear ALL of it. Sometimes it just seems like so much to deal with, plus it's hard seeing everyone all the time when you know stuff you wish you didn't. I know Pastor Wentz has been doing this for about 30 years, which means you've been right there with him. How do you deal with all the drama happening all the time? Does he tell most of it to you, or do you ask to not know everything? Is it hard for you to interact with people when you know stuff about their lives, sometimes things they don't know you know, sometimes things that they know you know, but that upset you?
>
> And also, how did you get spiritually filled up when your kids were really small? At just about every meeting we go to I'm babysitting the kids or trying to keep them quiet so they don't distract people. Even at the women's meetings I have the baby and have to nurse him during the meetings and stuff. And sometimes it's just as hard to enter into God's presence at home where there's

always so much noise and activity. So I was wondering what you did to get filled back up when you're always giving all the time.

I'd really appreciate it if you have any helpful tips.

Here's Paula's answer:

It is awfully hard sometimes to be married to a pastor. Sometimes it's better than others, sometimes it's VERY difficult, and sometimes, it's great. Like where we are right now, I'm loving it; I think maybe God gave us a nice place for a breather after the last one, but I'm also very cognizant that there are no guarantees, that anything could change at any time. I think the key is in, is it Philippians 4, where it talks about being content in any circumstance? I remember Rick Joyner referring to times of being abased and times of abundance, and being content in any of them. But that's not really what you're asking.

It varies according to the circumstances, as to what David tells me about people in the church. At one previous church, I was aware of EVERYTHING, mostly because David really needed to be able to talk to someone he trusted. Of course, he didn't tell me anything said in confidence in counseling situations, but pretty much everything else. That was hard on me, but I think it was better than if I had not known anything. We were able to help each other grow through the circumstances, and help each other stay focused on God. The biggest thing that helped me when I knew things about people that indicated they were not living up to the fullness of what they should be in Christ, was two things, actually. The first was to **keep my eyes on Jesus.** The second was, when I was tempted to look at someone else's sin, to turn instead and look at myself and how far I am/was from what I should be, and to begin to ask God's forgiveness for myself. It takes a lot of will power, and sometimes I could only begin to do this after I had allowed myself the freedom to express my own human responses

110

to David (but never anyone else in the church). **I think a lot of the circumstances we encounter in life are really mostly irrelevant in the big picture, but HOW we respond to them is vitally important.** And we have to be constantly seeking to see Jesus, and to love others as He does.

I have to admit, that I find this much easier now than ten or fifteen years ago. Many of the things you ask don't have hard and fast rules. A lot you'll just learn as you go through it and are able to say, "God, WHAT do I do now?" And **it may be different in different times.** At another church, I checked David's email for him to alert him to urgent things (this was before he spent a lot of time on email) - it was an important help for him, but it also brought me more stress. Now, he takes care of it all, and I am so much happier not to know things. So basically, I let him determine how much I need to know. If he seems to need to unload and share things with someone he knows won't talk to anyone else, then that's where I am. Otherwise, I'm happier not knowing things - UNLESS it is something that would impact the safety of myself, or the kids when they were home. For instance, someone he was counseling who might come to the house - I would need to know any possible safety related issues. Or, and this is a sticky one, because you never really know, if someone thinks that because they told David something, they think I know also. Then, if I see them, I would need to know to ask after them, but that can get really sticky because you don't always know what people's expectations are. So I generally don't let on that I might know something specific that is going on in their life, but try to ask open ended questions after their health or whatever, that gives them an opportunity to share if they want, and they know that I care about them. It's really tough, and again, something that you just have to ask God about in each situation, because they all vary. But generally, if you are guided by love and seeking to love others, you do the right thing.

It's really important to practice separating yourself and the family from the church. And especially, **continuing to maintain the atmosphere of a sanctuary in your house.** There are so many negative spiritual influences that will try and destroy your peace, as well as just the everyday stresses. One of the very biggest things that God showed us was to cleanse off those things before entering the house. I'm sure you've heard us talk about this - to command things that are not of God to be gone from any influence around us, to speak death to germs and bacteria and viruses, and to invite the Holy Spirit to cleanse us and surround our home with his presence. We did this whenever we came home from being anywhere (you pick up things even at church…). We do this even now, recognizing when one of us forgets, usually by a sense of a negative spiritual presence. This just helps in general in keeping everyone at peace at home, but also giving you that foundational base at home where you can regenerate and rest your spirit.

You know, you ask about how hard it is to interact with people when you know things that upset you. Yes it is. Again, I think the answer is love. (More and more, I'm hearing from God that it's all about love. And there is so much that I don't know about it, but at least I know this: God is Love. And that is so central to everything in the Christian life.) It applies even within our own families. Sometimes I have to forgive, again recognizing my own falling short of where I should be as a Christian, and love as Christ loves. As I begin to feel that kind of love, which is different from my love as a wife or mother or sister or daughter, I feel the pain and my heart aches for the other person, in love. **To see through the eyes of Christ brings it to a different plane,** a different reality, one which I think connects with the heart of God.

So yeah, if you need to vent about some of these people, do so to your husband, but probably not other people, and then I would suggest that you pray together for them. A good rule that usually does apply to every situation is that **if you talk about**

112

someone or some situation, ALWAYS end it with prayer for that person, along with a cleansing for yourself and asking God to keep you close to Him even in having to deal with those things, and asking Him to help you see them with His love.

You ask about the kids, and that's a tough one, too. When you have more than one child they can be a handful. When our kids were little, I purposefully did not do many things at the churches because I saw the kids as my primary responsibility. **The things at church might or might not get done, but I felt like I was the one who was there to meet the needs of the kids.** During those years, it was extremely difficult to get anything out of church for myself. Because you're always trying to keep track of the kids. So I basically decided that **it was more important for me to make the kids' experience at church one where they could connect with God.** I didn't try so much for myself, but instead tried to hold them, and let them develop that sense of peace in the Lord's presence through the comfort of sitting peaceably with me. Rather than fighting with them, I tried to provide them with things that would enable them to sit and enjoy (a lot of food!!!!), and then, if they were beyond their capabilities, I would go in another room with them and play, or sit while they played. A lot of times I got very frustrated. I couldn't see how I was possibly growing or being of any help. And I thought it would last forever. But I think that God blessed that time - first, with the kids, I think they developed a fairly healthy desire to know God because they knew him in peace and love in their experience in church. But I think God also blessed me through it in ways that I'm still not aware of, but in other ways that I am now beginning to recognize.

From what I've seen, you and your husband seem like great parents. You both have a very patient attitude towards the kids. The biggest encouragement I can give you is that **even though it is really hard right now, it won't last forever.** You two have such a desire to seek God and follow him, and I know that as you continue to do that, he will guide you in the specifics of how to get through all these frustrations. In another six months, you'll find it completely different. But it can be very difficult - as I said, there were a LOT of times I was extremely frustrated, and when we added the stresses of the church to the stresses of raising little kids, well, there was a reason we discovered the importance of spiritual cleansing before coming into the house - because it was all coming out as anger and negative behaviors.

If you ever get a chance to get away to a women's conference or something, I encourage you to do it – times like that can be lifesavers. Make sure your husband knows how important that is to you.

One of the things that had the biggest impact on my own ability to spend some time with God was when David began getting up with the kids and taking care of them in the mornings while I had some alone time in the bedroom. I'm not saying this will work for everyone, but for our schedules, it worked. He got up with the kids. I think they could pretty much get their own cereal. Then, everyone understood that Mom was not to be disturbed. So I could sit there in my bedroom, with the door closed, and even though I might hear some yelling or crashing of dishes, I wasn't responsible for it. It was exactly what I needed in order to cope at that time. I ate in peace, I had a little time with God, and then I could come out and take over with the kids. Then, David went off to have his quiet time, and went off to the church. So **maybe there is some time where your husband could be with the kids while you have some time alone at the house.**

You know, I think the biggest thing that helped me come through those years was the fact that David prayed for me, and sought God so deeply. At the time I might not have understood it as well, but now, looking back, I KNOW that anything good that has come out of us has been due to his prayers. So, I encourage you to **ask your husband to pray for you and your ability to cope**

with these demands. God will honor those prayers. And, for the same reason, I encourage you to **pray for him.** Because your connection with God is deep, and God will honor your prayers.

We'll continue praying for all of you, for God's blessings and love to surround you.

I hope this was helpful - it was nice just sitting here and answering it - almost like a visit.

Love,

Paula

Points to Remember

- Your responsibility is to God, your spouse, your children, and your church, in that order.
- God does not want you to sacrifice your family on the altar of your church work.
- The most effective way of teaching your people how to treat each other is letting them see how you treat your family.
- Never use your family as sermon illustrations without asking them first.
- Try to understand the pressures your ministry puts on your spouse and children, help where you can, and let them know how much you appreciate it.

10

MOVING ON

I planted the seed in your hearts, and Apollos watered it, but it was God who made it grow. – 1 Corinthians 3:6

Perhaps you serve in a tradition like mine, where a bishop moves pastors from church to church, matching needs with gifts. In other traditions, local congregations hire their pastors (and fire them), and pastors have the freedom to move as they wish. Perhaps your plan is to start a church, raise up someone to pastor it, then leave and do it again somewhere else. Even if you hope to never leave your church, one day you will become unable to do the work. How do you know when it is time to move on? How do you prepare yourself and your church?

When to Leave

Sometimes the decision of when to move on is made for you by someone in authority, or by your health or other personal situation. In most cases, however, you will need to go through a process of discernment. Even when the decision belongs to someone else, you have to know whether God wants you to accept it or try to change their minds. I strongly encourage an annual retreat to seek God about his direction for your ministry. Make this one of the questions you pray about.

For some pastors, the very idea of leaving a family of believers is almost unthinkable. You have poured your life into these people. It may feel like giving up, being defeated, even betraying a sacred trust. This attitude can be very helpful when you are called to persevere through difficult times in ministry. But it can become a hindrance if God really is calling you to something new.

The apostle Paul rarely stayed at one church for more than a year. Barnabas, pastor of the church in Antioch (Acts 11:22-24), moved on to plant other churches (Acts 13:1-3). **Paul recognized that different pastors might be appropriate for different stages in a church's life.** He wrote, *I planted the seed in your hearts, and Apollos watered it, but it was God who made it grow* (1 Corinthians 3:6).

I had been at my first church a little over three years when the bishop decided to move me to another congregation. I had grown to love the people, and as their pastor I felt God had given me a responsibility for them. But as I prayed about it, God showed me that I needed to widen my view.

If God, through the bishop, was calling me to become pastor of another church, that meant he was shifting my responsibility to the people of the new church. And God would not abandon the people of my old church. He would provide the right new leader to fulfill his plans for them.

This perspective helped me see beyond my own local church, and helped me be more objective later in my career when the time came to move again.

Sometimes the impetus to consider a move will come from a sense that your work in your current place is finished. You may feel that you have given the people all you have to give – or all they are willing to receive. If one day you find yourself really relating to Jesus' words about casting pearls before swine and shaking dust off your feet, maybe that's what is happening. Be very careful here. It could be time to move, but it could just be that you need a break, like the three month leave I mentioned in Chapter 8. **It would be a shame to give up on a good ministry just because your soul and body are exhausted.**

It may begin to seem that the people's vision for the future of their

117

congregation has moved in a different direction from your own, to the point where the two can't be brought back together. This doesn't necessarily mean somebody is wrong. It could be that God really is calling you and your congregation in different directions. If that's the case, God has someone in mind to lead the church where he wants it to go, and he has a place for you that will fulfill what God is calling you to do.

Sometimes the impetus to move has nothing to do with your current church. Things may be going great. But somehow you begin to feel drawn to something else – another church, another place, another form of ministry. Being drawn to a new ministry is an exciting and positive feeling, but it requires careful discernment. Is it a call from God, or a temptation from the evil one?

Depending on the way your church works, another congregation may ask you to leave your church and come work with them. An authority such as a bishop may tell you your skills are more needed in another congregation. Or you may feel that God is calling you to become an evangelist or a counselor or a teacher or a writer, rather than a local church pastor.

You don't want to run when God is calling you to stand. But what if God wants you to go? You don't want to stay and waste your gifts on a church that will not receive them. You don't want your continued presence to become an obstacle to God's next move in that place. And you don't want to deprive a potential new congregation of what God wants to do through you there.

Figuring all this out calls for great spiritual discernment. When things get tough, you have to know if God is calling you to stay and fight the spiritual battle, or make room for someone else, whose gifts and graces may be better suited to what the church needs right now. How do you know for sure?

Avoid talking about this with anyone in your own local church, at least initially. They are too close to the situation to see it objectively. They may have an agenda of their own. The best they can probably do is tell you what they think you want to hear. Instead, **find a small group of spiritually mature Christians from outside your church who can help you accurately discern God's direction** in this matter. It's best if at least some of them are pastors or Christian leaders who have been through similar situations in their own lives.

Finally, if you stick it out long enough, there will most likely come a time when you will retire. **Retiring from actively leading a church does not mean retiring from God's work.** God always has something for his people to do. For me, it was writing. I never seemed to be able to set aside time to write while I was the full-time lead pastor of a church. I felt God leading me to take early retirement so I could make that time. Other pastors volunteer as hospital chaplains or teachers. Others feel called to just spend time with God, through gardening or art or reading or travel or just sitting in God's presence. Don't feel guilty if that's what you wind up doing. After all, being with God is what we were created for. The key is, don't retire just because you feel worn out, or to get away from something. **Retire to something.**

How to Leave

I was once appointed as pastor to a church where the previous pastor was retiring after thirty-four years with that one congregation. When he started about thirty people attended each week. When he retired the average attendance was over six hundred. Many of those people had never known another pastor. His children had grown up in that church and were still active there, now bringing his grandchildren. He owned a home in the neighborhood. He loved that church, and he would never do anything to hurt it.

But he couldn't let go. Publicly he turned over the reins to me, but privately he continued to meet with people. He continued to mentor church leaders. And naturally, they continued to see him as their pastor, instead of me. When I made decisions or tried to lead the church in ways that were different from what he would have done, people resisted. Eventually that pastor and one of the key leaders of the church left and started a new church down the road. Almost half the people, and most of the leaders, went with them. A few years later the bishop moved me to a different congregation. Years later that church, that my predecessor loved so much and in which he invested so much of his life, continues to decline.

When you leave a church, leave. If God says stop being pastor of a congregation, stop. Trust God to take care of your old church; he won't move you until he has a plan for them. But that plan no longer includes you. If you stay around or keep coming back, you'll just get in the way of God's new plan. And you won't be available for what God wants to do with you.

There is one exception to this rule. Sometimes it works and sometimes it doesn't. That exception is when the long-term pastor of a church chooses and trains and grooms the new pastor. This process should be done carefully, prayerfully, with the full input of the other leaders of the church. It should take several years. During this time the retiring pastor should gradually turn over more and more authority and responsibility to the heir apparent, including preaching responsibility. Long before you officially step down, your successor should essentially be running the church.

When the day finally comes, have a big celebration. Perform some ritual or symbolic act, such as handing your successor your keys to the church office, to indicate the transfer of authority. Then stay out of the way. Don't talk to anyone unless your successor asks you to. Don't give advice unless your successor asks you for it. Even if you disagree with something, keep your mouth shut. Otherwise you can split the church.

Someone may ask, "What if I move on to another role? What if we all agree that I will turn over my day to day duties as pastor to someone else, but I will stay in the local congregation with a different ministry, perhaps using this church as a base for a traveling ministry of teaching or church planting or supervising other pastors?"

In theory that sounds good. However, I have never seen it work well. You are used to doing certain things and making certain decisions. If you remain in the same place, with the same people, simple human nature says it will be very difficult to stop doing those things and making those decisions, especially if people keep asking you to. And they will ask you to, because they are used to asking you. They know you know how to do it. They know you can probably do it faster and better than the new person.

You tell yourself you're just helping out. But what you are really doing is undermining the authority and confidence of the new pastor, and blocking their opportunity to grow into the job. And you're taking time away from the new thing God has called you to do.

If you are moving into a new form of ministry, even if you will continue to be affiliated with the church you had led, it is best for all concerned if you make a clean break in a new location.

No matter what the circumstances of your departure, **leave a blessing behind.** I saw a cartoon showing a pastor in his pulpit, with bags packed near the door and a waiting taxi visible through the window. The pastor was saying, "I've wanted to preach this sermon for a long time." Don't use your last sermon to defend yourself or "tell off" people who gave you trouble. That won't help the church. It will only make you look bad.

Instead, use your last days and weeks to bless people. Personally thank people for being part of the church, and for specific things they did that were helpful. Encourage them to support the new pastor, for the good of the church.

Go to your office and try to think like a new pastor coming in. What would you need to know? Organize things. Make lists. Throw stuff out. **Your successor will be building on the foundation that you laid, so make it as easy as possible to build well.**

Resist the temptation to warn the new pastor against certain church members. You may have had a bad time with them, but your successor might have a very different experience.

It's very important to make a public statement to the effect that, while you have been blessed and honored to be the pastor of this church, from this point on you are the pastor no longer. Encourage people to look to the new pastor for their spiritual needs and church leadership. Tell them you will not interfere. Then honor that word.

After all, **if God no longer needs you to pastor this church, he must need you someplace else. So get to it!**

When the Pastor Has to Be Removed

This is a difficult section to write.

One church I served had two services every Sunday morning, with a time for refreshments in between. We also hosted another congregation in another part of our building. One Sunday, during the refreshment time between services, the wife of the pastor of the guest congregation called me into another room and told me her husband was in jail. He had been arrested the night before for a serious crime.

Pastors are human beings. We are subject to the same frailties and temptations as anyone else. **Sometimes pastors fall.** And if the fall is serious enough, the pastor may have to be removed.

No one is immune. 1 Corinthians 10:12 says, *If you think you are standing strong, be careful not to fall.* Every local church or association of churches needs to **prayerfully create a written policy detailing the steps to take if there is a credible accusation of serious wrongdoing** on the part of a pastor. Do this before the situation arises. When you are in the middle of dealing with a scandal, with emotions running high and possibly reporters and police asking questions, that is not the time to be figuring out what to do.

Here are the steps I recommend.

1. **Make sure the church is protected** from loss or damage that may be brought on by a pastor's misconduct. For instance, in the United States, an accuser may file criminal charges, and may also sue the pastor. Beyond that, the church as an institution can be sued, and so can church leaders, on the pretext that they should have set up safeguards. Most American churches carry large insurance policies to cover legal fees and damages in the case of such accusations.

2. **Decide what transgressions warrant disciplinary action** within the church. Consider such things as doctrinal differences and actions unbefitting a Christian, as well as accusations of criminal, sexual or financial wrongdoing.

3. **Decide what will constitute a substantive accusation.** In my

denomination, for instance, an accusation of sexual misconduct must be submitted in writing and signed by the alleged victim before an investigation will take place. This is to protect pastors from spurious allegations.

4. **Decide which transgressions call for the pastor to be removed** from authority for the protection of the church while the accusation is being investigated, and which, if any, can be investigated while the pastor continues to serve.

5. **Decide what will be done to provide for the pastoral needs of the congregation** if the pastor needs to be removed during an investigation.

6. **Decide what will be done to provide for the needs of the accused pastor and family** during the investigation.

7. **Decide who will conduct the investigation**. Ideally this should be a body of objective outsiders who are familiar with the workings of churches, such as a group of other pastors.

8. **Decide what will be done when the investigation has been concluded.** For pastors who are found innocent, how will their names be cleared? If found guilty, what kind of discipline will be instituted, what kind of rehabilitation will be offered, and how will it be decided if and when they may return to being a pastor?

Planning like this is good and important, but it is worthless unless the pastor and congregation agree to abide by it. It is not unknown for a pastor who has been removed from one church to go off and start another one nearby, with many of the same people following. There's usually not a lot you can do if this happens, so forgive, learn, and move forward.

I pray you will never have to deal with these things, but **establish policies just in case.**

Points to Remember

- Very few pastors stay in one church their whole careers.
- God may be calling you away from a bad situation or toward a new opportunity; just be sure it is really God calling and not your own fears or ambitions.

- When you leave, go as you hope the pastor you are following will leave the place you are going.
- Have a policy for situations that may result in a pastor being forced to leave.

11

BASIC RULES FOR PASTORS

I compiled this list some years ago, to remind myself of what is important. The order is more or less random.

1. Worship until the joy comes
2. Surround yourself with prayer
3. Keep the main thing the main thing
4. Read, believe and do the Bible
5. Love the people
6. Keep a personal Sabbath
7. Put your family first
8. Over-communicate
9. Tithe
10. Read
11. Believe
12. Do more gainers than drainers
13. Never click "send" after midnight
14. Remember who you work for
15. Have fun
16. Don't get too comfortable
17. Never bind yourself with anything that causes you to sweat (Ezekiel 44:18)
18. Reach out to "the other ones"

19. Remember "faith" is spelled R-I-S-K
20. Keep your objectivity
21. Accentuate the positive, eliminate the negative
22. Strengthen yourself in the Lord
23. Stretch yourself
24. Exercise your faith
25. Go on to perfection
26. Pre-pray the day
27. Don't limit God to your theology
28. Eyes forward
29. Don't do good programs, do life-transforming encounters
30. Go with the flow of the Spirit

III

LEADING A CHURCH

The Old Testament describes in great detail how the tabernacle was to be built, priests and Levites organized and rituals conducted. Similar regulations about the church are nowhere to be found. Apparently God wants us to prayerfully use our creativity and intelligence to adapt Biblical principles to our own situations. Here are some options and ideas to help all your ministries and administrative functions work together to fulfill God's three-fold purpose in your particular church.

12

AUTHORITY AND DECISION MAKING

It seemed good to the Holy Spirit and to us to lay no greater burden on you than these few requirements. – Acts 15:28

All true churches recognize God as the ultimate authority. They don't all agree on the best way to hear and do what God is saying. Who has authority to state God's direction? Who decides what to do about it? Who actually does the work, and how? Our understanding of how God speaks to his people, and how we work to carry out his will, largely determines how we organize our churches.

Every church faces two basic questions, which can be expressed in different ways. **Where does God want us to go, and how does he want us to get there?** What does God want us to be, and what does God want us to do? What is God's strategy for our church, and what are his tactics for implementing that strategy? I call the first of these questions directional, and the second operational.

Directional Authority

Every church can't excel at every ministry. Not even the largest church has enough people and resources to do everything that can be done. And some things are mutually exclusive. For instance, you can keep all your people in one congregation, or you can send some of your people out to plant new congregations. Who decides which you will do? Who has the authority to tell your congregation what direction God wants it to take at a given time?

Some churches believe God gives direction through an authority outside the local congregation. It might be an individual such as a bishop or an apostle, or it might be a group such as a denominational body. Perhaps all the pastors in a region get together and pray for God's direction for their area.

Some churches believe God's direction should come from the pastor, with no other input. Certainly pastors should always be praying for God's guidance. But if the pastor is the only person in the church who knows how to hear from God, it seems to me the pastor is failing and the church is in trouble! No individual, including the pastor, has all knowledge (1 Corinthians 13:9). *There is safety in having many advisors* (Proverbs 11:14). 1 Corinthians 14:29 says that when someone believes they have a word from God, the others who are experienced in hearing God's direction should weigh what is said. We see this in action with the Jerusalem council in Acts 15.

In congregational churches, final authority rests in the whole church meeting together. Some restrict their voting membership to exclude new Christians who may still be largely influenced by worldly values and ways of thinking. Between congregational meetings, a group of leaders work with the pastor to keep things running.

Regardless of the specific model, most churches depend on a group of mature leaders to join the pastor in discerning God's direction. In some the pastor has the final decision, advised by the leadership team. In others the leadership team decides, advised by the pastor. Sometimes authority is split, with the pastor ruling in areas such as worship, and the leadership team in things like finances.

Often the form of church government seems to reflect the dominant political philosophy and culture more than theological considerations. Churches that originated in cultures ruled by kings tend to be comfortable with centralized authority. Churches that started in democracies, such as America, tend toward a congregational model. **All kinds of churches can do good ministry.**

Vision and Mission

Somebody said, "If you keep on doing what you've always done, you'll keep on getting what you've always gotten." Or, in words attributed to Albert Einstein, "The definition of insanity is doing the same thing over and over again and expecting a different result."

Whether directional authority rests in an outside person or body, the pastor, a group, or the whole congregation, it's important to **periodically step back and take a fresh look at your church's direction, and whether that is still where God is calling you.** Otherwise you may keep doing the same things over and over again, even if they stopped working years ago.

What do you think God wants your church to look like five or ten years from now? What does he want you to be known for? What does he want you to be doing? What kind of people does he want you becoming? To put it in the language of the business world, what is your vision?

What do you think God wants your church to accomplish? What specific part of "thy will be done on earth as it is in heaven" has God assigned to you? In other words, what is your mission?

Your vision describes what God wants your church to be. Your mission is what God wants your church to do. When these are clear they give your church direction. You can simply **look at every program and idea and ask, "How will this move us toward our vision? How will this help us accomplish our mission?"** If you don't have a good answer, why do it?

Strategic Planning

Clear visions and missions don't just happen. Every year or two you need to get your church leaders together to seek God's direction for your church.

Don't call it a meeting. Call it a vision retreat or a time of discernment, to indicate that this is special and important. Include your official leaders, but don't stop there. **Include informal influencers,** the ones other people listen to before they form opinions. And try to include one or two representatives of the people you hope will form the future of your church, such as new Christians or young adults. Make your group big enough to include the voices you need to hear, and small enough to have good discussions.

If possible, meet somewhere other than your church or usual meeting place. A park or a restaurant or even a room in another church offers a change of scenery that can really make a difference in how people see and think about things.

Many pastors find it helpful to have an outside person, such as a neighboring pastor, lead the process. They may say exactly what you would have said, but a different voice makes it sound fresh. Your people may think, "This expert is saying the same thing our pastor said. Our pastor must be really smart!" And it's good for you to sit back and let somebody else take the lead for a change.

Start with prayer and Bible study. Focus on God's purpose for the church, or how to discern God's leading.

Ask the group to **list the strengths** of your church. Focusing on strengths rather than problems builds faith and new ideas.

Talk about the community where God has placed you. Ask God to reveal, through prayer and discussion, why he put your congregation there. What can your church, with its specific people, strengths and resources, offer your community, with its specific people, needs and opportunities?

Develop a simple sentence that gives a picture of what God wants you to become in the next few years. This is your vision statement. Develop another simple sentence that describes what God wants you to do for the next few years. This is your mission statement. If your time away accomplishes nothing more than these two statements it will be well worth it. Publicize those statements in the church, and keep them before the people. They'll give your leaders and people a sense of direction that will bring unity and teamwork.

Action Steps

Now that you know where you are going, **how will you get there?** Some leaders find it helpful to make a list of goals. Others find such a list artificial and constraining, preferring a more spontaneous approach. God can provide direction and guidance either way. Choose what works for your personality and leadership style. Just be sure you can communicate it all to those who do things the other way.

If you choose to list goals, make them as helpful as possible. A good church goal has seven characteristics, answering seven questions. Every goal should be:

1. **Prayer-based** – Did God inspire or approve this idea?
2. **Specific** – What exactly are we planning to do?
3. **Targeted** – How will it advance our vision and mission?
4. **Defined** – How will we know when we have achieved it?
5. **Supported** – Are the people we expect to do this excited about it?
6. **Timed** – When will we evaluate and adjust, and what is our final deadline?
7. **Worthwhile** – Will the benefits, tangible and intangible, be worth the cost in time, energy, resources, and the lost opportunity to do other things?

Even if you prefer not to write down a list of goals, keep these questions in mind. Use them to evaluate projects and ideas. They will keep the more spontaneous personalities from going off in the wrong direction, and they will help reassure and motivate those who like to see plans.

Operational Authority

It's important to dream dreams and plan plans, but somebody has to keep things running day to day. Directional authority decides the big picture, like the general style of your worship service. Operational authority decides the details, like what songs you will sing this week.

Operational decisions should be made by those doing the work. As long as they stay within your directional guidelines and policies, let your people use their initiative and creativity. As pastor, you don't need to be involved in every detail. Let whoever handles church money decide what bank to use. Let whoever cleans your meeting space decide what kind of broom to buy. Let whoever is in charge of the children set up the rotation of child-care workers. Once general direction and guidelines are set, the pastor and church leaders should only get involved if there is a problem.

Some pastors have trouble delegating. But **it's important to let others do the work**, even if you know you can do it better or more efficiently yourself. People learn and grow by doing things, and you free up your time to do the things that only you can do. If somebody does something differently than you would have, stop before you correct them. Prayerfully ask yourself if the difference between their way and your way is worth the negative effect your criticism will have on that leader's confidence and motivation. Most of the time it won't be. If it really is important, correct gently and in love.

Meetings

If a decision involves more than one person, you need to communicate. In very simple cases email or a quick phone conversation may be enough. Often, though, it takes a meeting. When more than one person is working on a task, or when what one person does affects another person's area of responsibility, there's no substitute for face to face conversation.

Vision Meetings

There are basically two kinds of meetings. The first are where you discern God's vision and guidance and prayerfully seek new ideas. I call those vision meetings.

Vision meetings can be about a big question like the direction of the church, or a specific issue like new ways to involve children in worship. The vision question should be the only agenda item. Formal parliamentary procedure has no place here. Instead, **encourage anything that generates new ideas.**

Ask God to guide you, then start brainstorming, mind mapping, journaling, doodling, all together or in smaller groups – whatever works for you and your people. Don't stop to evaluate or discuss any one thing until you have a good long list of ideas. This can be hard, because as soon as an idea is mentioned, most people start thinking about how it might or might not work and how much it will cost. The problem is, if you deal with ideas as they come up, you may choose one idea and move on before a better idea has a chance to be considered. God is a creator, and he made us in his image. This is a time to let your people explore their creativity. Evaluate, prioritize and plan only after you have given yourself a lot of options to consider.

Management Meetings

Vision meetings are exciting, but they don't actually make anything happen. That takes management meetings, where people share information, make plans, assign tasks, and attend to the many details of implementing the vision.

In thirty-four years of ministry **I've never had good success trying to combine management and vision meetings.** They involve different ways of thinking, different processes, and often different people. Visionaries are impatient with the details of management meetings, and hands-on people can feel like visioning meetings are unrealistic nonsense. Know which kind of meeting you need, and structure it accordingly.

Elements of a Successful Meeting

Notice

Before any meeting people need to know five things:

1. Who is invited
2. When and where to show up
3. What will be decided
4. What they will be expected to contribute
5. What to do if they can't be there

Find a consistent and effective way to get this information out.

Attendance

Be clear about who is expected at the meeting. Announce whether others may attend and how they may be involved. May they speak in the discussions? May they participate in decision making?

Most pastors are glad to have any interested people attend church meetings, and usually it's a great way to learn and get involved. However, in some cases this may not be a good idea. Confidential issues should always be discussed in a closed meeting with only those who need to be involved. And sometimes people want to attend a meeting so they can push their own agenda. As with all policies, it's best to settle these points before a specific issue arises that may influence your judgment, or appear to.

Leadership

As pastor, you don't need to be the one leading every meeting. In fact, as your people grow in Christian maturity and leadership skills, you don't even need to attend every meeting. Encourage your people to take leadership. It helps them grow and frees up your time.

God-presence

Every church meeting should start by inviting God's presence and guidance. After all, it's his church, his people, his money, his ministry. When problems arise, as Pastor Kenneth Hagin used to tell his leaders, God is not up in heaven wringing his hands and saying, "Oh no, what are we going to do?" Make sure you do something right at the beginning that reminds everyone that this meeting is a God thing. Help people set aside worldly distractions and ways of doing things, and personally invite God to come and guide you.

Here's a quick and effective way to do this:

1. Read aloud a short passage of Scripture
2. Read it again, perhaps from a different translation
3. Allow 30 seconds of silence for everyone to identify a word, idea or image that stood out to them
4. Take a minute for everyone to share that with the person next to them
5. Have several volunteers share what their partner said
6. Have one or more people pray, incorporating some of those thoughts as they invite God to join you, ask his guidance, and offer yourselves for his purposes

Agenda

Management meetings need an agenda listing everything you need to accomplish. (If you don't know what you need to accomplish, don't have the meeting.) As the meeting goes along, the agenda reminds everyone how much you still need to cover. Every group has some people who just like to talk. When one of these folks starts telling stories or going off on a rabbit trail, the leader can gently call attention to the agenda to get the meeting back on track.

Structure

There is no one right way to structure a meeting. Vision meetings should allow a lot of room for creativity. Management meetings need a way to keep people focused. Some meetings start with everyone reporting on their area of responsibility, followed by any old or new business that was not covered in the reports. Sometimes you may want to deal with an important issue first, so the decision is not rushed. Other times you may prefer to get small things out of way before dealing with a big issue. Make sure your agenda reflects the structure you want.

Decision making

Where the pastor makes all the decisions, meetings are for providing information and, when asked for, advice or recommendations. At the other extreme, some systems require unanimous consensus for any decision to be final. In the middle are churches where decisions are made by voting, either among the leadership team or by the whole congregation.

All three of these methods have their strengths and weaknesses. The first allows for fast decisions, and may be necessary in churches where the pastor may be the only spiritually mature, experienced or informed person. However, this can be very draining for the pastor, and it may not allow much opportunity for others to grow. It can also create a lot of temptation for the pastor to become autocratic and even self-serving. As the saying goes, "Power corrupts."

Consensus sounds very humble and spiritual, but I believe it is based on two fallacies. First, it assumes that *unity in our faith* (Ephesians 4:13) requires unity in our opinions. Second, it assumes that all present in a meeting are sufficiently mature Christians that they are consistently led by the Spirit and never give in to their own biases or desires. Even Jesus didn't have that among his own twelve chosen apostles. A requirement of unanimous consensus allows one person with a different opinion or motivation to block the entire church.

That leaves voting. Some say voting promotes divisiveness, but I think it just reveals it. As the deacon said to the pastor in the hospital, "Pastor, the church board hopes you get well soon, by a vote of five to four."

Many churches say they make decisions by voting, especially in historically democratic cultures. In my experience, even in these churches a formal, counted and recorded vote is rarely taken. Instead, the right answer becomes clear as the issue is being discussed. As pastor, if you let it be known that you feel strongly about an issue, your reasoning and your respect will usually prevail. In other cases, as facts are presented and questions answered, a *de facto* consensus emerges. As things become clear, someone says something like, "It seems like what I'm hearing is this. Everybody in favor?" If someone objects, they discuss it some more. If no one objects, they consider it a vote. And it is, in the sense that everyone had an opportunity to talk, and the opinion of the majority became clear. But this way people who don't feel strongly one way or another are not forced to take sides, and no one has to go on record as opposing the leader or the majority.

I believe this is the decision-making model used in the first Church Council in Jerusalem (Acts 15). Everyone spoke, then James summed it up and put the conclusion into an official statement. Smart leaders listen to King Solomon: *Without wise leadership, a nation falls; there is safety in having many advisers* (Proverbs 11:14).

If people seem to be evenly divided on a major issue, find a way to delay the decision if possible, or decide ahead of time that this decision will require a two-thirds or three-quarters majority. You don't want to make a decision that requires the whole church to be on board, only to have half of them walk away and leave you hanging.

Some churches recognize prophets who are known for their ability to hear from God. In many cases, if they say God has spoken to them about an issue, that settles it. A word from God can guide the pastor, create consensus, or sway a vote. The apostle Paul tells us to eagerly seek this gift (1 Corinthians 14:1), as it can be a real blessing. But it must be handled carefully. 1 Corinthians 14:29 tells us not to blindly accept prophetic words. Instead, a group of mature Christians should weigh every word that claims to come from God, because 1 Corinthians 13:9 says *we know in part and we prophesy in part* (ESV). A true prophet will humbly welcome this scriptural caution.

Prophets need to understand that their responsibility ends with accurately delivering the word to the appropriate person, usually you as pastor. It's not up to the prophet to make sure that you do what they think you should do about their word, or to denounce you as unspiritual if you don't (see Acts 21:7-14). But with these cautions, you should urge and train every person in leadership, and indeed in your church, to follow 1 Corinthians 14:1 *Let love be your highest goal! But you should also desire the special abilities the Spirit gives—especially the ability to prophesy.*

Record keeping

Make sure someone is making an official record of your decisions. I don't know how many times I've had church folks ask me, "What did we decide about this? Who was supposed to do that? What date did we set? How did we do it last year?" My answer was usually, "I don't remember. Did anybody write it down?"

There's a lot of power in taking official minutes. If there's a dispute about what happened in the last meeting, people will go by whatever is written. That's why one of the first actions of many meetings is to review and approve the minutes of the previous one. That way if the secretary made a mistake it can be corrected. A review also reminds people of unfinished business, and if someone missed the previous meeting it helps them catch up.

Assignments

One of the most frustrating things that can happen in any organization is when some important thing doesn't get done, because everybody thought someone else was going to do it. Whenever you make a decision make sure you also clearly decide who is responsible for doing whatever needs to be done to make it happen. If there's a deadline or a need to report back to someone, be sure that's clear as well.

Next steps planning

Make a habit of asking, "What's next?" If an activity brings new people into contact with your church, how will you follow up with them? If a Bible study gets people excited about studying scripture, how will you capitalize on that excitement before it dies away? Always be thinking at least one step ahead.

Approval and oversight

Some operational decisions made at the working level may need to be approved by someone with a larger view of the church's situation. Your money and volunteers are limited. Be sure everyone knows which ideas can be done immediately, and which ones need some kind of approval.

Especially with new workers, there may be a need for oversight. They may have the best intentions in the world, but if they misunderstood what they were supposed to do, or other obligations arose, or they just didn't have the ability, you might be very glad you made a progress check.

Reporting

When an important decision has been made or an event has been planned or carried out, don't keep it a secret. Let your people know. Celebrate.

We tend to think, "I know about it, so everyone else must, too." But everyone else wasn't in the meeting. Everyone else may not have been part of the program. People get excited about their church when they feel like it's making a difference. But if they don't know what you are doing, they won't know the difference you are making.

Even better, when it's appropriate, publicize your activities to the community. The only thing better than your church folks feeling good about your church is for the community to feel that way.

Evaluation

Once your event or activity has happened, don't just move on. Evaluate. How did it go? Were the results worth the trouble and expense? What worked well? What could be done better next time? Should there be a next time? How will you follow up?

Points to Remember

- Be clear about who has the authority to make various kinds of decisions for your church.
- Be clear about what God wants your church to be and do, and support only what leads to that.
- Re-evaluate regularly.
- Work toward only doing what only you can do; delegating lets others grow.
- Do visioning and managing in separate meetings.
- Make meetings effective.
- Keep clear records of decisions and responsibilities.

13

WORSHIP SERVICES AND CELEBRATIONS

Honor the LORD for the glory of his name. Worship the LORD in the splendor of his holiness. - Psalm 29:2

When most people think of church, they think of the weekly worship service. It's where visitors visit, and it may be the only spiritual activity of the week, even for many Christians. That's why some pastors call the main worship service "the most important hour of the week."

For others, their first contact with church is being invited to a wedding, baptism or funeral. These celebrations help people recognize God in the most important events of their lives.

Worship Space

You can have church anywhere – in a house, under a tree, in a cathedral, wherever two or three are gathered together in Jesus' name (Matthew 18:20). But you do gather someplace. Whether you own your own building, rent space for a few hours a week, or just make do with what you can find, wherever your church gathers, there are some things you should think about.

Function

To the extent you can, **lay out your worship space based on how you're going to use it**. In some churches the sacraments are central, so an altar is the focal point. Others focus on the preached word, so a pulpit is front and center. Churches where musical worship is the priority provide plenty of room for musicians and singers.

What is important in your service? Where will you do it? How much room will it take? As you place chairs and furniture, make sure people can see and hear your speakers and musicians, leave room for singers and sacraments, and think about exit routes in case of fire or other emergency.

Flexibility

In one church I served, the sanctuary was up a flight of stairs from the building entrance. A few years before I came there, they spent a lot of money to install an elevator. They were very happy with it until they had their first funeral. No matter how they maneuvered, the elevator was just a bit too small to hold a coffin! Luckily, there's a back door with fewer stairs. They bring coffins in that way.

Winston Churchill said, "We shape our buildings, thereafter they shape us." One thing you can be sure of is that after you have your worship space set up something will happen that you didn't think about – like those coffins. **The more flexible your space is, the less you will have to shape your services to fit it.**

Symbols

Crosses, candles, a Communion table and other physical symbols can help set your worship space apart as a place dedicated to God. Colors often have symbolic meanings. If you come from a church that has a tradition of these symbols, make sure you know their history and why they are important, and use them to help teach your people. If you don't have such a tradition, don't just dismiss the idea. **Symbols of various kinds can be powerful communicators** reminding us of God's presence and the basic truths of our faith. You don't have to adopt anyone else's symbols, though there are some that are pretty universal among Christians. But I encourage you to prayerfully study the role of symbols and how you might use them. If you don't, you may find that some to-you insignificant part of your service or decorations has taken on a symbolic meaning for your people. Heaven help you if you unwittingly change something that has become a symbol of someone's faith!

Decorations

Some churches decorate their worship spaces as opulently as they can, to demonstrate that God deserves the very best. Some decorate with banners and plaques as a way of communicating and reinforcing points of faith. Some don't decorate at all, not wanting to distract people from pure worship.

Most churches that use decorations put up special ones for Christmas and Easter, and sometimes for secular holidays as well. This can certainly enhance the spirit of the season. However, well-meaning volunteers can sometimes decorate with items that, unknown to them, come from a secular or even pagan background. They may carry a meaning inappropriate for church. It's a lot easier if you can catch these ahead of time, instead of having to ask someone to remove a decoration they may have put a lot of time into.

How you decorate your worship space says a lot about your theology and your spiritual priorities. Don't display something just because a church member donated it. The things people see as they worship help shape their experience of God. Consider them carefully.

Comfort

There's a saying, "The brain can absorb only as much as the seat can endure." The same is true of the spirit. If you don't normally sit in the congregation, try it out. How is the seating? How is the temperature? The airflow? Is the sun in anyone's eyes? You don't need to make things so comfortable that people fall asleep, but **most people won't come back to a place where they aren't comfortable** – emotionally, relationally and physically.

Child care

Many congregations welcome babies and small children in the service. Others prefer to offer nursery care and Christian education (often called "Sunday School") or "children's church" during the worship time. Much of this depends on your culture, but here are a few things to consider.

Keeping children in the service allows them to experience worship with their family. Children should see their parents publicly worshiping God. And children pick up a lot, even when they don't seem to be listening. As a preacher, if I can keep the attention of the children then I know the adults will listen and understand.

On the other hand, crying babies and squirming toddlers can be a real distraction, especially for their mother. Church may be her only chance all week to focus on something adult for herself. She may decide that if she doesn't get anything out of it, why make the effort to go?

Taking children out of the service can be good for the children as well as the parents. It allows you to provide Bible lessons in a way appropriate for their age. If they enjoy it they'll ask their parents to bring them back, and they may invite their friends.

On the other hand, if children are not in the service that means the adults who are teaching or caring for them also have to miss the service. And it means the children have no model for adult worship. I once taught a week-day class of 13-15 year olds. One day I took them into the sanctuary to talk about symbols and sacraments. One girl, whose parents had brought

146

her to church regularly for most of her life, said this was the first time she had ever seen any of these things. Her only experience of church was the children's program.

If children are not in the service with their parents, have a way to reach them if a problem arises. And if your church is large enough that you can't count on everyone knowing everyone else, it's important to have a way to make sure children are picked up only by their parents or other authorized adults.

Worship Services

Most churches have their main weekly worship service on Sunday morning, to celebrate the resurrection of Jesus. Some denominations meet on Saturday morning, in recognition of the Sabbath. Some churches have added a Saturday evening service, for people who work on Sunday or just like to sleep late. And many churches meet Sunday mornings, Sunday evenings, and Wednesday evenings, and faithful members are expected to attend all three.

The Bible doesn't specify when or how often to gather for worship, though once a week seems like a minimum expectation. To keep things simple, I'm writing as if your main worship service is on Sunday morning. If it's at a different time, just make a mental substitution as you read.

People come to church from all different kinds of situations, backgrounds and expectations. They need to worship God and grow in their knowledge and faith and commitment. They need to receive prayer, share testimonies, be comforted and be challenged. They need to seek and receive forgiveness, offer themselves for service, connect with each other, and be equipped for the work of ministry. That's a tall order for an hour or so!

Your weekly services are the main time your people come together as the church. That means they should reflect the church's three purposes: to be a comfortable home for God to live among his people, to raise up God's adopted children to be like their big brother Jesus, and to invite everyone to join God's family through powerful demonstrations of love. In other words, you need to be sure your services include time for worship, for discipleship training, and for encouraging your people to carry God's presence beyond the walls of your meeting place.

How do you put all that together in one service a week, or even two or three? It would be a lot easier if the Bible told us exactly what God wants in a church service. Unfortunately, it doesn't tell us. But people will be glad to!

People who grew up liking church know how a service should be: exactly like the services of their fond memories. People who had a bad experience likewise know what they want: anything different. Even people with no previous church experience will have opinions.

Many churches shape their services to please their members. Sometimes the people demand it; sometimes the pastor just likes to make people happy. But even if the members agree on the kind of service they like, it's usually not something outsiders want.

Other churches shape their services to attract non-Christians. The pastors have taught their people to sacrifice their own preferences, when necessary, in favor of reaching the lost. This is a huge improvement over, "It's my church, I want it my way." If the choice is between Christians being comfortable and non-Christians being saved, it's no contest. But it still misses the fundamental question, because the focus is still on people.

The first purpose of church is to be a home for our heavenly Father to dwell among his people. So the first question in designing a worship service is not, "What do I like?" or even, "What will attract unbelievers?" The first question must be, "What does God want?" **When we worship God the way he wants to be worshipped, he will take care of everything else.**

The closest thing to a Biblical description of Christian worship is 1 Corinthians, chapters 11-14. Paul sums it up in verse 26.

When you meet together, one will sing, another will teach, another will tell some special revelation God has given, one will speak in tongues, and another will interpret what is said. But everything that is done must strengthen all of you.

According to Paul, a worship service should not be a few people performing while everybody else watches. Everyone should have a part, as the Holy Spirit moves them. In the surrounding verses Paul tells how to do this in an orderly way. Beyond that, it seems that how we fashion our worship services is pretty much up to our own God-given creativity.

That said, there are some basic elements that should be considered in every church service.

Basic Elements

Service flow

I heard about a prayer meeting where one brother prayed, "Oh Lord, send us a spark. Just send us a spark of your Holy Spirit fire." The next person passionately added, "Yes, and Lord, water that spark!" Too often, that's exactly what happens.

1 Thessalonians 5:19 says, *Do not stifle the Holy Spirit.* I've been in services where the singing and praying have created a beautiful atmosphere of worship and God's presence, and then it's all disrupted because the next thing that happens is an announcement about needing helpers for the church dinner. Worship is a spiritual exercise, but it reaches our spirits through our minds and emotions. That works better when there's a logical or emotional flow from one part of the service into the next. If there isn't, we can pour water on the spark of Holy Spirit fire.

Liturgy

Liturgy is the order in which things happen in your service. Some churches carefully plan out the order of worship and write it down in a handout so everyone can follow along. Others feel that limits the spontaneity and creativity of the Holy Spirit. But even those churches often do essentially the same things in the same order every week. They have a liturgy; they just don't write it down.

149

The Holy Spirit can inspire planning and writing on Wednesday just as much as he can inspire spontaneity and speaking on Sunday. One is not more spiritual than the other. Either can leave room for the Spirit to move, and either can become rigid and dry. Pray, try different things, and see how God leads you. Personally, I like to have something written, even if I'm the only one who sees it, just to make sure I don't forget something important.

Spirit-led order

You may have gathered that I am fascinated by 1 Corinthians 14:26-33. These verses imply a potential for chaos. Verse 30 even gives instructions for interrupting the speaker! Yet Paul closes by saying, *God is not a God of disorder but of peace.*

For a mature congregation, maintaining this peaceful order should not be a problem. Unfortunately, visitors and new Christians will not always understand what is happening and how things are to be done. Most of us have experienced that awkward time when someone is giving a prayer request or a testimony of praise or even an announcement, and they just go on and on – maybe even saying inappropriate things. It's up to you as pastor to gracefully maintain order, and direct the service where the Spirit wants to take it.

Time

How long should a worship service last? There are a lot of strongly held opinions around that simple question. I visited a church attended by thousands where services were strictly held under an hour, and an even larger church where they routinely went three hours or more. Much depends on the expectations of the people, which are usually based on what they were used to in the church where they grew up.

If you minister in a place where people expect a church service to last a certain length of time, it's probably best to go along, unless you strongly feel that God is leading you to do something different. For some reason this can be one of the hardest traditions to break.

Whatever you decide, unless something extraordinary happens it's good to be consistent. People want to be able to plan the rest of their day. If they invite a guest, they want to be able to tell them what to expect. Even Spirit-led spontaneity usually happens within a broadly predictable time frame.

Music

Music has been a part of worship since the beginning. Jubal, *the first of all who play the harp and flute,* was in the eighth generation from Adam (Genesis 4:21). King David, a musician himself, appointed singers to serve at the temple day and night (1 Chronicles 9:33). King Jehoshaphat even sent the choir in front of his army as they went to battle, which says a lot about the role of music in spiritual warfare (2 Chronicles 20:21-22). Paul describes music as an integral part of New Testament worship (1 Corinthians 14:26).

Some churches talk as if worship is defined by music: "First we worship, then we hear a sermon." Music is important, but it's not the only way to worship. Giving tithes and offerings is clearly worship. Prayers, statements of faith, the sermon, even announcements should be done in a way that helps people experience and respond to God's presence – in other words, as worship.

As a preacher who is also a musician, I've become painfully aware that some people endure the music to hear the sermon, while others put up with the sermon for the sake of the music. This is not just true of people in the congregation. I've seen song leaders leave the room once the sermon started, and I've known pastors who thought the purpose of music was to get people on their feet for a minute so they could stay awake during the sermon. Wherever you fit in that spectrum, remember that probably half of your people are on the other side. Plan your services accordingly.

What is the purpose of music in a worship service, anyway? Actually, there are many purposes. Paul refers to *psalms and hymns and spiritual songs* (Ephesians 5:19; Colossians 3:16). Apparently, even in the first days of the church there were different kinds of music for different purposes.

Music can turn our thoughts from the world. It can create an atmosphere for worship. It can be calming and soothing, or stirring and inspiring. On a very functional level, musical interludes can help the service flow by smoothing transitions.

Some songs target the mind, with lyrics that teach Bible truths in a way that sticks in the memory. Others target the spirit; simple words and tunes repeated over and over allow people to focus on God instead of the words and notes.

Because the role of music in worship is so varied, and because people have such different ideas about it, tensions are bound to arise. In fact, some pastors jokingly refer to their music team as "the war department."

Here are four common areas of potential conflict.

1) There can be a tension between *Make a joyful noise* (Psalm 100:1 ESV) and *Play skillfully* (Psalm 33:3).

Some people don't sing during the congregational singing. Usually it's because somebody told them, perhaps decades ago, that they don't have a good voice, or they can't carry a tune in a bucket. Often these people wish they could join in with the congregation, but they're afraid they'll distract people or mess up the sound. *Make a joyful noise* (Psalm 100:1 ESV) is the verse for these folks. Anybody can make a noise, right? So encourage them to sing, at least quietly. Remind them that nobody is listening to them. The ones who sing are listening to the music, and the other non-singers are too concerned about their own sound.

On the other hand, the verse for your music leaders is, *Play skillfully* (Psalm 33:3). Musical talent, whether vocal or instrumental, is like any other natural ability. It needs to be developed. Teach your musicians that studying and practicing is an offering to God.

How skillful should someone be before you ask them to sing or play in church? Different pastors answer that in different ways.

I've been in churches that were known for excellent music. The leaders required auditions for new members, and only those who met high standards were accepted. If your music program is one of the reasons visitors come back to your church, this approach makes sense.

I've also been in churches where the congregation gracefully endured musical presentations that fit more into the "joyful noise" category. These churches put relationships first. They continued to let Aunt Edna sing solos, even though her voice lost its charm years ago, because everybody loved Aunt Edna and they didn't want to hurt her feelings.

It's up to you to prayerfully decide which approach you will take. Your vision and mission statements should be helpful with this kind of decision.

2) There can be a tension between *Ask for the old, godly way* (Jeremiah 6:16) and *Sing to the Lord a new song* (Psalm 149:1).

Most Christian movements have their own musical heritage. If you are part of a traditional denomination, you may have a stockpile of hymns hundreds of years old. New churches use newer music. But time keeps marching on. In America, much of the music called "Christian contemporary" dates from the 1980s and before. What was once new has become "the good old songs."

One common traditional American order of worship is sometimes called a "hymn sandwich:" one hymn at the beginning, one hymn just before the sermon, and one hymn at the end, with everything else sandwiched between them. The person who selects the hymns usually tries to tie them in with the theme of the sermon, so the people are singing words that reinforce the teaching. If you are part of a denomination with a distinctive doctrinal heritage, singing the old hymns can be a great way to keep that heritage alive.

More modern orders of worship usually start with a solid block of congregational singing (usually called the "worship time") that can extend for half the service. There may be little or no music the rest of the time. The songs are usually selected more for their effect in helping people enter into worship than for the content of the lyrics. A common pattern is to start with fast songs to get people engaged, sing one or two medium songs for transition, and end with slow songs, which are often seen as "more worshipful," to help people feel God's presence and express their love. Many churches find this spiritually effective. Others consider it nothing more than psychological manipulation.

I've been blessed to serve some churches where people wrote their own songs. I love to encourage people to explore their gifts in this way. It can be a powerful affirmation of your teaching to hear it reflected in the lyrics of a new song.

Again, your vision and mission statements should help as you prayerfully discern the role and kind of music God wants your particular church to use.

3) There can be a tension between worship and performance.

Some think the only way to worship through music is to sing. But many people find music performed by a soloist or group to be just as worshipful. Even background or transitional music should contribute to worship.

I used a word here that has a bad connotation in some churches. "Performance" can be a handy way to refer to any music not sung by the entire congregation. But it can also refer to an attitude where performers draw attention to themselves and the music, rather than using the music to draw attention to God.

Obviously the second meaning has no place in a church service. Musicians who are used to performing in the secular world, where a charismatic stage persona and an attention-grabbing musical style are positive things, may not immediately understand this, and their performances can indeed distract from worship. But I've known some churches that went so far to avoid a performance mentality that they didn't allow talented instrumentalists to play solos. Personally, I think that's a mistake. All kinds of talents and abilities should be dedicated to God and used at their highest level for his glory. What matters is that the musician - or preacher or anyone else – be focused on honoring God more than impressing people.

I don't like to limit the kinds of music that can be used for solos or special pieces, as long as they are worshipful. But songs meant for the congregation to sing are different. The goal is for the people to express their worship in song. Make it as easy as possible for them. Simple words, easy tunes, singable ranges and, most of all, well-loved songs encourage people to release their inhibitions and sing their praises. In congregational worship, the musicians are there to help the people sing.

154

Your worship leaders should be your lead worshipers, leading the congregation into worship by their own example of worship. This raises a question: should unbelievers or new believers be allowed to join the worship team? Some churches see the music program as an evangelistic draw to musical unbelievers looking for a place to sing or play. Others feel that anyone who is placed before the congregation will be seen as a representative of the church and its beliefs and values, and therefore only mature Christian believers are appropriate. Either way can work. My own feeling is that anyone seen as a leader in the worship service should meet the standards of your other church leaders. If your worship team includes a group where individuals aren't highlighted, that may be a good place to get unbelievers involved.

4) There can be a tension between religious style and popular style.

I grew up at a time when the stereotypical church musical instrument was the pipe organ. A few progressive churches were beginning to experiment with electric guitars and drums in hopes of reaching young people. For many others, this was total heresy. Numerous sermons proclaimed, "Rock and roll is of the devil!" It's kind of interesting to remember that Martin Luther, the father of the Protestant Reformation, set many of his hymns to the tunes of popular drinking songs. And the organ itself was resisted by some when it was first introduced into churches – although pastors liked it because they only had to deal with one musician instead of a whole orchestra! (See "war department" above.)

In many places, some kinds of music are traditionally considered "religious," and others are not. In religious settings, religious people often want to hear religious music. People who didn't grow up in church usually prefer popular styles.

Despite the protestations of those pastors of my youth, no instruments or types of music are inherently more spiritual than others. Paul's words about food apply equally to music: *Since everything God created is good, we should not reject any of it but receive it with thanks. For we know it is made acceptable by the word of God and prayer* (1 Timothy 4:4-5). To my mind, saying Christian music should not use certain rhythms, because those rhythms have been used in nightclub music, is like saying Christian churches should not be made of bricks, because nightclubs have been made of bricks. Of course, in any culture there may be certain musical forms that have become associated with images and habits of worldliness, non-Christian religions, or even the occult. If something you do musically is likely to produce ungodly thoughts and ideas in anyone, it's probably best not to do it.

Offerings and announcements

Many churches act as if offerings and announcements are unspiritual interruptions, the unseemly business side of the institution disturbing the real purpose of the gathering.

I have to say I've struggled with that some myself, especially with regard to announcements. But the fact is, you have to have some way to let people know what is going on. And your church needs some amount of money to carry out its mission. The weekly worship service is the logical place to take care of these needs.

But I think it's a mistake to think that offerings and announcements can't be worshipful. Throughout time and around the world perhaps the one common theme in all religious observances is people making offerings, whether it's money or animal sacrifices. In fact, I would go so far as to say the essence of worship is offering ourselves to God. Insofar as our financial gifts represent that, the giving of tithes and offerings may be the most worshipful thing we do. And since announcements often involve ways for people to offer God their time and service, they are a legitimate part of worship.

Some churches make a point of saying that first-time visitors are not expected to donate to the church. Some don't take offerings as part of the service at all; these churches usually have a box of some kind at the back of the church, and people are expected to drop their tithes in as they enter or leave. These practices are largely in reaction to polls that say that, in America at least, many people feel churches are always asking for money. However, I don't believe that's the best solution.

I once visited a very large church where, when the time for giving offerings was announced, the people responded with cheers and applause. They had been taught that the offering was an opportunity to express to God their love and faith. They also took literally Malachi 3:10,

> *"Bring all the tithes into the storehouse so there will be enough food in my Temple. If you do," says the LORD of Heaven's Armies, "I will open the windows of heaven for you. I will pour out a blessing so great you won't have enough room to take it in! Try it! Put me to the test!"*

They were cheering for the opportunity to receive a blessing.

You don't have to get your people to stand up and cheer for the offering, but don't treat it as if you're embarrassed about it. Consider introducing it with a brief Bible passage or teaching on God's promises and faithfulness. Teach your people the joy of trusting God with their finances.

Now for announcements. How do you let your people know about upcoming events and opportunities? Many churches print them in papers handed out at the weekly service. Others project them on screens. Either way, people have to read them – and many of them won't.

If you really want the congregation to know about something, somebody has to stand up and say it in church.

I'm not sure there's a perfect way to make announcements during a church service, but decades of wrestling with this problem have given me some insights.

- **Don't place announcements where they will shift focus away from God** and what he is doing in the service. Most churches find the beginning of the service best, although people who come in late may not hear the announcements.
- **Don't announce things about individuals** without getting their permission first.
- **Don't let announcements get repetitive** from week to week. If you do, people will start to ignore them.

- **Don't announce things that only pertain to a limited group**, unless you are hoping to attract new people.
- **Don't just read the written announcements**. If you do, the people will stop listening.
- **Don't use guilt** to get people to attend an event. If something isn't meeting the needs of enough people to make it stand on its own merits, perhaps you shouldn't be doing it.
- **Don't use shorthand** and insider language: "Faithbuilders will meet in the Grace room this week at the regular time, newcomers welcome." If I'm a newcomer, I have no idea what that means.
- **Don't let announcement time get too long**. TV commercials and radio news headlines convey a lot of information in 30 seconds or less. Learn from them.
- **Make announcements interesting.** Use visual aids, testimonies, and photos or videos if you can. But watch out, these can eat up a lot of time.
- If you have written announcements, **highlight only the most important or time sensitive** during the service, and encourage people to read the rest.
- **Use different people to give announcements**. If speakers are excited, the people will be, too. But be sure they're prepared and practiced, and don't try to say too much.

The Christian life is not just believing doctrine and feeling spiritual. It's a faith that needs to be put into action. Announcements are where you give your people opportunities to do that. Give them the thought they deserve.

Special days

Special days can keep your weekly services from falling into a routine. Some special days are celebrated throughout Christianity, like Christmas and Easter. Others are national or cultural. And every church comes up with special days of its own.

Some pastors feel like too much attention to special days interferes with their freedom to choose what to preach and how to design worship services. Others find that special days inspire their creativity. Remember, no matter how you feel about special days, there will be those in your congregation who feel the opposite. You need to minister to them, too.

The ancient church created a calendar of seasons and holy days that repeated each year. Starting four weeks before Christmas, it sets times to focus on preparing for Jesus' coming, the incarnation of Christ, the inclusion of the Gentiles, self-examination and repentance, the sacrifice of Jesus, his resurrection, the coming of the Holy Spirit, and the ministry of the church in the world. Some ancient denominations still follow the Julian calendar for their religious holidays and therefore celebrate holy days on different dates than most, but the essence of the celebrations is the same.

The events highlighted in the church year don't always fall on Sundays. Special services to recognize these days can be very powerful. In particular, if your main weekly services are in the morning, an evening service breaks people out of their routine and can make them more spiritually open. Evening services also allow much creative use of lighting, whether from candles, spotlights, or other sources.

These are the most common special services. I list them mainly to be helpful to those who are not familiar with them, and to spark your creative thinking. Observe them or not, as you feel led.

- **The four Sundays before Christmas** – Also known as Advent. Many churches use a setting of five candles, usually four in a circle surrounding a larger one in the center. On the fourth Sunday before Christmas they light one candle. Each week they light an additional candle. On Christmas Eve they light the center candle, representing the light of Christ come into the world.

- **Christmas Eve** – In America this is the most attended service in most churches. Many churches begin it at 11:00pm, so by the time the service is over, it's technically Christmas morning. A popular tradition for many is to distribute candles to everyone who attends. Then, usually at the

159

end of the service, all the lights are turned off and the flame from the Christ Candle is spread from person to person until the room is ablaze with candle light. You won't have to preach it for your people to see the powerful symbolism.

- **Christmas Day** – Most churches have services on Christmas Eve or Christmas Day. Few have both, but that is more for practical issues than liturgical or theological reasons.

- **Watch Night** – The night before New Year's Day. While the world is celebrating in its worldly ways, a night of prayer for the coming year can be especially meaningful.

- **Ash Wednesday** – The first day of Lent, which is the season of reflection and repentance leading to Easter. The tradition is to mark the foreheads of believers with ashes mixed with water, to symbolize repentance. Often the ashes come from burning left over palms from the previous year's Palm Sunday (see below). A more recent trend has been to distribute notepaper to the congregation, inviting them to list the sins and sorrows they wish to be rid of. A small fire is lit in a safe container, with a fire extinguisher nearby. People drop their papers into the fire before receiving the ashes.

- **Palm Sunday** – The Sunday before Easter, celebrating Jesus' triumphal entry into Jerusalem (Matthew 21:1-11). Many churches distribute bits of palm fronds to the people.

- **Holy Thursday** – The Thursday before Easter. Also called Maundy Thursday (a Latin name of uncertain derivation), it commemorates Jesus' last supper with his disciples before his betrayal and arrest. Celebrations almost always feature the Lord's Supper. Many churches include some form of foot washing ceremony (John 13). The service often ends by removing any joyous decorations or symbols from the sanctuary, and draping a black cloth over the cross.

- **Good Friday** – The day of Jesus' crucifixion. There are three different traditional ways of honoring the sacrifice of Jesus on this day. 1) Many churches have services remembering "The Seven Last Words of Jesus" – the seven things Jesus said as he hung on the cross, as found in the four gospels. Often this service starts at noon, the traditional time of the crucifixion, and goes until three o'clock, when Jesus died (Matthew 27:45-50). This is a great opportunity for neighboring churches to join together, with different pastors preaching on the different "last words." 2) A traditional evening Good Friday service is Tennebrae, or the service of darkness. The room is lit only by candles, often fourteen. The Scripture accounts of the betrayal and death of Jesus are divided into a series of readings equal to the number of candles. After each reading one candle is extinguished, until at the end the room is in darkness. Traditionally at this point a large noise signifies the stone being dropped into place to seal Jesus' tomb. People leave in silence. 3) Some ancient denominations celebrate "the stations of the cross," retracing Jesus' path from his condemnation before Pilate to his crucifixion. While some of the events are apocryphal, there can be surprising emotional and spiritual power in physically walking from point to point, periodically stopping to remember and pray.

- **Easter** – Many churches have a special early morning service, usually outdoors in a place where the sunrise can be seen. The service begins in the dark. Pastors try to time it so the sun rises over the horizon as the good news of the resurrection is being proclaimed.

Liturgical churches use different colors to symbolize the different church seasons. These can be valuable teaching tools for those who are visually oriented.

Whether you decide to embrace the church year, borrow part of it, or ignore it completely, be sure your decision is prayerful and informed. Know what you are following or giving up, and why.

Secular and patriotic holidays are also important to your congregation. In most cases they are spiritually neutral; they may not help your people's faith, but they probably won't hurt. And they can be an opportunity. A special service tied into the theme of the holiday might attract people who normally wouldn't attend church. For instance, in America the second Sunday in May is Mother's Day. On that day we often see people who don't normally attend church. They came to honor their mothers.

On the other hand, don't let a holiday overshadow the purpose of your service. Celebrating and honoring our mothers is a good thing, but in some churches it almost seems like mothers become "god for a day." Pray for the right balance.

The third kind of special days are those you create yourself. Sometimes these give certain groups a special role in the service, such as Children's Sunday. Sometimes they emphasize certain aspects of Christian life, such as World Communion Sunday or Bible Sunday. Sometimes they spotlight certain programs or needs of the church, such as Missions Sunday, Stewardship Sunday, or the International Day of Prayer for the Persecuted Church. Sometimes they are designed to honor groups that provide service to the community, such as Teachers Sunday or Firefighters Sunday. All these offer special opportunities for your people to invite their friends and neighbors who don't normally attend. And they are a great time for your sermon to show how the gospel speaks to everyday life.

Visitors

The first time someone visits your worship service you have four goals: make them feel welcome, make them feel comfortable, make them feel you care about them, and make them glad they came. If you can accomplish these four things the first time they visit, the odds are good that they'll come back.

Make them feel welcome

A welcome feeling should start the moment they see the place you meet. Is it inviting? Is it obvious where to go and what to do? If you have a parking lot, is there special parking set aside for visitors, near the door?

Every visitor should be greeted by a friendly, smiling person the moment they come in, if not outside. If the visitor is not dressed appropriately or starts to sit in the wrong place, this is NOT the time to mention it.

If the visitor is there at the invitation of one of your people, they probably already feel welcome. That's a great head start.

Make them feel comfortable

How much of what happens in your service is only known to people who have been there a while? People won't feel comfortable if they don't know what to do or can't follow what's happening. If you sing songs or use a prayer that "everyone knows," print or project the words anyway. Visitors will feel lost without it, and even your regulars may appreciate the reminder.

Unfortunately, not everyone has the same comfort level or expectations. Some people come to a new church hoping no one will notice them. They feel uncomfortable if they are singled out. Others feel the opposite. If they aren't greeted by several different people they'll say your church is unfriendly. Train your people to be sensitive to the Holy Spirit as they greet people.

Make them feel you care about them

When you greet visitors, don't stop with a simple hello. Teach your people to introduce themselves, ask questions, and follow up with conversation.

Find a non-intrusive way to gather names and contact information from your visitors, but don't be pushy if they are hesitant. If you do get contact information, be sure to use it within the next day or two to let them know you are glad they visited. Offer to answer questions or be of service. Be sure to invite them back.

The point is to make them feel like you care about them as people, not just numbers to build up your church or potential givers to support your budget.

Make them glad they came

Most regular church-goers have no idea how hard it is for someone to visit a church the first time. Add that to the many other things they could be doing on Sunday morning, and their visit represents quite a commitment. Make sure that when they get back home they'll feel glad they came.

How do you do that? It depends on two factors: your service and your people. If your service left them feeling encouraged or inspired, or that they learned something relevant to their lives, they will probably come back. If your people left them feeling that your church might be a place where they could make friends, or find support, they will probably come back. If both happened, you will almost certainly see them again.

Sacraments or Ordinances

An important part of many worship services is celebration of The Lord's Supper, also called Holy Communion or the Eucharist. Depending on your traditions and facilities, you may also have the privilege of celebrating baptisms as part of a church service.

Sincere, knowledgeable, Bible-believing Christians see these things in a variety of ways. I have no intention of trying to push a particular theology. If you are part of a denomination or tradition, please follow those teachings and practices. If you are on your own in this regard, study the Bible and ask God to guide you. I just want to give a broad overview, and raise some practical considerations in the context of a worship service.

First the question of terms: some traditions refer to Baptism and Holy Communion as ordinances. Other traditions call them sacraments. Generally speaking, "ordinance" emphasizes actions by which people symbolize their commitment to God, while "sacrament" emphasizes God's response of grace and blessing.

Some ancient churches add five additional sacraments: confirmation into the faith (for those who were baptized as infants), confession of sins, marriage, ordination, prayer for the sick, and prayer for the dying.

Most churches practice these without considering them sacraments or ordinances.

Baptism

Broadly speaking, where baptism is seen as a sacrament, people of any age can be baptized. Those churches believe you're never too young to receive God's grace. They see baptism as a New Testament parallel to circumcision, a sign that the parents are members of the family of God, and they want their child included. They point to passages such as Acts 16:15, which refer to entire households being baptized. Churches that see baptism as an ordinance symbolizing a personal commitment to Christ quite logically withhold baptism until people have reached an age where they can reasonably make such a commitment.

Churches that don't baptize babies usually have some way for parents to publicly dedicate their child to Christ. Churches that do baptize babies usually provide an opportunity for them to later make a public confirmation of their commitment to Jesus. Either way the end result is the same: through either baptism or dedication, babies of believers are recognized as part of the church family; through either baptism or confirmation, people old enough to make a commitment to Jesus have an opportunity to publicly do so.

Some churches teach that baptism requires total immersion under water. You can do this in church if you have the facilities – an inflatable swimming pool works fine. Otherwise any large enough body of water will do. Other churches pour water over the head and catch it in a basin, or sprinkle water on the head. Churches that baptize babies generally use one of the latter methods. Both date back to the early centuries of the church, if not to its very conception. In fact, some scholars argue that there was not a large enough body of water in Jerusalem to immerse the 3,000 new believers who were baptized on the day of Pentecost (Acts 2:41), and therefore infer that it must have been done by sprinkling or pouring. This is another of the many places good Bible-believing Christians understand things differently.

However you do it, when you baptize a person, they are joining the family of God. And the family should know they are being joined! Therefore, **baptisms should be celebrations**, open at least to other church members, if not the public. In fact, an important part of the ceremony should be a promise from your people to help their new brother or sister grow and mature in the Lord. Baptism is not a graduation, it's a beginning.

One practical point: if you are baptizing someone by immersion, be aware of what they (and you) are wearing. Some clothes that are entirely appropriate when dry may become embarrassingly inappropriate when wet.

Whatever your theological views on baptism, it is an important spiritual step. Most pastors teach a class or do individual pre-baptism counseling beforehand, to be sure people understand the commitment they are making.

The Lord's Supper

As with baptism, different churches have different understandings and practices of the Lord's Supper. If you are part of a tradition, follow those teachings. If not, find out what you can about the various views and practices, and ask God how he wants you to do it. Here are some of the options.

Some churches celebrate the Lord's Supper every time they gather. Others may celebrate it only a few times a year. Generally, those that celebrate more often see it as a means of grace that should not be neglected. Others feel that frequent celebration causes people to take it for granted, to the point that it may no longer be meaningful for them.

Some churches allow anyone to participate, some restrict participation to all baptized Christians, some to members of their own church or denomination, and some are even more restrictive. In some traditions anyone may preside at the celebration, while others restrict that privilege to ordained clergy.

As for the elements, some churches use leavened bread, some unleavened. Some churches use wine, others unfermented grape juice. "Ordinance" churches tend to see these as representing the body and blood of Jesus.

"Sacrament" churches tend to see them as actually being or becoming the body and blood of Jesus, at least in a spiritual sense.

In some churches the people come forward to receive the elements. In others the elements are passed among the people where they sit. In some traditions everyone drinks from the same large cup, in others they dip their bread in the large cup (an ancient practice called "intinction"), and still others use small individual cups.

I'd like to suggest a few practical tips that apply to every celebration of Holy Communion, no matter how it is understood or carried out:

- Prayerfully **consider the spiritual flow** of your service as you decide when in the order of worship you will celebrate the Lord's Supper.
- Be sure to **include some explanation** of what Holy Communion is and why you celebrate it.
- Be sure you **tell everyone what they are expected to do**: when and where to move, when to eat or drink, etc. If you don't, visitors will feel lost. Even regular attenders appreciate being reminded.
- **Be aware of hindrances** to participation. No one who has a desire to receive, and who is eligible according to your tradition or understanding, should be prevented because of a physical barrier or disability.
- Be sure you **allow enough time.** Don't rush people; give them time for a spiritual experience.

A last point: I believe many people overlook the healing power of receiving the Lord's Supper. Jesus said of the bread, *This is my body, which is broken for you* (1 Corinthians 11:24). Isaiah 53:5 says, *With his wounds we are healed* (ESV). The wounds by which we are healed were received in the broken body of Christ, which is the bread of Communion. Whether you understand this as a symbol that builds faith for healing, or as a tangible impartation of grace, the connection to healing is something that should be lifted up.

Weddings and Funerals

Weddings and funerals are the most important events in many families. They are also one of the main church activities likely to have non-believers in attendance. Train yourself to think of these celebrations, not only through the eyes of the participants, but also the guests or mourners.

In particular, prayerfully look for a way to **include a simple but clear gospel message**. A Christian marriage is a celebration of two redeemed, transformed people who want to spend their lives following Jesus together. A Christian funeral is a celebration of the fact that for those who have put their faith in Jesus, death is not an end; it's a door to a whole new wonderful life, and God is with us on both sides of the door. These truths bring hope and joy that should be proclaimed.

As for the details, follow your own customs and traditions as far as they are compatible with Christian belief. If you are ministering in a place where the traditions come from a different religion, prayerfully decide whether it is best to modify them just enough to make them acceptable to Christians, or whether it is better to change them completely to mark the fact that this is a distinctively Christian service. Talk to other Christian ministers in the area. If you can all have a unified approach, that gives the best witness.

Some pastors only perform weddings or funerals for people who are part of their own church. Some will not marry people who have been divorced, or who live together before marriage. Other pastors see weddings and funerals as opportunities to reach exactly those people with the good news of Jesus.

Again, if you are part of a denomination that has strict rules about such things, follow those rules. Otherwise, ask God to show you what he wants you to do. Personally, I do not consider a divorce that happened before a person became a Christian, or a divorce on biblical grounds (the spouse committed adultery), to exclude a person from marrying again. The same goes for an innocent person who was divorced against their will.

For me, most of the work of a wedding happens before the ceremony. I require several sessions of pre-wedding counseling. I focus on practical tips on how to have a good marriage, using Bible verses wherever possible. If I don't already know the couple are good Christians, I present a clear gospel message and invitation to faith. Most couples appreciate the time and personal attention.

As for the wedding itself, perhaps the biggest issue is getting people, including the bride and groom, to look past the bustle and excitement. Find ways to keep the focus on the meaning of marriage and the necessity of keeping Jesus central.

Speaking of bustle and excitement, consider asking one of your church folks to serve as wedding coordinator. It can save you a lot of time and busy-work. In churches where I did a lot of weddings, I even had the coordinator handle the rehearsals. After all, I already knew my part!

In many ways funerals are similar to weddings. Again, people can get so caught up in what needs to be done that they don't stop to really experience their feelings. If the primary mourner is the kind of person who always takes care of things, encourage them to let others take care of them for a change.

Funerals provide a unique opportunity for talking about eternity, and this life as our only chance to prepare for it. Pray about how God wants you to grasp this opportunity. But please don't tell people that their loved one is going to hell, even if you know they weren't a Christian. I have never known anyone to be drawn to the Lord by such a message, but I have known several who were driven away by it. Besides, you don't know whether, in God's grace, the deceased may have come to the Lord with their dying breath.

Most people, pastors included, tend to be attentive to the mourner for about six weeks. Then they move on. Plan some kind of long-term follow-up. In particular, a recognition of the one-year anniversary of the death can mean a lot.

Points to Remember

- The first consideration is not what you like or what will attract people, but what God wants.
- The Bible gives great latitude in how we design our worship spaces and services; give prayerful thought to every aspect of them.
- Some people endure the music to hear the sermon, others endure the sermon to hear the music.
- Every part of the service can and should be done worshipfully.
- Make visitors feel welcome, comfortable and important.
- Don't overlook the evangelistic potential of weddings and funerals.

14

PREACHING

How then will they call on him in whom they have not believed?
And how are they to believe in him of whom they have never
heard? And how are they to hear without someone preaching?
– Romans 10:14 ESV

What's the first thing that comes to mind when you think of a pastor? Probably, it's preaching. In every church I've served there were people who just called me "Preacher." In this day of videos and podcasts, there's still amazing power in face-to-face, in-person communication, especially when it's anointed by the Holy Spirit of God.

Why Preach?

Preaching the word of God is an awesome responsibility. When you stand in front of people and preach, they expect to hear not only God's Word, the Bible, but God's words to them personally. Some of the worst experiences of my ministry have come when I temporarily lost sight of that. If you start taking preaching lightly, or begin to see it as just a job or a routine, you may sound just as good to your own ears, but the power will be gone and your people will know it - and if you keep it up, they'll be gone, too.

The first, last and continuing rule of preaching is, **soak it in prayer.** Don't write something pretty or important-sounding and ask God to bless it. Don't proclaim your own opinions and expect God to anoint it. **Find out what God wants these particular people at this particular time to hear and understand and do, and make that as clear and compelling as you can**, with God's help. Then leave the results to God.

Every sermon should do four things: **proclaim a truth, explain its meaning, apply it to life, and encourage action.** Every pastor naturally leans more toward one of these than the other three - for me, I love the explaining part, and I have to consciously remind myself to include the other three. Bible passages and topics differ in how easy they are to understand or how much people need to be encouraged to follow them. But you need to include some proclamation, explanation, application and motivation or your sermon won't be complete. And this doesn't really come under preaching, but if you are motivating your people to do something, provide a way - church program, volunteer opportunity, resources - for them to do it.

In other words, every sermon needs to answer four questions about your Bible text: What does it say? What does it mean? What does God want me to do about it? What is going to get me out of my chair to do it?

You notice I assume your sermon is based on a Bible text. You don't have to start by reading a passage, though that's an excellent way to begin. But **if what you say isn't what the Bible says, you may be lecturing, you may be arguing, or you may just be spouting off, but you aren't preaching.**

Using the Bible

Preaching starts with the Bible.

I often hear preachers say, "I just read the Bible and say what it says." If that's all there is to it, why do so many who "just say what the Bible says" wind up saying such different things?

The Bible is the inspired, inerrant word of God. But the way God chose to convey his inspired, inerrant word is through a collection of writings from dozens of authors, writing over fifteen hundred years or more, in a variety of cultures and literary styles, and three different languages – none of which most pastors can read.

The fact is, **it's not always obvious what God is saying.** And you know what? I believe God wants it that way. Jesus spoke in parables so that only those who cared enough to ask him would understand (Matthew 13:36; 15:15). The riches of the Bible are like gold: a few nuggets lie on the surface where anyone can find them, but only those who are willing to dig will strike the vein.

Successful gold miners know the rules that lead to finding rich ore in the ground. Successful preachers know the rules that lead to finding God's truth in the Bible. Here are a few of the most basic rules.

Read meaning out of the Bible, not into it

Don't start with your opinion and then look for passages to support it. **Start with the Bible and look for God's opinion.** If you really want to find what God says about something, these rules will help you find it. Of course, by picking and choosing verses, and ignoring the rules, you can make the Bible seem to say anything you want. But it's a dangerous thing to say, "Thus saith the Lord," or even "Thus saith the Bible," when what you really mean is, "Thus saith my own opinion" (see Jeremiah 14:15).

God doesn't contradict himself

If a passage seems to contradict another passage, or a fact from science, history or archeology, then you don't understand the passage, or what it seems to contradict, or both. Keep praying and studying. Look for a way of understanding it that allows all the seemingly contradictory parts to be true. In the meantime, don't focus on the problems. As the American humorist Mark Twain said, "It's not the parts of the Bible I can't understand that bother me. It's the parts I do understand." Focus on obeying the parts you understand. The more you do, the more you'll understand, and the part you don't understand will shrink.

Let the Bible interpret the Bible

If one part of the Bible isn't clear about a subject, see what else the Bible has to say about it. Put it all together and come to an understanding that accounts for all the Bible says.

Context, context, context

Realtors say there are three keys to the price of a house: location, location, and location. The three keys to a Bible passage are context, context, and context. Literary context is the words that precede and follow the passage you're looking at. Historical context describes the events surrounding the writing of the passage. Cultural context describes the values, customs and beliefs of the culture in which it was written. Any or all of these can shed important light on what the original author was trying to get the original readers to understand.

Meaning, principle, application

On the surface it seems like the task of Bible reading is to understand what the words mean and apply them to your life. Unfortunately, this skips an important step. Sometimes directly applying the words would work fine in the age and culture in which it was written, but it doesn't work at all in a different age or culture. This is why understanding the cultural context can be so important.

The missing step is to determine the principle underlying the words. Then you apply the principle in a way that makes sense for your time and culture.

For instance, at the ends of several of his letters Paul tells the Christians to greet one another with a holy kiss. In that culture a kiss was a commonly accepted greeting of affection and fellowship. In many cultures today the same meaning would be conveyed by a handshake, or possibly a hug. In these cultures, attempting to kiss another person could lead to a grave misunderstanding. Here, offering a handshake instead of a kiss is not disobeying the Bible, it's obeying the principle Paul was really getting at.

Don't be dogmatic about anything the Bible isn't dogmatic about

Some things in the Bible are very clear, such as salvation by grace through faith. Other things are not so clear, such as when Jesus will come back. Where the Bible is clear, stand firm for the truth. Where the Bible is not clear, allow people their opinions.

Where the Bible isn't clear, consult Christian teaching, your spirit and your mind

If the Bible is clear you can stop there. But some passages aren't clear. Read how other Christians have understood them. Listen to God in your spirit. Learn all you can about the question, then consider what seems reasonable. And if you have this much trouble understanding a passage, be generous with those whose similar struggles lead them to interpret it differently.

Literal, figurative, allegorical

In America we have a phrase to describe when rain is coming down very hard. We say, "It's raining cats and dogs." We all understand what that means because we say it all the time. But imagine someone two thousand years in the future, speaking a different language, trying to understand that phrase. Should they take it literally - were we claiming that actual cats and dogs were falling from the sky? Is it allegorical - were we trying to convey some spiritual truth using rain, cats and dogs as symbols of something else? Or is it figurative – an idiom that everyone in our time, language and culture understood through common use?

All these types of writing were used by those who wrote the Bible, and more. Special literary types such as poetry, wisdom, and apocalyptic writing have their own rules of interpretation. For instance, sometimes prophesies had an immediate fulfillment as well as a future meaning.

In most cases, if you read the Bible the same way you read any other book, your common sense will tell you if something is meant to be taken literally. When Jesus said, *"I am the vine"*(John 15:1), nobody thinks he was inviting people to pick grapes from him. But when the meaning is not so obvious, consider what kind of writing you are dealing with.

Use study tools, but remember they aren't inspired

Christians have been studying the Bible for almost two thousand years, and Jews have been studying the Old Testament for almost as long again. Take advantage of their work. Cross-references, concordances and search functions on digital Bibles can help you let the Bible interpret the Bible. Bible encyclopedias and handbooks can tell you about historical and cultural context. Commentaries can teach you what other Christians have learned and thought about a given passage. A good study Bible will give the most important of this information on the same page as the Bible text. And of course the internet is a wealth of information. Use all of these tools in your study.

But remember, the Bible is inspired, but the study helps aren't. As with anything else of human origin, some will be more useful than others. Follow Paul's advice in 1 Thessalonians 5:21 *Test everything, hold fast what is good* (ESV).

Freely use what you find in your sermons, but if you use someone else's words, be sure to give them credit. If you let people think someone else's work is your own, you've crossed the line from research to stealing.

Approaches to Preaching

Now that you've studied the Bible, it's time to proclaim it.

There is no one correct way to preach a sermon. Listen to great preachers, study their ways of constructing and delivering sermons, but don't pick one to copy in every detail. If you could become just like someone else, one of you would be redundant. And the world would be deprived of the uniqueness of you. As you keep learning and trying different approaches you'll gradually develop your own style that fits the gifts and abilities God built into you.

There are many different approaches to proclaiming God's word. Like many other things, your preaching style is a combination of choices in a number of different areas. You can picture each one as a line, with opposite extremes on the ends, and a whole range in between. As I describe them below, think about where on the line you usually fit. I'll tell you where I tend to land on each one, just as an example. Remember that one end is not better or worse than the other, although as in most things, extremes in preaching are probably best avoided. When we finish, picture it all together and you'll have the shape of your unique style of preaching. But stay flexible. In any given situation or sermon God may lead you to move one way or another in any of these aspects. And if you naturally favor one end, remind yourself not to neglect the other, because there will be people listening who hear better from that end.

Emotional or intellectual

Some preachers aim at informing the mind. Others aim at moving emotions. Pure information can be dry, while pure emotion can have little lasting effect. Personally, I'm much more comfortable with an intellectual or analytical approach. I have to consciously remind myself to consider emotion.

Prepared or spontaneous

Some preachers do a lot of study. They outline, write and rewrite their sermons. Others just stand up and start talking, trusting the Holy Spirit to supply the words.

I believe the Holy Spirit can inspire words being written just as surely as he can inspire words being spoken. Haven't you ever read a daily devotion and thought, "God sure knew I needed that today!" even though it was written months or years ago?

On the other hand, spontaneous words can have an immediacy and freshness of delivery that is hard to duplicate when you're reading a manuscript. Of course, even the most ardent supporters of "speaking from the heart" prepare themselves through prayer and Bible study, even if they don't plan out specific words.

I've moved back and forth on this through the years, sometimes writing full manuscripts, sometimes outlines of varying detail, and sometimes just a few bullet points, but I always prepare in some way.

Some preachers plan their sermons weeks or months ahead of time, perhaps preaching series of sermons, perhaps following the church year or a calendar of Scripture passages called a lectionary. Others wait each week, sometimes until they stand up to preach, to see what God puts on their heart. A plan allows you to do advance preparation and advertise what you will be speaking about. Deciding each week allows you to preach on current events and needs without disrupting a sermon plan. I've tried all of these, and I still go back and forth on it.

Evangelism, discipleship or exhortation

Some preachers see their main job as leading people to become Christians. Their sermons focus on salvation. Others see their main job as helping Christians grow more and more into the image of Christ. Their sermons focus on understanding the faith and living it out. Others see their job as urging people to do what they already know they should do. Their sermons focus on encouragement and motivation.

Sometimes discipleship preachers neglect a compelling invitation to Jesus. Sometimes evangelistic preachers wind up with a church full of Christians who know they're born again, but not much else. Sometimes exhorters fail to build a solid foundation of truth to support their calls to action.

I praise the Lord for the evangelists and exhorters. My own gifts run more toward teaching and equipping, so I consciously remind myself to include in my sermons a simple gospel invitation and encouragement to practical action. Which of these emphases do you need to remind yourself about?

Narrative or linear

Narrative preachers use stories to convey their messages, like the parables of Jesus. Linear preachers teach *precept upon precept, line upon line* (Isaiah 28:10 ESV), like the Sermon on the Mount. Stories engage interest and can be more memorable than outlines, but a systematic point by point explanation can be clearer than a story. I naturally think in outlines, but I try to use simple stories as illustrations because I know some of my listeners connect better that way.

Topical or expository

Topical preaching starts with a topic, and pulls together what the Bible says about it. Expository preaching starts with a Bible passage, and explains and applies it. I use both. I enjoy walking a congregation through a Bible passage, or even a whole book of the Bible in a series of sermons. But when a specific subject needs to be addressed, because it's in the news or something is making it relevant to my church, I preach a sermon or series about what the Bible says on that topic.

Eternal truths or current events

Some pastors focus solely on teaching Bible doctrine, trusting that mature Christians know how to take the eternal truths of the Bible and apply them to what is happening in their lives and their community. Other pastors emphasize life situations and current events, knowing that newer Christians need to be taught how to think Biblically about the events of their lives and the world. My own approach is to teach Bible truths, and use current events and everyday life to illustrate and apply them.

Engagement with the world or separation from it

Some pastors feel like the church should be a place where people can rise above the social and political opinions that so often divide people in other contexts. Others believe God calls the church to be a prophetic voice, speaking truth to power.

As you prayerfully consider whether God wants you to preach on a social or political topic, these questions might be helpful: Is there a moral issue here that is clearly addressed in the Bible, or is it strictly a political or philosophical disagreement about the best way to do good? If the government doing something that negatively affects Christians or a minority, is God calling you to address it, or does he want you to focus on getting people saved? How important is it to God that you not risk alienating those already in your congregation, or not risk getting the church closed down? Does God want you to be a public face for this issue, a behind-the scenes worker, or a silent prayer warrior, or does he want you to leave this issue for another part of the body of Christ to deal with?

I have good Christian friends and colleagues, and even members of my own family, who see some political questions very differently from the way I do. I know they love God, I know they understand the Bible, I know they know how to receive God's guidance in their lives, yet sometimes our politics are completely opposite. What am I to make of that? I have to conclude that God doesn't necessarily want every Christian to see every issue the same way. If I believe God wants me to vote "Yes," and you believe God wants you to vote "No," I have to believe we may both be right. God may have his reasons for letting an election be decided 55/45 instead of being unanimous.

Personally, I try not to let my congregation know my personal political views. When I feel led to address a moral issue, I preach the relevant Bible truths and let people make the political connection. Other than that, I leave politics alone. But I have many preacher friends who make their politics very clear, and I trust that's how God is leading them.

The whole Bible or your favorite passages

Some preachers make a real effort to preach all the doctrines of Christianity from all parts of the Bible. Others feel that God has called them to emphasize a specific message, perhaps an important truth they feel is not well understood.

In my own ministry I've found that many people in the churches I've served have not been taught much about the Holy Spirit. In attempting to correct that I probably preach more about the Holy Spirit than many other pastors. In general, though, a local congregation needs a well-rounded diet of spiritual truth. One of the values of the lectionary is that, if you commit to preach from the prescribed Bible passage each week, it will force you to cover parts of the Bible you might otherwise neglect.

It may be that there are some areas of the Bible you just don't feel qualified to preach about, at least not yet. One way to address this is to invite guest preachers who can talk about those things. It will round out what your congregation hears, and you will learn something yourself.

If you feel strongly that God has given you a specific message to share, you may be called to be a traveling teacher, visiting various churches and preaching the same thing everywhere, rather than pastoring a congregation that needs to hear something different every week.

Holiness or grace

Holiness preachers emphasize the need to live obedient lives pleasing to God in every way. Grace preachers emphasize God's unconditional love and forgiveness. Obviously both are true, but both can also easily be misunderstood. Preaching holiness without preaching grace can allow people to think they earn forgiveness and salvation by their good works. Preaching grace without preaching holiness can allow people to think they can get away with anything without eternal consequences. I try to be right in the middle on this one.

The chosen few or every tribe and tongue

Some preachers focus on the differences between Christians and non-Christians, or even between their church and other churches. This can build a sense of identity and community, but it can also allow people to be judgmental about other groups, or feel they are better than everybody else. Other preachers emphasize God's love for everyone. This can build openness and tolerance, but it can also allow people to feel that all religions are equally valid. I probably tend a little toward the second side, so every now and then I make it a point to emphasize that Jesus Christ is the only way to God.

Speaking for God or teaching people to hear God

Some preachers believe God has called them to tell people what God wants them to do. Others feel God wants them to teach people how to hear God for themselves. The first can be good with a congregation that is fairly new in their faith, or when God actually has spoken strongly to the pastor, but it can really open the people up for manipulation from unscrupulous preachers. Personally, I tend pretty strongly in the second direction on this one, but beware: people can think God is telling them some pretty strange things.

Some Don'ts

Don't preach "at" specific people

It can be tempting to use a sermon to send a message to one person, or a small group of troublemakers. Resist that temptation. The rest of the congregation will either know who you're aiming at and take sides, or they'll think you're aiming at them and resent it. And they'll be cheated of hearing what they need to hear. Besides, it usually doesn't work anyway.

One pastor had a member who always thought the sermons applied to other people. One Sunday there was a snowstorm and this member was the only person who showed up. The pastor thought, "Aha, now I've got him!" and preached a sermon aimed right at the person. When he was done the member said, "Great sermon, Pastor. Too bad the people who needed to hear it weren't here!"

Jesus said if you have something to say to a person, say it to them one-on-one (Matthew 18:15-17).

Don't use the pulpit to advance a personal agenda

The pulpit is a sacred place devoted to proclaiming God's word. There's nothing wrong with pursuing your own ideas and projects, and there are many legitimate means for doing that. The sermon is not one of them. The only agenda that should be advanced through preaching is God's agenda.

Don't use anyone in a sermon illustration without asking them first

This includes your family. Different people are sensitive about different things at different times. Even if you are holding someone up as a shining example of right, still ask them first. And never, ever use something told you in confidence, even if you think you have sufficiently disguised the person or situation. There is no quicker way to destroy trust.

Don't try to cram too much into one sermon

This is one of which I'm often guilty. I know what I want to say because I've been studying it and thinking about it all week, if not for years. I tend to forget that my listeners haven't been doing the same. Some of them may be completely unfamiliar with what I'm talking about. They need me to break it down for them. Some of the best preachers spend an entire sermon explaining and illustrating one point in a number of different ways. If you find that you are rushing to say everything you want to, maybe it would be better to break your message into several sermons.

Don't talk beyond people's ability to listen

Some congregations start fidgeting if the sermon goes beyond fifteen minutes. Others feel cheated if it's less than forty-five. I was disappointed to discover that very little of that difference is due to the skill and ability of the preacher. Much of it is cultural expectation. At least as much has to do with the environment - it's hard to keep people's interest if they are physically uncomfortable.

And people won't keep listening if you run out of things to say. One Sunday a parishioner told me, "Your sermon had a great ending. Unfortunately, you kept talking another ten minutes."

If you find your sermons are running a little long, go back and see if you are "running off on rabbit trails." Side issues can confuse your listeners and distract them from your main point. Every sermon should have one clear goal. Anything that doesn't contribute to that goal should not be in that sermon. Take the side issue and make it the main point of another sermon.

Somebody said, "The main thing is to keep the main thing the main thing." Most people will only remember one thing from your sermon. Make sure it's the main thing.

Points to Remember

- Soak your preaching in prayer.
- Every sermon should proclaim a truth, explain its meaning, apply it to life, and encourage action.
- Learn and use the time-tested rules for interpreting the Bible.
- Study great preachers and sermons, then develop your own style.
- Don't misuse the privilege of preaching.

15

MINISTRIES

For we are God's masterpiece. He has created us anew in Christ Jesus, so we can do the good things he planned for us long ago. – Ephesians 2:10

Paul says the pastor's number one job is *to equip God's people to do his work and build up the church, the body of Christ* (Ephesians 4:12). "Ministry" is just another word for doing God's work, serving God by serving the people he loves.

When a church grows beyond a handful of people, they will naturally start dividing themselves into ministry groups. Some will work with the children, some will share musical skills, some will take care of the building, and so on.

As your church grows, it becomes helpful to formalize these ministry groups. You can avoid a lot of trouble later on if you have written policies outlining what each group does, how they relate to each other, how people become a part of the group, and so on. For instance, are members elected – by whom? Or appointed – by whom? Or do they just volunteer – approved or overseen by whom?

These rules are particularly important for those who handle church money or have legal responsibility for church property. Most denominations and established churches have detailed policies for these things. If yours doesn't, read some from other churches for ideas.

There are basically three kinds of ministries. The first focuses on a task to perform. The second focuses on a group to serve. The lasts oversee the resources that support the first two. I'll list the most common kinds of ministry groups and give a thought or two from my own experience.

Pastor beware: every one of these groups will want you involved in their ministry. That's a good thing, but it can also be bad. It's good that the groups feel their ministry is important enough for the pastor to be part of everything they do. It's bad because they can easily take up all your time. This is the place to remember what the apostles said when they set up the first ministry group in the Jerusalem church:

"We apostles should spend our time teaching the word of God, not running a food program. And so, brothers, select seven men who are well respected and are full of the Spirit and wisdom. We will give them this responsibility. Then we apostles can spend our time in prayer and teaching the word." - Acts 6:2-4

Train, support, resource, encourage and oversee your people, but beyond that, let them do their ministries, and you do yours.

Task-Defined Ministries

Every congregation should fulfill **the seven main functions of a local church: worship, member care, discipleship, serving, evangelism, societal transformation, and prayer.** Your church may combine some of these or sub-divide them, but you need to address these seven functions in some way. Task-defined ministries do this.

The job of ministry groups is not to do the ministries, but to organize and promote the ministries so everyone can do them. For instance, often church members feel that only the people in the evangelism group have to do evangelism, and the rest of the congregation are off the hook. Sometimes even the group members begin to believe that. As pastor, keep reminding your people that every Christian is responsible for the work of the church.

By the way, where I've use the word "group," many churches say "committee," "team," "board" or "council." Prayerfully consider the terms you use, because each word carries connotations. "Committee," "board" and "council" can imply that this group legislates and plans work for other people to do. "Team" implies a group that works together, which some people can take to mean that those not on the team are not involved in the work. I'm using "group" as the most generic term, but it may not be the best word for your church.

Worship ministries

Every pastor knows a worship service doesn't just happen. If there will be music, somebody has to plan and rehearse. If you are celebrating Communion, somebody has to prepare the elements. If you use candles or flowers, somebody has to find them and set them in place. If you designate people to read Scripture or hand out bulletins or receive the offering, somebody has to schedule them. If you decorate for special seasons, somebody has to get the decorations, put them up, and take them down. The worship ministries group plans and coordinates all these things, and the myriad other logistical details involved in your worship services.

Member care ministries

Jesus said, *"Your love for one another will prove to the world that you are my disciples."* (John 13:35). As we've said before, God created human beings to be his family. The church is the people who are trying to live that out. The more people do things together, the more they get to know and love each other, the more they feel like a family. Some of the things they do together might just be for fun. Others might involve accomplishing a task, like a church work day when people come together to wash windows and fix up the building. Sometimes a member needs a little help, like meals for the family of a new mother. When a member misses church for two or three weeks, somebody should check on them to see if everything is alright. The member care ministries group plans and coordinates these activities.

Some churches have formal membership lists, with specific criteria and responsibilities. Others consider everyone who attends church to be members. Formal membership can help assure that only mature Christians who agree with your theology can vote in your meetings or serve in leadership. It may also give some leverage if church discipline is required. Informal membership can be more attractive and inclusive – and it's certainly a lot less paperwork.

Discipleship ministries

There's a lot more to becoming like Jesus than listening to a sermon every week. The discipleship ministries group coordinates Bible studies, Sunday School classes and other opportunities for people to develop their souls and grow in their faith. A big part of this is encouraging people to have a daily prayer and Bible reading time. Providing written resources, such as a daily devotional magazine or website, can be very helpful.

Before I became a pastor, I found that my greatest spiritual growth came in small groups of other Christians. We helped each other know God, understand the Bible and live the Christian life, with not a pastor in sight. Such groups can meet in homes, at work during lunch hour, in coffee shops, or wherever and whenever works.

Some of your most effective leaders might turn out to be people you would never expect, like housewives, students or retired people. Train, resource, recognize and encourage them. Don't micromanage, but do stay aware of what is happening in the groups, because situations will arise from time to time that will require your attention as pastor.

Evangelism ministries

Evangelism moves people from having no knowledge of Jesus Christ to knowing about Christ, recognizing their need of Christ, and finally putting their faith in Christ. Their journey doesn't stop there, but the task changes from evangelism to discipleship.

Ideally, the journey to faith parallels a journey to involvement in your church. When people don't know about your church, you want them to become aware of it and view it favorably. That involves advertising and public relations. When people visit, you want them to have a good experience. That involves seeing that your members, building, worship service and programs make a good impression. When people go home their first Sunday, you want them to come back. That involves follow-up. The evangelism ministries group plans and coordinates all of these things.

Pastor Adam Hamilton says every church member should be able to answer three questions: Why do people need Jesus? Why do people need church? Why do people need my church? The ability to answer these questions, and the confidence to share those answers with non-Christians, requires training and motivation. Coordinating that is another job of your evangelism ministries group.

Aid ministries

Aid ministries, sometimes called helping or mercy ministries, demonstrate God's love in practical ways. It may be as simple as helping an elderly person in care for their home. It may be feeding homeless people, or clothing orphaned children. Needs are everywhere. As church people work together to help others, they grow closer to each other and to God. They often say it's one of the most rewarding things they ever do. Finding, planning, publicizing and coordinating these opportunities to serve is the task of the serving ministries group.

A note of warning: in some settings, offering help to those outside the church may be seen as an attempt to bribe them to become Christians. Be aware, and pray hard before violating local customs.

Social influence ministries

Jesus taught us to pray for God's will to be done on earth as it is in heaven. Where earth is not like heaven, God's will is not being done. Christians are called to pray and work to correct that.

When the problem is with individuals, we are to *patiently correct, rebuke and encourage your people with good teaching* (2 Timothy 4:2). When the problem is with systems of society or government, we are to influence those in power to bring earthly "kingdoms" more in line with the Kingdom of God. Social influence ministries, sometimes called peace and justice ministries, work to make the congregation more aware of social issues and plan responses, often in coordination with other churches and organizations.

Some pastors feel that the church should not be involved in trying to change society, but just focus on individuals. It's true the church has a poor track record when it tries to take over the role of secular government. But it's also true that most of the world's advancements in human rights, such as the abolition of slavery in England and America, have come about through Christian influence in society.

One note of caution: on many social issues there is a fine line between righteousness and politics. If a person feels no need to try to help when large segments of the population are hungry or oppressed, that's a question of righteousness, by any Biblical definition. If people want to help, but disagree about the most effective way to do it, that's not a question of righteousness, but a matter of politics. Keep a careful eye on your social influence ministries to be sure they don't stray into the area of politics.

Prayer ministries

Prayer should be the ongoing activity of every Christian. It should underlie, guide and cover every ministry of the church. Because of that, many people don't think of establishing a separate ministry for prayer. But the fact is, a recognized group devoted to practicing and promoting prayer may be the most important ministry group your church can have. Prayer accesses the most powerful force in the universe.

The first task of a prayer ministry group is to teach and promote prayer, not just as a private personal exercise, but as a ministry that objectively changes the world to a new reality. The second task is to practice prayer themselves. Some people have a calling to intercession. Pastor, if you're smart, you'll identify those people, organize them into prayer groups, encourage them and recognize them. Some pastors recruit a special prayer group to pray specifically for the pastor. That can be a real blessing.

Group-Defined Ministries

Group-defined ministries are among the first ministries that develop in most churches. Whether it's caring for children, getting the teen-agers together, or visiting shut-ins, certain groups of people need special attention. Clubs and support groups can also be a great "side door" into the church, a way for your members to invite friends who would be wary of a church service.

Infants, children, teens, young adults and the elderly have different abilities and needs, so Sunday School classes and fellowship opportunities are often broken up according to age. Some churches expect all ages to participate in the main worship service, while others provide alternatives for some age groups. Often, the responsibility for providing all these ministries falls on the one age group I didn't mention – active adults. Don't forget to provide for them while they are providing for everyone else.

In modern society, churches need to take special precautions to protect the children in their care, and to protect members who work with children. It's not unknown for child predators to stalk churches looking for their next victim. It's also not unknown for perfectly innocent church workers to be charged with molesting the children in their care. You need a system in place to protect both. The most basic element is a requirement that two adults must always be present in any children's class or ministry. You also need a way of knowing who is authorized to take a particular child out of your care.

Age Groups

Infants and pre-schoolers

Don't discount the ability of even very young children to learn about God. Babies can learn to associate Jesus and church with feeling good and secure. Toddlers can learn songs and Bible stories. Some people treat the nursery as just a place to warehouse children while their parents do church stuff. It can be so much more.

On the practical side, safety and cleanliness are your top priorities for this age group. If the parents don't feel confident that you will take good care of their child, they won't use your children's ministry, and they may even leave your church.

Children

Don't underestimate the spiritual potential of children. They have a way of asking questions that get right to the heart of a matter, and their simple faith can lead them to pray powerful prayers. Make opportunities for them to practice what you teach them. And encourage them to invite their friends. Children can be great evangelists.

Teens

Many churches focus their youth groups on games and food, with little spiritual content. Churches can't compete with the secular world in the area of entertainment. But many teens are very interested in the deeper questions of life. They want to know that their lives have meaning, that they can make a difference. When teenagers become committed to a cause, they go all the way. Ask God to show you how to tap into that passion.

Young adults

Most adult needs are based around life situations, which we'll talk about in a moment. Some churches have specific groups that focus on young adults as an age group. Don't try to organize activities for these groups. They are fully capable of doing that themselves. Just facilitate and support them – and as always, keep an eye on what they are doing so you can head off potential trouble, such as a false teaching infiltrating the group, before it arises.

The elderly

In some cultures, as people get old enough that they are no longer physically able to do the kind of work they used to, they begin to feel useless. This is a great time to encourage them to become part of a prayer ministry. Even if they can't get out to prayer meetings, they can certainly pray. Their age gives them the wisdom and experience to pray in detail about things that are going on in the church. Encourage them that God may have spent their whole lives preparing them for this most important ministry.

Life Situation Groups

Grouping people by age is an easy and often effective way of tailoring ministry to certain shared needs, but there are other groupings that should not be ignored. For instance, people in a particular life situation may share similar needs. Many churches have groups for women, men, singles, parents of small children, or widows and widowers. Each situation has its own unique set of challenges to living the Christian life. Sometimes it's helpful to be around people who understand what you're going through. Sometimes it's just more fun to be with people when you have something in common.

Support Groups

Support groups are a specialized kind of life situation ministry. Some events or situations leave people needing special help that is best provided by others dealing with the same issues, perhaps with a trained facilitator. People struggling with addictions, dealing with grief, raising a child with disabilities, healing from various forms of abuse, women facing emotional aftermath from abortion, these and many more can benefit from meeting together to support each other. Some of these groups are short-term, others may last a lifetime. All are opportunities to demonstrate the love and power of God to people who may be unusually aware of just how much they need it.

Interest Groups

Interest groups and clubs can be great ways to get people together for fellowship and demonstrate how God fits into every area of life. Groups can be organized around hobbies, sports, almost anything. Every church activity doesn't have to be overtly spiritual. One of the best ways for people to come to the Lord and grow in discipleship is to just spend time with mature Christians. Interest groups are a great opportunity to do that.

Support Ministries

Does your church meet in a building? Do you receive tithes and offerings? Do you spend or give away money? Is anyone other than the pastor involved in making decisions or carrying out ministries? Do you make copies, order supplies, or keep records?

If you are like most pastors, the answer to all these question is yes. Caring for all these details may not seem like ministries, but they are, and vital ones at that. These are what I call resourcing or support ministries. You could say **they make all the other ministries possible.** They support all the other ministries by providing the resources that allow them to function.

There are basically four resource areas that need to be responsibly handled if your church is to function smoothly: **money, property, personnel and administration.** In smaller churches all these areas may be handled by one group, sometimes called deacons or elders, sometimes called an administrative board or church council or presbytery. In other systems each area has its own group. I'll talk more about these areas in upcoming chapters.

Support ministries all face a common temptation: getting priorities backwards. It's way too easy to start looking at evangelism as a way to get more people to support the church budget, instead of remembering that the purpose of the budget is to win people to Christ, and carry out other ministries. It's way too easy to ban children from certain areas of the building because they might mess it up, instead of remembering that the building is just a tool for ministry, including ministry to children. Keep your people focused on what really matters.

As pastor, Ephesians 4:12 says your job is to equip the people to carry out the ministries. That makes you the main resourcing and support minister. In other words, a big part of your job is to **make sure your leaders and workers in all kinds of ministries are trained, equipped and encouraged.**

The Ministry Matrix

Task-defined ministries focus on doing a specific ministry task, usually for the whole range of people. Group-defined ministries focus on ministering to the needs of a specific group of people, usually with the whole range of ministry tasks. **The ministry matrix is a way of reminding your task-based ministries of all the different groups they need to serve, and your group-based ministries of all the different ministries they can be involved in.**

Let's draw a ministry matrix for your church and we'll see how it works. Take a piece of paper and list all your task-defined ministries in a column down one side. Then list all your group-defined ministries across the top.

Draw lines across the paper between each task, and down the paper between each group. The grid you've just drawn is your ministry matrix.

Here's an example:

	Children	Youth	Women	Addiction Support
Worship				
Member Care				
Discipleship				
Evangelism				
Aid				
Social Influence				
Prayer				

This is how it works. Say your worship ministry group is planning a special Easter service. As part of their planning they can look across the columns and ask themselves, "Will children understand this service? Is there a place for them? What about the teenagers? Would the women's group like to coordinate a meal afterwards? Is there anything in the service that could especially help people overcoming addictions, or potentially pose a problem for them?" Every task-defined ministry group can do the same. Basically you are asking two questions for each group. First, **how will our event or our overall ministry serve this group?** Second, **is there a way this group can help us with our event or ministry?**

Going the other direction, each group-defined ministry should go down the page and think about what their group needs from each area, and how they can be involved in it. For instance, the children's ministry group should periodically ask, "How are we teaching the children to worship, and involving them in our worship services? Do we follow up when a child stops coming? How well are we helping our children grow up as good disciples of Jesus? Are we winning children to Christ and teaching them to share their faith? How can children be involved in our service projects? How can we help our children think in a Christian way about what's going on in the world? Are we teaching our children to pray effectively, and do we appreciate the power of their prayers?" Again, you are asking two kinds of questions for each area of ministry. First, **is my group being ministered to in this area?** Second, **how can my group be involved in carrying**

out this kind of ministry?

Ministry Planning

Most churches find it helpful to get all the ministry leaders together once a year to plan events for the next twelve to eighteen months. Probably the most common way to do it is also the least effective. That's to have a meeting in the same place and time slot where you usually have meetings, pull out a calendar, and pencil in all the things you did last year. If you want to totally exclude creativity and new ideas, that's a good way to do it.

I'm guessing you don't want to totally exclude creativity and new ideas. In fact, you may even be in favor of them, at least a little. In that case, your goal isn't just to put some events on the calendar. Your goal is to find out what God has in mind for your church for the coming year, and through you for your community. Here are some ideas I've found helpful. We covered some of these in Chapter 13, but I've repeated them here to keep them all together.

Meet someplace different

It's amazing how a simple change of scenery can spark creativity. It doesn't need to be anything fancy. Maybe your town has a library with a meeting space available to the public. Maybe there's a park with a pavilion. Perhaps there's another church in town with a room they would let you use. The point is to get your people's thinking out of the same old rut. That's a whole lot easier if you're not in the same old place.

Allow plenty of time

It's hard to explore new ideas if everyone is watching the clock. Allow at least half a day. A full day, with a break for lunch, is better. If you can do it, an overnight retreat with your leaders can be a wonderful way to combine planning with fellowship and spiritual growth.

Invite a guest facilitator

Just as a change of scenery can spark creativity, so can a change of voice. Somebody said, "An expert is somebody who gets off an airplane with a briefcase." You don't have to fly someone in. Perhaps you and a pastor friend can trade off facilitating for each other. We listed some of the reasons for this in Chapter 13.

Appoint one official note taker

Everyone should take notes, but be sure you designate one person to keep the official version. That way, when Charlie says, "My notes say we're going to do that on the 20th" and Sue says, "I wrote down the 27th," you have a place to go for an authoritative answer.

Start with a brief Bible study

After your opening prayer, don't just dive right into filling the calendar. Take some time to remind everyone what this meeting is really all about: discerning the specific things God wants you to do in the coming year to fulfill the three purposes of the church. A time of interactive Bible study around those areas can help people refocus. This can be especially important if some of your leaders have jobs that involve similar kinds of planning activities, but very different goals and priorities.

Revisit your vision and mission statements

If you have written vision and mission statements, take a few minutes to review them. Remind yourselves of what they say and why you wrote them that way. Consider asking your leaders if anyone feels there is anything about them that might need to be re-evaluated or updated. One of the main reasons for having these statements is to help you decide whether any given event or program is fulfilling your church's calling. Before anything goes on the calendar, you should be able to say how it helps advance your vision and mission.

Evaluate the last year

What worked well? What didn't? What could you improve? What might not be worth doing again? Almost every program or event has a life cycle. First it's new and exciting, then it becomes routine, then it becomes "the way we've always done it," then it begins to lose effectiveness. Finally it's time to put it to rest, and invest your time and resources elsewhere. That can be a hard decision, but a necessary one. When people stop coming because they want to, and only show up out of a sense of duty, that's a good sign that you probably need to start looking for something new. On the other hand, I've always felt that if even a few people want to continue an activity, as long as it doesn't take resources that could better be spent elsewhere (including the pastor's time), there is no reason to make them stop.

Dream

I always like to include some time for dreaming. It's sometimes called brainstorming. This is where you ask your group an open-ended question: What is your dream for our church for this year? If money and workers and time were not a problem, what would you like for us to do this year to move us more toward being who God made us to be and doing what God made us to do?

The process is simple. First, everyone throws out ideas while somebody writes them down in a place where everyone can see them. After the ideas stop or a set time runs out, the group chooses a few ideas that seem worth further investigation.

It's amazing how exciting and creative this process can be. But it only works if one very important rule is followed: during the first stage, when ideas are being tossed out, no discussion is allowed. Every idea gets written down, no matter how crazy or impossible it might seem.

The first few times you use this process you will have to work hard to enforce this rule, but be strong. If you don't, people will grab the first idea that is suggested and start talking about whether they think it will work, how much it will cost, who would be in charge, and how some other church tried it and it didn't work. You'll use up all your time, and people will be discouraged from suggesting other ideas. Make sure you get all the ideas out on the table before you begin sorting them out and evaluating them.

Seek synergy

Use your ministry matrix. Look for how the different areas of your church can work together. How can an educational activity also involve fellowship? How can a fellowship activity also involve evangelism? How can the men help with a woman's activity? How can a children's activity involve worship? Be creative. Don't let the lines between your ministries become walls.

Avoid scheduling conflicts with local events

I once served a church where many of the most active people were also rabid Washington Redskins football fans. I quickly discovered that if I wanted anyone to come to a meeting or event, I better not schedule it when the Redskins had a game.

In your community, what draws crowds may be sports or school events or civic activities or even another church's annual affair. Before your planning meeting, task someone with finding out as many of these dates as they can, so you can take them into account in scheduling your own events. Of course, you also want to avoid conflicts within your own church.

Agree on who is responsible

How many times have you heard this exchange? "Weren't you supposed to do that?" "Oh no, I thought you were going to." For each activity, be sure everyone is clear about who is in charge – especially the person in charge.

When more than one person is involved, be sure everyone knows who is supposed to do what, the due date, and who they should tell when they have done it or if a problem comes up.

Send a summary to all participants

You can put everything on a calendar, list planned activities in chronological order, or group the activities according to who is responsible. However you do it, make sure your records include who, what, when and where for every planned event.

Report to the congregation

Your people want to know what their leaders have planned for them. Reporting back makes them feel like their church is active and alive. It lets them get church events onto their own calendars. And it's a great opportunity to encourage people to get involved in particular activities.

Set your budget later

We'll deal with budgeting, and the pros and cons of a written budget, in Chapter 17. I bring it up now because experience shows that if you set your budget before you plan your ministries, your financial expectations will limit your dreams. And remember what Jesus said: *Where your treasure is, there your heart will be also* (Matthew 6:21 ESV). How you spend your money reveals your priorities. If you set your budget first, your spending priorities will most likely have been set with a money mindset rather than a ministry mindset. Remember, money is just a tool to help you do ministry. Let your ministry goals drive your budget, not the other way around.

Make long-term plans

Besides annual planning meetings, **it's important to have some long-term goals in mind.** What does God want your church to look like in three years? Five? Ten? Naturally, the farther out you get, the less certain and specific you can be, but you do need to have some kind of direction in mind. Especially when it comes to acquiring a building, or buying equipment, or hiring a staff person, knowing your ministry priorities is vital. Do you need a kitchen or a classroom? An organ or a drum set? A youth pastor or a custodian?

In my experience, many people have unspoken assumptions about what the church is all about and where it should be heading. They are unspoken because everyone assumes everyone else sees things the same way. When you reach a decision point and people discover that other people have different ideas, they can feel surprised and even betrayed. A long-term plan can start these discussions without the stress of an impending decision.

Long-term planning, sometimes called strategic planning, is a long process. Consider the needs and resources of your church and the needs and resources of your community. Look for places where they intersect. Remember that your people are your greatest resource, other than the power of prayer.

Points to Remember

- Train, support, resource, encourage and oversee your people, but beyond that, let them do their ministries, and you do yours.
- The job of ministry groups is to organize and promote ministries so that everyone can do them.
- What you call your ministry groups can determine how people see them.
- Some ministries focus on tasks, others on people groups, others on support and resourcing.
- Gather your leaders to evaluate, plan and coordinate ministry activities

at least once a year.

16

LEADERS AND WORKERS

That the leaders led in Israel, that the people volunteered, bless the Lord! - Judges 5:2

Author Gene Edwards makes a fascinating case for the idea that the Apostle Paul did not select leaders for the churches he founded. He came to a city, preached the gospel, and gathered those who responded. Then he left town, often under duress. When he visited again a year or so later, he took note of those everyone else turned to for decisions, and named them leaders. In essence, he was just officially confirming what the people had already sorted out for themselves.[i]

In any group of people, some will lead and some will follow. Leadership is one of the natural gifts God builds into certain people (Romans 12:8). As a pastor, one of your most important responsibilities is to **recognize the people God has prepared to lead your church and ministries**. **Then train and equip and support and encourage them** to be the best leaders they can be. And I wish I didn't have to say this, but it can be just as important to protect the church from self-appointed leaders who would take you in the wrong direction.

Some churches become large enough to hire paid staff for certain positions. This chapter was written with volunteers in mind, but much of it applies to paid staff as well. If your church is at the point where you are considering hiring someone, praise the Lord! I encourage you to read some of the numerous good books that will help you with issues specific to that task.

Finding Leaders

Jesus said, *"Seek the Kingdom of God above all else, and live righteously, and he will give you everything you need"* (Matthew 6:33).

In the context of the Sermon on the Mount, *everything you need* refers to food, clothing and shelter. But I don't think it is stretching things too far to say that if God will provide these necessities of life for individuals, he will provide the necessities of life for a church on the same basis. Good leaders are a basic necessity of life for every church. If you are sincerely seeking to advance God's kingdom through your church, God will provide the leaders to help you do it.

Becoming a leader

Some people would say you don't "become" a leader, you either are one or you aren't. They believe leaders are born, not made. To a large degree I think this is true. But in a church or other organization, even the most naturally gifted leader needs to be recognized, and granted authority to lead in a defined area.

There are four ways that usually happens in churches. Many churches use different ways for different positions.

The fastest and most direct way to officially identify leaders is for the pastor to appoint them. The downside of appointing leaders is that everyone knows exactly who made the decision. If it looks like you're playing favorites, or if it turns out to be a mistake, they know who to blame.

Some churches elect leaders at annual congregational business meetings. The advantage is that everyone has a chance to be involved in the decision. Depending on how your church makes other decisions, this may be the best way for you, at least for the most important positions. But let me raise a few cautions. In a small church, people may feel pressured to vote for their friends – "I didn't get to do that job because so and so voted against me." In a big congregation, some members may not know some candidates. If you have a lot of new Christians in your church, they may not have the Christian maturity to make an informed decision. If you have more than one person running for one important position, there's a potential for division. And if you only have one slate of nominees for the congregation to vote on, the decision is not really being made by the congregation, but by whoever created the slate.

In some cases, new leaders are chosen by the existing leaders. This can be a middle ground between appointment and congregational election. Presumably, your leaders are mature Christians who know the Lord, know the people and know the needs of the church, so they should make a good choice. And for the pastor, if a new leader doesn't work out, it can be very helpful to have a group of leaders standing with you in the decision.

Finally, many people become leaders in the church simply by volunteering. People who volunteer for leadership positions can be a real blessing. Volunteering shows that they are interested, they are available, they feel qualified and they are motivated. For most positions in the church, that's pretty much all you need.

However, there are a few positions where hard experience has taught me to be wary of volunteers. In particular, if someone seems eager for a job that gives them access to the church's money, watch out. **If someone seeks a position that gives them any kind of control over you as pastor, through your pay or your living or working conditions or even whether you keep your job, be careful.** If someone seeks a position because they think it will make them a big shot in the church, look for someone else. Graciously suggest another area in the church where they can volunteer. If they genuinely want to serve God, they will be happy to consider it. If they get angry and threaten to leave the church, don't try too hard to stop them. Their reaction just proves that their motives were not good, and you and the church are better off without them.

As your church grows, at some point it will be a good idea to create some kind of personnel committee. This is one of the support ministries we mentioned earlier. Their job is to:

- Pray for wisdom
- Know the leadership needs of the church
- Know the people of the church
- In confidential discussions, prayerfully match potential leaders to leadership needs
- Make their recommendations to whomever makes the final appointment or election
- Pray for the leaders

In some churches this committee is also responsible for training, equipping, resourcing, supporting and evaluating leaders once they are in place.

Three quick bits of advice regarding your personnel team: First, don't publicly nominate someone without asking them first. If they decline the nomination after it's been announced, you'll look disorganized, and everyone will be embarrassed. Second, don't assume people will do a job forever. Ask them once a year if they are willing to continue. Third, don't let individuals on your personnel team offer a position to someone until the whole team has agreed. If the offer has to be rescinded because of confidential information, or because someone else offered it to another person first, or you found a better candidate, again you look disorganized and everyone is embarrassed.

Biblical qualifications

The Bible has a fair amount to say about what the kind of person God wants leading his people. Paul advises Pastor Timothy, *Never be in a hurry about appointing a church leader* (1 Timothy 5:22). Once they've been put in place, it's almost impossible to remove them without causing hard feelings and dissension in the church.

Jethro, Moses' father-in-law, advised him to appoint leaders to serve as judges under him to settle minor disputes among the people. Jethro suggested he look for *"capable, honest men who fear God and hate bribes"* (Exodus 18:21). The apostles had similar criteria for those they put in charge of the food ministry: people who are *"well respected and are full of the Spirit and wisdom"* (Acts 6:3). Paul expands on this in 1 Timothy 3:1-12.

Essentially, all these passages agree that character is the most important qualification. Jesus said of false prophets, *"You can identify them by their fruit"* (Matthew 7:16). That's equally true in the positive; you will know good character by its fruits: *love, joy, peace, patience, kindness, goodness, faithfulness, gentleness and self-control* (Galatians 5:22-23).

In addition to asking people to do certain ministry tasks, some churches officially recognize those who have achieved a certain level of Christian maturity. They may give them a title, such as "elder," so everyone will know who they are. Sometimes this recognition carries with it certain duties. Other times it's a way of honoring and recognizing a small group of key people in the church who can be called on as needed, especially for prayerful advice and spiritual support. If your church honors people in this way, pay special attention to the Biblical qualifications.

Ability

Obviously you don't want to give a person a job they are unable to do. That's not fair to the church or to them. So it seems natural to choose someone whose job or education parallels the responsibilities of the church position you're trying to fill.

In many cases that makes sense. A professional musician might be an obvious choice to lead your church music program. A retired teacher might be perfect to head up your children's ministry.

On the other hand, **a person's secular employment may not indicate the best place for them in the church.** Somebody who spends five days a week working with small children may really want to be around adults at church, instead of automatically being stuck in the nursery. And sometimes the difference in outlook between the world and the church is significant. For instance, an accountant's job may require a zero-sum mentality that is just the opposite of the faith-filled, God-will-provide outlook you want for your church finances.

Remember what happened to Samuel when God sent him to Jesse's house to find the next king of Israel.

> *When they arrived, Samuel took one look at Eliab and thought, "Surely this is the LORD's anointed!" But the LORD said to Samuel, "Don't judge by his appearance or height, for I have rejected him. The LORD doesn't see things the way you see them. People judge by outward appearance, but the LORD looks at the heart." - 1 Samuel 16:6-7*

If secular training and skills aren't necessarily indicators of the right person for a job, what about spiritual gifts? After all, 1 Peter 4:10 says, *God has given each of you a gift from his great variety of spiritual gifts. Use them well to serve one another.*

Some churches put a lot of store in "ministry according to gifts." They may use spiritual gift questionnaires. The hope is to find the place of service where each one *can do the good things he planned for us long ago* (Ephesians 2:10).

I'm a big believer in spiritual gifts. I'm not such a big believer in indiscriminately using spiritual gift tests, for two reasons. First, many of the tests differ in how they define the different gifts, or even how many there are. Romans 12:6-8, 1 Corinthians 12:7-10, and Ephesians 4:11 are the three lists usually cited, but passages such as 1 Peter 4:11 and Exodus 31:1-6 could also be considered.

Second, some people, even some pastors, take the results to mean that they should not try to do things in areas where they didn't get a high score: "I scored low on 'evangelist,' so I don't have to share my faith."

The Great Commission doesn't say, "Make disciples of all nations, but only if you scored high on 'evangelist.'"

If you can find a test that accurately reflects your own understanding of spiritual gifts, go ahead and use it. Just make sure you know what the test is measuring and what the results mean. And make sure your people understand that while they might be better at some things than others, they aren't excused from living a well-rounded Christian life.

"Ministry according to gifts" has a complementary philosophy: "Whom God calls, God equips." Few pastors are accomplished writers, speakers, counselors, worship designers, intercessors and administrators when God calls them. I know I wasn't. But all these and more are essential skills to be a successful pastor. As I offered myself to God for pastoral education and training, he equipped me for the job to which he called me. He'll do the same for you, and the people he has called to be your leaders.

Secular training, ministry interests and spiritual gifts can all be indicators of who God is calling to lead and work in your church. Where specific skills are lacking, God will supply them – if the person is willing to pray and work toward that, and if you as pastor are willing to resource and encourage them.

Cultural considerations

Some cultures have values or traditions that must be taken into account in who you choose to put in positions of leadership. Note that when I say "cultures" I don't just mean countries or ethnicities. In America, rural Pentecostal churches have a very different culture from urban mainstream churches, and in both those examples the white church culture is different from the African-American or Hispanic or Asian church culture. Most people are so immersed in their culture that they have to make a conscious effort to even be aware of it.

Different ethnic and church cultures may have very different views of who is acceptable in what positions of leadership, totally apart from how they interpret Bible verses that touch on the same thing. Ask yourself: in my culture, who would be acceptable in this job? A single person? A divorced person? Is a certain minimum age expected? A certain gender? Is there anything else I should consider?

And now the big question: do I feel called by God to violate these cultural expectations in the name of Jesus? Sometimes God does that. If this is one of those times, go for it! But be aware of the cultural expectations you are breaking, so you can prepare for the reactions.

In short, look for people who

- Love God
- Love your church
- Habitually put time and energy into learning and growing in the Lord
- Support your vision for the church
- Have a passion for a given area
- Are teachable
- Have time to do the job

Term limits

Some churches make a policy that people can only serve in a given position for a certain amount of time. Then they have to step aside, possibly moving to a new position, possibly just taking time for a rest. Sometimes this is a blanket policy that applies to every position in the church, sometimes it only applies to specified positions.

Those who favor term limits argue that they make room for new people with fresh ideas and energy. They give those who have done a job for a while a chance to rest, or move on to other areas of ministry. Term limits can help keep people from getting entrenched with too much power over a given area of ministry. And new people may be more willing to take on a task if they know it's not a lifetime commitment.

On the other hand, there's no substitute for experience. If a person has a passion for a certain ministry, or if they have unique skills, forcing them out may make them feel no longer wanted, and it may leave the church in a difficult situation. Once again, there is no right answer for every church, but God has the right answer for yours.

Working with Leaders and Workers

You've discerned who God has prepared to lead your church and work in the ministries. Now, as pastor, how do you most effectively work with them?

Some pastors are micro-managers and control freaks. I tended to the opposite extreme, what I called "delegation to the point of abdication." Neither of these are good. Go too far in the first direction and your leaders will never learn to think for themselves, and you won't have time for your other work. Go too far in the other direction (I speak from experience) and your leaders will feel abandoned, and you won't know if they're doing what you want them to.

Each of us pastors have our own natural leadership style. Each of your leaders and workers have a style of leadership they respond best to. Your natural style and theirs may not always match. On top of that, some situations demand different leadership styles than other situations.

To most effectively work with your leaders and ministry workers, you have to **adjust your natural style to the needs of the situation and the person.** That's a skill well worth learning, but way too much for me to try to address here. So I'll just share a few lessons about working with leaders and workers that apply pretty much across the board.

Spend time with them

Getting the ministry done is the second-most important reason for choosing leaders. The most important reason is to help them grow as Christian disciples and develop their leadership skills for the future. That takes spending time with more mature Christians, and especially with you as pastor. Christian faith is more than knowing the Bible or giving mental assent to a list of doctrinal statements. It's a lifestyle. As the saying goes, Christianity is more caught than taught. Your people learn facts from your sermons and classes, but they learn life from watching you. That takes time together.

You need to know your leaders and workers will do their job. You also need to trust that they won't head off in some direction of their own, but will be loyal to you and the church. And they need to trust that you will listen to them and support them. The only way to build that trust and loyalty is to build your relationships. Spend time praying together for each other and the church. Spend time in Bible study. Spend time working together. And don't forget to spend time having fun together. Aside from praying together, fun may be the best relationship builder of all.

Encourage them

Let them know you believe in them, appreciate them and will be there for them when they need you. Learn what kind of encouragement means the most to each person.

Train them

People are often more willing to take on a responsibility if they know training is available. Training gives both you and them confidence that they can do the job, and do it the way you want it done.

Every position in your church should have a written job description. You should also keep records of what was done in the past, how it was done, and where to find needed materials or information.

Make sure you provide on the job training, either from the person they are replacing or from you as pastor. This is usually a simple four-step process:

1. I do it, you watch me
2. I do it, you help me
3. You do it, I help you
4. You do it, I watch you

After that you leave the person to do the job. You just check on them occasionally, or when they ask for help. For some common ministries you may be able to find books, online training or even classes, for those who like to learn that way. Use your judgment for each person.

Resource them

There are few things more frustrating than being asked to do a job and not being given the tools or materials or information to do it. Know what your people need – ask them every now and then – and make sure they have it. This may mean making the case for them to whoever decides your spending priorities. Of course, your church may not have the money to provide everything for every ministry. As pastor you have the big picture. You know all the needs of all the ministries, and all the resources available. Your leaders will look to you to prioritize them, and to encourage those leaders you can't fully resource.

Protect them

As a pastor, you are on the front lines of spiritual warfare. Your leaders and workers are joining you there. Your first line of defense, of course, is prayer. But there are also practical steps you can take to protect yourself and your people from temptations and accusations. Here are a few of the most basic ways to protect from accusations of misconduct, and potential lawsuits:

- Be sure you and your leaders are aware of local laws, and follow them
- Always require at least two adults, or one adult and one teenager, wherever children are present
- A man should never counsel a woman alone; if confidentiality requires privacy, someone else should be close enough to hear a call for help
- A man should never visit an unrelated woman alone in her home
- Where laws or insurance call for it, require signed consent forms from parents for their children to participate in activities, drive with adults other than their parents, or have their pictures published or posted on the internet; be sure your forms have the proper wording and keep

copies in a safe place
- Be sure group leaders, especially of children, are aware of any special dietary needs or medical conditions
- Consider clergy malpractice insurance
- If you own or lease a building and allow other groups to meet there, require them to follow the above guidelines, especially if children are involved
- Find out what other precautions your laws require or your insurance company recommends

Give feedback

Your leaders won't know how they are doing unless you tell them. Point out what they are doing well. Be specific. Give constructive criticism where necessary; good leaders will appreciate it. Solomon, who knew a thing or two about leading people, wrote, *Correct the wise and they will love you* (Proverbs 9:8). Most people want reassurance that they are doing what they were asked to do.

Celebrate them

Good leaders and workers don't do it for the glory, they do it to serve God and the church. Still, they deserve to be publicly recognized for their service. You might consider an annual dinner in honor of church volunteers, perhaps coupled with a "worker of the year" award. Public recognition can be especially important for someone who has served a long time and is retiring due to age or illness. A plaque or certificate or some kind of memento they can display can mean a lot. If you own or lease a building, you might consider some kind of memorial, listing the names of people who have given extraordinary service.

When necessary, replace them

Sometimes, even when you've followed all the steps outlined above, you'll discover that one of your leaders or workers is just not getting the job done. It could be that you missed God's guidance in selecting them. More often, it's because circumstances changed in their lives – they have a new baby, their job is requiring longer hours, they are having health issues, or maybe they're just getting too old.

Before you do anything else (except pray), **talk to them**. It could be they're not even aware that they aren't performing up to expectations. If that's the case, a little constructive feedback, sandwiched between words of encouragement and appreciation, may be all they need.

If it's more than that, try to find out what the issue is. Often people are aware that they aren't doing as well as they had been, and they feel bad about it, so be sure you sound caring and supportive, not critical. If it's a short-term life situation that will be over soon, it's probably best to just wait it out. If it's more than that, they may well be glad for the opportunity to be relieved of responsibility. Figure out together whether they need to be replaced immediately or whether they can continue until you find a replacement.

The situations I find hardest are when a person has become ineffective but doesn't know it, or doesn't want to step down. For the sake of the church I have to find someone else to do the job, but for the sake of the person I don't want to hurt their feelings. Praise the Lord, this hasn't happened often. I have only two bits of advice for this situation: pray for wisdom, and try to preserve the person's dignity.

The exception to this is when the person is hanging onto a position in order to exert influence, often against the pastor. **Before you run into such a situation, create a policy** about how people can be removed from positions. And if possible, have your leadership team take the actual step of removing the person. Otherwise, it might just look like a personality conflict with you.

Be aware ahead of time that if you have to take this step, you are likely to lose not only that person, but their friends as well. Be sure you are hearing God clearly. But if it has to be done, it has to be done. **Never let one person or clique hold the church hostage.**

Communication

One of the biggest sources of problems in leadership teams is poor communication. It's also one of the easiest ones to correct. The effort you put into establishing good communication policies, and developing them into habits in your leaders, will more than repay itself in smooth operations and lack of conflicts. Don't forget to include these policies in your orientation for new leaders and workers.

No blindsiding

"Blindsiding" is a term from American football. It refers to unexpectedly being knocked down by something you can't see coming.

As pastor, people expect you to be aware of everything that's going on in your church. You can look really bad if someone asks you about something and that's the first you heard of it, or if you fail to provide a pastoral response in a time of need because nobody told you about it.

Often, you won't know those things unless one of your leaders says something to you. Make sure they know how important that is. Don't let them assume someone else will tell you. I always say I'd rather be told something three times than not be told at all. In the same way, if you become aware of something one of your leaders needs to know, be sure they know it. Nobody likes to be blindsided.

Centralize scheduling

You can't be in two places at one time. Two groups using the same space at the same time is chaos. Two groups using the same resource at the same time is a tug of war.

None of these is a good thing. All of them can be avoided by centralizing your scheduling. Make sure your church keeps one centralized calendar of activities, and designate one person to be responsible for putting things on that calendar. Stress that no event, room or a resource is considered scheduled without going through that one person.

Be clear, complete and concise

Sermons, stories and chatty letters are great in their place. Their place is not messages intended to convey information and coordinate activities. When you are communicating with your leaders about your expectations, their responsibilities, or upcoming events, be clear, complete and concise. If your communication is written, via print, email, texting or social media, reread it before you publish or send it. If you'll be talking in person or on the phone, plan it out ahead of time. **Ask yourself if there is any way it could be misunderstood** – generally if something can possibly be read the wrong way, somebody will. Ask yourself if you included all the necessary information. Don't assume somebody knows something just because you already told them; it's much safer to have all the information in one place, even if it means repeating something. Take out unnecessary words and irrelevant remarks that can muddy the waters. And train your leaders to follow these rules when communicating with you and each other.

Say who, what, when, where, why and how

In journalism these are the basic elements of reporting, and they are equally important in planning activities or assigning responsibilities. Who is responsible? Who is invited? What will happen? What is needed? When is the event – date, time, duration? When do things need to be done? Where will it happen? Where should people be? Why is this worth your leaders' and workers' time and energy? How should it be done? How will it look when it's finished? All of these questions may not apply to every communication, but you'd be surprised how many of them will.

Acknowledge communications

I get frustrated when I send someone an email or text or leave a phone message, and I get no response. Is the person gathering information for a reply? Should I assume they will comply with my request? Did my message get lost in cyberspace? Are they sick? Are they mad at me for some reason, and giving me the silent treatment? There's no way of knowing.

Don't do that to your people. Give some kind of response, even if it's just "Thanks for the information" or "I'll look into it" or "I put it on my calendar." And insist your people do the same.

Reinforce the vision

Use your communications to remind your leaders of what your church is all about. Most email providers allow you to automatically include a line or two at the end of each message. This could be a key Bible verse, or your church's mission statement. If you print a church newsletter or bulletin, include your vision statement in the masthead. You could start sermons with, "In keeping with our church's vision, …" Keeping your vision before your leaders and your people reminds them why they do what they do. It builds unity, and helps new people catch on.

Over-communicate

Have you ever had a conversation like this? Member: "Why wasn't I told this was going to happen?" Me: "Well, I'm sorry, but we announced it in church three weeks in a row, printed it in the newsletter and the bulletin, and put it on the church Facebook page." Member: "Yes, but why wasn't I told?"

Just because you put out a communication doesn't mean the other person received it. The more important a message is, the more you need to be sure it was received, understood, and won't be forgotten.

Be careful about confidential information

In our modern world, it's becoming more and more apparent that email and social media may not always be secure. Paper messages can be left where others can see them. Spoken conversations, in person or on the phone, can be overheard. When you are discussing confidential information, be careful. When someone feels that you have betrayed a confidence, it can be very hard to regain their trust.

When Leaders Do Wrong

We'd like to believe that the people we prayerfully choose to work with us in leading God's church are all mature, committed Christians who will never do anything wrong. The sad fact is, that's not always the case. Don't feel bad if it happens to you; even Jesus had two of his chosen twelve leaders fail. Peter was ultimately restored, but Judas was lost forever. If it happened to Jesus, it can certainly happen to you.

So what do you do when a leader does wrong? First, **don't go off half-cocked.** As best you can, make sure they actually did the wrong they are accused of. Paul advised Pastor Timothy, *Do not listen to an accusation against an elder unless it is confirmed by two or three witnesses* (1 Timothy 5:19).

What if the wrongdoing is confirmed?

Several years ago a young pastor I know asked me for advice on how to handle a situation where a church leader was found guilty of a serious moral failure. I'll share with you an edited version of my answer to this pastor. You can adapt and apply these principles to any kind of moral lapse.

Hi Pastor,

The situation you describe is a very difficult one.

I can't give a specific response, because I don't have all the details, and sometimes even in two seemingly identical situations God will lead in different ways. But there are some basic principles that should always apply. The best thing is if a church develops a policy for how to handle a situation like this while it is still hypothetical, so your response won't be colored by personalities and relationships.

The ultimate goal is that the fallen member will be restored to the Lord and, if possible, people who were harmed, and that the church and all involved will all be stronger for the experience. It is important to keep in mind that restoration is the goal, not punishment or making an example, though there may be some value in that as well.

If the person has not been removed from all positions of leadership, this should be done immediately. It doesn't have to be done publicly, or the reason made public - that is a matter for discernment - but it does need to be done. If a different reason is needed for public consumption, a variety of things can be said that are true, such as the person is coming under a lot of stress lately and needs a break, or they feel they need to take time to focus on their family.

If the sinner is repentant, that is a major first step. If not, then Matthew 18:15-17 and, if necessary, 1 Corinthians 5:1-5 come into play. This must be done very carefully and prayerfully, to be sure all the facts are known and that everyone's motives are pure. The goal is always to show God's love, even when discipline is necessary.

However, it is important also to protect the church. One of the most destructive things that happened in my ministry at one church was in a similar situation when the other members of the leadership team sided with the person who had the moral lapse, protesting that I was treating the person wrongly because I made the person give up their position of leadership. Then they told others in the congregation, to the point that much of the church was taking sides over the issue. So you need to be sure before choosing the people for Matthew 18 action that they agree with you on both the morality and the process, and that they will publicly support you in conversations with other church members. This can be especially important if it is a situation where the congregation doesn't know the real reason. I have been in situations where a lot of misinformation was being told about me by the person being disciplined, but because of confidentiality I was not at liberty to tell my side of the story. So it is important that the other members of the leadership team are on board with you as much as possible before taking action.

If the sinner is repentant, a confession is important, at least to all those who already know about it or should know about it. If it is not known to the church as a whole, it is a matter for serious prayerful discernment as to whether it should be made public. The answer may be different in different cases.

In all this, especially where it is not known to the church at large, you need to prayerfully weigh the value of working to rehabilitate the person quietly, versus the value of giving the church an example of discipline. And of course you need to weigh how likely it is that something like this can in fact remain not widely known.

Of course, the sinful actions must be completely stopped, as a precondition for anything else. If the person is not willing to do that, they are not repentant, by definition.

All the above can happen fairly quickly, but it just sets the stage for the real work, which is restoration to the Lord and the church, and where necessary and possible, reconciliation with others who may have been harmed. I say "if possible" because reconciliation is a two-way street.

It is probably good at the outset to set a certain minimum amount of time for the process, sufficient to see whether it seems like the repentance and restoration will be lasting. Certain requirements should also be laid out that the person must meet before being restored to any position of responsibility in the church.

One requirement should be to meet with you and/or another church leader regularly, perhaps once a week. The agenda should include Bible study, accountability and prayer. The Bible studies should start with passages particular to the specific sin, and spread outward to dealing with temptation, holiness of heart and life, and discipleship in general.

Accountability questions should be decided on within the first few meetings, and asked and answered every time. Prayer can spread outward in generality to go along with the Bible study, while always including prayers for strength to overcome particular temptations.

It may well be that this particular sin was all that happened, but it also may be that there are other problems that made it harder to resist this temptation. If so, these also have to be prayed about and dealt with.

The decision to restore the person to responsibility should never belong to you as pastor alone. It should only be on the advice of a group of mature Christians within the church, whose objectivity is above question. This is for two reasons. First, you may be swayed by friendship for the fallen member, or an over-active mercy gift, or even by the church's needs for the person's skills. Second, in case things go wrong again, if it was a group decision, it will not be as easy to blame you. The other side of it is that if a group is involved, any friends of the sinner who may be pressuring for an earlier restoration will have to persuade the whole leadership team rather than just you.

Restoration to responsibility should be done gradually, beginning with less important or influential positions, and on a trial basis.

Again, this entire process must be a demonstration of Christian love. There should be a specific ending point, so it doesn't feel like it will go on forever. When that point is reached, it is important to celebrate the restoration of the fallen member, as publicly as is appropriate given how widely the situation is known (see 2 Corinthians 2:5-8).

I hope this is helpful. I realize it got to sounding kind of academic. I was trying to make it as general as I could, not knowing any details. Please let me know if it helps.

Blessings,

David

Points to Remember

- One of your most important responsibilities is to identify, train, equip, support and encourage leaders.
- Make public, at least within your church, who your leaders are and the area and extent of their authority.
- Leaders should love God, your church, and you, and be growing, passionate, teachable and available.
- Spend time with your leaders, support them, communicate with them, and hold them accountable.
- Before it becomes necessary, adopt a church policy detailing what to do if a leader does wrong.

[i] Gene Edwards, Beyond Radical. 1999, n.p.

17

MONEY AND PROPERTY

Go to Hilkiah the high priest and have him count the money the gatekeepers have collected from the people at the Lord's temple. – 2 Kings 22:4

Some people might think money is not spiritual enough for a book about ministry. The fact is, as long as we are ministering in the world, we will have to deal with money. Even Jesus had a treasurer (John 13:29).

Money in itself is neither good nor bad. It's a medium of exchange, a tool for getting things done – including God's things in the church. Contrary to what many believe, the Bible doesn't say "money is the root of all evil." It says the love of money is the problem (1 Timothy 6:10).

It's unlikely that anyone reading this book is obsessed with the love of money. Being a pastor is not a good way to get rich. But you do have to deal with money, and money that is not your own. When God's people give their money to God, they put it in your hands. That's a heavy responsibility. And the devil would like nothing better than to find something about the way you handle that responsibility that he can use to accuse you. Mishandling money can destroy your witness, your ministry, your church, even your life.

Raising Money

Before you can handle money you have to get some. If you are just starting a church in your own home, for the first little while you may not have any appreciable expenses. But even if you don't outgrow your house, you will be wanting to carry out ministries that will cost money. Perhaps you need more chairs, or a musical instrument. Perhaps someone in your church loses their job, and other folks want to help pay their rent. It's almost impossible to carry on much ministry without using the tool of money. Where does that money come from?

Should the church ask for money?

In America, one of the common excuses people give for not attending church is, "They're always asking for money." Most of the people who say that would find another excuse if that one didn't work, but unfortunately there is enough truth in it that everyone understands what they are saying, and many agree.

Some churches give the impression that the main reason for evangelism is to gain new givers. Some seem to always be just a few dollars away from having to close their doors. Some imply that God will punish you if you don't give, or make you rich if you do. Institutional survival, guilt, fear and greed can all be effective motivators, but they are not fitting for followers of the God of love who created and sustains the universe.

On the other hand, it does take money to carry out most ministries.

Beyond all that, giving is the main way we learn generosity and trust. The sixth fruit of the Holy Spirit in Galatians 5:22, often translated "goodness," also carries the sense of generosity. You can't learn peace unless you have conflict, you can't learn patience unless you have trials, and you can't learn generosity unless you are asked to give.

Some pastors and church leaders routinely ask individuals for contributions for specific purposes, especially for large expenses that are not part of the normal operating budget. Others don't feel comfortable doing

227

that. I think the difference is mainly a matter of personality. If you're not comfortable with it, as I'm not, consider having one of your leaders do the asking.

A colleague told the story of visiting a woman of very limited means, during a time when he was trying to raise money for a special project. He knew the woman had little money, so he decided not to ask her to contribute. Instead, she asked him about it. She was hurt and a little angry at not being asked. She had been looking forward to being part of the project through her small contribution. She felt she was being left out. The lesson is, **never decide for someone else whether or not they might want to give.**

Having a very wealthy church member may not be the blessing it sounds like. If every time the church needs something, Brother Bigbucks donates it, the church can come to see Brother Bigbucks as their source instead of God. This can also make the rest of the people feel like their own giving is not needed. And of course it can give Brother Bigbucks an inordinate amount of influence over what the church does and doesn't do.

Cast a vision

Some people will support an abstract idea like "making the budget," but many will not. Most people need to be able to visualize what they are being asked to support. Help people see what their gifts will accomplish. Don't talk about a program; describe before and after pictures of the people who will be helped by it. Don't talk about a bill; describe what is being done with what the bill pays for, or what won't be done if the bill isn't paid. Moses described God's tabernacle so clearly that the Israelites could see it in their minds, and they contributed so much to its building that Moses had to stop them from bringing more (Exodus 36:4-7). If your people catch the vision of what God is calling your church to do, they will bring more than enough, and be excited for the opportunity.

Publicize results

Casting a vision talks about the good you hope to do with your people's gifts. Publicizing results talks about the good you did with what they already gave. It's the other side of the coin, and it's important for two reasons. First, if people never hear about what you did, they may wonder if you did anything at all. That can cause them to wonder if giving to your ministry is really good stewardship, or whether they should look around for someplace else to give. Second, when people do hear the good you already did, it makes them more willing to give again. It gives them confidence that you will indeed put their gifts to good use.

Teach about giving

Some things don't lend themselves easily to vision casting. How do you cast a vision about insurance bills or cleaning supplies? How do you keep people giving to pay off a mortgage when the shine has worn off the building? More importantly, how do you get people to spiritually grow past only supporting things they are excited about? The answer is in teaching what the Bible says about giving.

I bet I know what word is in your head about now: "tithe." Right? When you talk about Biblical giving, that's what comes to most people's minds. But it doesn't stop there.

Some pastors teach that Biblical tithing applies to all believers; others say it was only for the Old Testament. Some teach that the full tithe should go to the local church, calling additional giving "offerings;" others say it's fine to spread your tithe around. Some say the tithe should be figured on gross income, including any amounts that may be deducted from your pay for taxes, health insurance, retirement or other programs; others say the ten percent is figured on net take-home pay, the amount you actually get when you cash your paycheck.

I've wrestled with all these questions in my ministry, for others and in terms of my own tithing. I told you about my own experiences with it in

Chapter 8. As I said there, **it is very important for you, the pastor, to tithe, and it's important for the church to know you do.** How can you teach what you don't practice?

It seems to me that whether tithing is part of the law that Jesus fulfilled, or whether it still applies in the church age, is a theological technicality that involves covenants and dispensations and other areas where good Christians differ. In practice, all I am and all I have belongs to God. In fact, doubly so: he created me, and then when I was lost he bought me back with the blood of Jesus. So for me, the issue is not that ten percent of what I have belongs to God. He owns the whole one hundred percent. The question is, how much does God want me to turn over to the church or other ministries for their part of God's work, and how much does he want me to control in my personal stewardship, to keep myself and my family healthy and growing and fitted for our part of God's work?

People ask me if the "storehouse" in Malachi 3:10 is the local church, or whether they can use part of their ten percent to support another ministry. I tell them Biblical scholars differ on that question, and I try to help them discern what God is saying to them. People ask if they should tithe on gross or net pay. I usually respond, half-jokingly, with something I read once: "That depends. Do you want to get blessed on the gross or the net?" I try hard not to be legalistic, but to help each person hear from God for themselves, because this is an area where I believe God may tell different people to do different things. Jesus told the rich young ruler to sell all he had, but did not say that to his rich friends Lazarus or Joseph of Arimathea.

I will say this: **I never had anyone try tithing who wasn't glad they did.**

By the way, make sure your people understand that a tithe is ten percent of their increase, whatever it is and wherever it comes from. If their income is zero, they shouldn't feel bad about not contributing to the church, because a tenth of zero is zero. On the other hand, if they bought a house years ago and sold it this year for a big profit, they should tithe the profit.

Tithing is good for the church, but it's vital for your spiritual growth. It's one of those things, like fasting and speaking in tongues, that makes no sense to your mind and doesn't feel good to your body. When you do it anyway, you demonstrate to your mind and body that your spirit is in control – and the Holy Spirit who lives in your reborn human spirit. Getting your human trinity of spirit, soul and body in proper order frees you for wonderful kingdom usefulness and blessings.

The Bible is full of passages about the blessings of giving. Preach on these passages. But don't focus on the money part. **Focus on learning to trust God.** Don't hide the blessings that are promised to those who give, but be careful not to let it sound like a get-rich-quick scheme.

Some churches have a short teaching about giving every Sunday before they receive the offering. Others don't have an offering during the service at all. In my tradition we have a prayer before the offering, where I always quote a Bible promise about giving. Ask God what will best honor him in your situation.

There are good books and courses available to teach a Christian approach to handling money. These usually start with how to get out of debt, but go on to other areas, including the blessings of giving. Some churches make these available as part of their Christian education program.

Giving is one of those areas where it's really helpful to support your teaching with testimonies from your members. People often feel like the pastor has a vested interest in getting them to give more, and in many cases they are right. But when regular church folks talk about how they have been blessed by trusting God with their money, it makes an impact.

In my opinion, **one of the biggest mistakes you can make is to avoid talking about money.** It's a huge part of the everyday reality of your people's lives. If the church doesn't teach them a Christian approach to money, the world will gladly jump in and take advantage.

Faith-promise giving

Many people say they can't afford to increase giving out of their current income, but if God were to provide additional money they could give that. For a faith promise, people ask God to show them an amount of money they are to ask God to provide to them, over and above their normal income, to be earmarked for a special project. Then they promise to pray regularly that God will provide that money, and that they will recognize it. They promise that when the money does come, they will pass it on to the special project. I have never seen people as excited about giving as when God brings in the extra money and they are able to give it.

Money back tithe guarantee

This may sound like a gimmick, but I include it here so you can decide for yourself. In Malachi 3:10 God instructs the Israelites,

> *"Bring all the tithes into the storehouse so there will be enough food in my Temple. If you do," says the LORD of Heaven's Armies, "I will open the windows of heaven for you. I will pour out a blessing so great you won't have enough room to take it in!"*

Then God adds an unprecedented invitation: *"Try it! Put me to the test!"*

I don't remember where I first heard of a tithe guarantee, but I have tried it in several churches. The church finance committee challenged non-tithers to start tithing, and offered a money-back guarantee. If a non-tither started giving a full ten percent to the church, and then felt that they were not being blessed, the church would refund the difference between their tithe and what they used to give. I have never known of anyone asking for a refund. Instead, the new tithers were blessed with increased faith, and the church was blessed with more faith-filled members.

Electronic giving

If your church or your members are connected to the internet, consider a way for people to give electronically. Members often appreciate the simplicity of setting up an automatic transfer from their bank to their church, and your treasurer will appreciate being able to rely on that regular income. And you can never tell who might respond to a "donate" button on your website.

Annual and capital campaigns

Annual giving campaigns provide a way to teach about giving while getting an idea of next year's income. Some churches purchase packaged programs, others put their own together. Some pastors preach the key sermons themselves, others prefer to bring in a guest preacher. Some churches have people sign "pledges" promising to give a certain amount, others are more comfortable with "estimates of giving" that are not seen as a commitment. As the year goes on, some churches follow up with reminders, especially if "pledged" amounts are falling behind; others see that as pushy. There is no one best way for all congregations, and it can be one of the touchiest decisions you will make. Pray!

A capital campaign is like an annual campaign, but more so. Instead of an every-year plea for help to make the budget, a capital campaign might be a once-in-a-lifetime event. It's not every year that your church buys property or builds or enlarges a building. Your campaign needs to be carefully and prayerfully planned and followed through. Do some research on what has worked and not worked for other churches or non-profit groups in your area. In particular, if you will be borrowing money or using a bond program, make sure you understand all the legal ramifications for your church, your leaders and yourself. Some pastors have found themselves held personally responsible to immediately pay the entire debt if the church was unable or unwilling to make payments.

Fund raisers

Some churches feel that charging money or even suggesting a donation for anything connected with the church is inappropriate, but in many churches fund raisers are an honored tradition. The youth may put on a car wash. Women's groups may have a bake sale. The whole church gets involved in the annual church dinner and rummage sale or musical program. The community is invited, for a price or donation. It's good fun and fellowship, people who may hesitate to come to a worship service are introduced to the church in a less threatening way, and money is raised for a good cause. If you are uncomfortable with the idea of fund raisers please skip ahead to the next section.

In my experience **the success of your fund raiser depends largely on two things: the cause, and publicity.** You could have the greatest event in the world, but if people don't know about it they won't come. Figure out who you want to attract, and advertise in a way that will attract them.

And be sure to include something about the cause in your publicity. If people know the proceeds will go to something they consider worthwhile, like helping the homeless or victims of a disaster, they will make a point of being there. And it will give them a positive opinion of your church. But if you tell people what you plan to use the money for, be sure that's where it goes. If there's a possibility that the needs might change or that you may raise more money than you need for the publicized cause, make sure people understand what you will do with any extra money you receive.

Some churches that own buildings supplement their giving by renting out space. This can be an easy way to bring in extra money, but beware of the hidden costs. Financially, your utility, maintenance and insurance costs can go up. And there's the opportunity cost: any space you rent to someone else is space you can't use for your ministry, at least not at the same time.

It's never a good idea to count on fund raisers to support your normal ministry operations. They are too uncertain. And if your people have the idea that their tithes and offerings aren't needed, they'll stop giving them. That's not good for your security or their spiritual growth.

Estate giving

Two easy ways for people to give are often overlooked. One is to leave something to the church in their will. The other is to name the church as beneficiary for a life insurance policy or similar instrument. Some people may be in a position to give various kinds of property or investments. Faithful givers who have supported your ministry during their lives will usually be quite open to ways to continue that support after they die; most of them just never thought of it before.

Endowment funds

An endowment fund is a sum of money the church invests, with the idea that the interest or dividends produced each year will be available to fund certain ministries. The principal is not to be touched, but allowed to grow, except in the case of a few special circumstances spelled out in the endowment charter.

As with many things, good Christians differ about the wisdom, value or even morality of endowment funds. Those who favor them point out that they can provide money for needs beyond the church's normal operating budget. They can be a way for wealthy church members to support your ministry after they die. And they provide a reserve for a major capital expense or emergency.

Those who oppose church endowment funds generally cite three reasons. They may feel it's not right to tie up a large amount of God's money in an account for the future when there are so many needs in the present. They may be concerned that the church will begin to look to the endowment fund as its source of security rather than God. And with a large endowment fund, people may begin to feel that their own giving is unnecessary, which can limit your ministry and stunt their spiritual growth.

Remember to thank people

I was amazed to read that many American church members say they have never once been thanked for giving money to their church. Oh, the pastor might say something from the pulpit thanking the congregation in general, and there might be a line in a form letter, but that's not really a thank-you. Many church folks don't feel that the church is grateful for their giving. For some people, what they give to your church might be a big sacrifice. Yes, it's expected, yes, they grow through it, and no, they aren't doing it in order to be thanked, but still, everyone appreciates being appreciated. Especially when someone gives significantly more than usual, or gives something you know represents a real sacrifice, make a point of personally thanking them. It's only common courtesy. And it may keep someone from moving their giving to another ministry where they feel their gifts are more needed.

Keep track of giving

Like many pastors, I used to make it a point not to know who gave how much to the church. Giving was supposed to be a private affair between the person and God. And some people were concerned that, if I knew how much people gave, I would favor those who gave more.

Then a colleague told me a story. This pastor always kept up to date on his people's stewardship. One day he noticed that a certain woman's giving had significantly increased over the past few weeks. He mentioned it to her, thanked her, and asked if there was something he should know. She said that indeed there was. She used to go to church out of duty or habit, and her giving reflected that. A few weeks previously she had a life-changing experience of God's presence and love. She responded by increasing her giving. Praise the Lord! The woman didn't realize it, but she was in a place where she really needed pastoral guidance to spiritually build on this experience. **Because of his habit of keeping up with his people's giving, my friend found out and provided that guidance.**

It's just as important to be aware of drops in giving. If someone's offerings suddenly stop or significantly decrease, it's usually for a reason. Perhaps they lost their job, or were hit with unexpected bills, or are experiencing some other crisis where they could really benefit from their pastor's support. Or perhaps they are unhappy about something in the church. (That "something" could be you. At one church I served, one of the money counters told me that a church member had attached a note to that week's offering saying, "Apply this money to anything except the pastor's salary.") Whether it's a life situation or a church complaint, being aware of it is the first step to ministering to the person.

Should you publicize donors?

The end of Acts 4 describes how some Christians who owned property sold it and donated the proceeds to help provide for their less fortunate brothers and sisters in Christ. It names Barnabas, "Son of Encouragement," as one who was especially recognized as a model of Christian generosity. Knowing about his giving inspired others to give, and many people were blessed as a result. Many pastors conclude from this that givers should always be publicly recognized.

Unfortunately, the story doesn't stop there. Acts 5 tells the story of Ananias and Sapphira. They wanted everyone to think they were as spiritual as Barnabas, but they didn't want to give as much, so they lied about the amount. The results were tragic. Many pastors conclude from this that givers should never be publicly recognized.

The trick is finding some means of recognition that will teach and inspire your people without discouraging those who don't have large amounts to give, and without tempting people to imitate Ananias and Sapphira.

Protecting Money (and Yourself)

Paul wrote to Timothy, *The love of money is the root of all kinds of evil* (1 Timothy 6:10). One of those evils is the temptation to steal money or otherwise use it improperly. Another evil is the suspicion that money is being stolen or improperly used, even if it is not. It's important to have church policies that protect the Lord's money, and also protect you and your people from temptation and suspicion. Here are some simple things you should always do.

Keep careful records

At any time you should be able to quickly find out

- How much money the church has
- Where it is
- Where it came from
- Whether any is earmarked for a particular purpose
- What was done with previous money

As much as possible, use standard bookkeeping or accounting techniques. Always have more than one copy of church financial records, kept in different places.

Have at least two people from different families count money

They can catch each other's mistake, they can defuse temptation, and in case of questions or accusations they can serve as witnesses on each other's behalf.

Keep church money in a church bank account

Never let people keep church money in their home or in a personal bank account. Even if you have to pay a fee for a separate account, this precaution is well worth it.

Separate responsibility for receiving and depositing money from spending or disbursing money

I know it seems easier and more efficient for one person to handle all the financial transactions, but it also makes it easier for that person to be tempted or suspected. The people who receive, count and deposit church money in the bank should always be from a different family than those who are authorized to spend money.

Moneys paid or given to the pastor should be overseen by a group or committee of people who are not relatives of the pastor

All financial dealings between you and the church must be open and transparent.

Have clear policies about purchases or other uses of church money and resources

Policies should spell out

- Who can spend money or authorize expenditures
- How much they can spend
- What they can spend it for
- How they will know if the money is available
- How they should report the expenditure
- Whether anyone else has to approve the expenditure

Those responsible for a specific area of ministry should be authorized to spend money for that ministry. That way small expenses don't have to wait for approval at a monthly meeting. For expenditures above a certain amount it's a good idea to require approval from your church leadership group. They can weigh the proposed expense against the church's overall finances and priorities. And of course, make sure everyone understands that just because the budget says they can spend a certain amount of money, that doesn't guarantee that the money is actually there to spend. If money is tight, the treasurer should let people know to hold back on spending for a while.

On the other hand, sometimes failing to spend money when necessary can be as harmful as spending it foolishly. A little spent on maintenance now may save a lot in repairs later. And under-funding ministry and evangelism can be a sure way to keep your church from growing.

Have oversight mechanisms to assure accountability

An independent annual audit should be performed on all church accounts. This can be as simple as asking another church member to check over the records. It should be someone who does not currently handle church money and is not closely related to anyone who does. Bigger churches may wish to engage a professional auditor. This may seem like a lot of unnecessary trouble, and perhaps expense. Unfortunately, way too many church treasurers have fallen to the temptation to "borrow" church money, especially if they told themselves they would pay it back. An audit can help your members (and you!) resist temptation, and it can prove your innocence if someone else thinks you succumbed.

Building a Budget

Some churches say, "We don't need a budget. We operate on faith." That sounds good, and I'm all in favor of faith, but that statement is not accurate.

If your church receives any offerings or spends any money, you have a budget, even if you think you don't. Your budget may not be written down and voted on, but when a new idea or unexpected need arises, I'll bet there is someone who can tell you whether you will have enough money to do it. That person did a quick mental calculation involving what you are committed to pay out and what you can expect to come in, and came up with an answer about the proposed new expenditure. In other words, they consulted the budget they keep in their head. Of course you can always try to raise new money for new projects; that's outside a budget. But you don't know if you need to do that until you have consulted your budget.

In its simplest form, a budget is just a statement of how you expect to spend the church's money over a given time. It includes fixed expenses and discretionary spending.

Fixed expenses are what you are committed to pay on a regular basis – things like building payments, insurance, utilities, and salaries. Not making your fixed expenses can cause big problems, like losing your building or your pastor.

Discretionary spending is what you'd like to do with what's left, but if you can't make the payment it's not the end of the world. This is things like ministry materials and missions support. If possible, you should also put something away for an emergency or a future big project.

There is a major irony here that I hope you noticed. The consequences of not making fixed expenses can be big and sudden. For that reason, available money almost always goes to the fixed expenses first. Ministries can be left unfunded. But **all the things the fixed expenses pay for are just tools to enable the ministries.** They are meaningless if ministry is not happening. To paraphrase James, what good is it, my brothers and sisters, to say, "Look, we have a wonderful building, paid up and insured," if you can't afford to do any ministries in it?

Strictly speaking, a budget is just about spending. But some way or other **your plan for spending money needs to be connected to the amount of money you expect to have available** to spend. Unfortunately, God rarely grants a special prophetic revelation about the church budget. So some churches go on faith: "If God leads us to do something, he will provide the means to do it." Others develop elaborate research-based financial projections. Most churches look at how much they got last year and how much they think that might change. As the year goes on, they use their budget to encourage giving, and they use giving results to adjust their plan.

Let me pause for a moment to share a word about basing your budget on faith. I'm all in favor of faith. That's how I live my life. But we have to be careful, because sometimes what we call faith is actually wishful thinking, or even presumption. The Bible tells us, *If we ask anything according to his will he hears us* (1 John 5:14, ESV). Notice the condition: "according to his will." Financing a church on faith is the same as any other form of exercising faith: first you have to find out what God wants. If God is not calling your church to open a food pantry or buy a building, he is not obligated to pay for it.

I don't want to dampen anyone's faith. But it has to be properly exercised Biblical faith. And God can lead different churches to exercise that faith through different financial processes.

Back to the budget. **Why do some churches write out their budgets, and others don't?**

There are two main reasons I've heard for not creating a written budget. The first is that it can take a lot of time and hard work. Particularly in a small church without much change going on, that work can seem wasted, because the odds are this year's income and expenses will be pretty much the same as last year's.

The second reason is fear that someone will use a budget as an excuse for not spending money that really should be spent. "Yes, that's an exciting and promising new ministry idea, but we can't do it because it's not in the budget." I've heard that many times over the last 35 years of ministry. But I don't think it's a sufficient reason to forgo the advantages of a written budget. A budget is a guideline, not a straitjacket; whoever made it can adjust it.

By the way, there are two good ways to deal with the "it's not in the budget" argument. One is, when you make your budget, allot a certain amount of money to be used for future new ideas. Then, when the idea comes, the money is already there. The other way to handle it is to seek funds outside the budget, from fundraisers or special offerings. If the idea is really good, and you present it properly, people will support it. If people don't support it, perhaps it wasn't really a great idea.

Here are some of the reasons **I encourage all but the smallest churches to create a written budget every year.**

A written budget puts your priorities in a concrete form

People spend money on what is important to them. A colleague used to say, "Don't tell me what's important to you, show me your checkbook." If a church claims to be all about helping the poor, but they spend all their money on beautifying their building, where do their priorities really lie?

There are two kinds of leaders: dreamers and managers. Dreamers respond to needs and problems with grand ideas. Managers respond to needs and problems by counting resources. Both are important. They balance each other. But, at least in a church setting, it's important to keep them in the right order. A written budget reveals whether your spending matches your stated vision and mission.

The purpose of a church is to minister to God and his family and to invite others to join in. **Money is one tool for accomplishing that ministry.** God may or may not guide you, in your particular situation, to try to maintain a healthy bank account, but that should never become more important than a healthy ministry. So, as we discussed in the section on ministry planning, let your leaders exercise the dreamer side of their minds in ministry planning before they use the manager side to set a budget.

As you set your priorities, remember that failing to spend money when necessary can be as harmful as spending it unnecessarily. This is especially true in the areas of leader training and appreciation, visitor follow-up, outreach, insurance, and building maintenance. On the other hand, there is almost always a point of diminishing returns, beyond which spending more will not result in significant improvement.

A written budget forces annual review and evaluation of your ministry

Ideally, your budget should be based on the results of your annual ministry planning. If you didn't do ministry planning, updating the budget is a natural time to ask whether various expenses were worthwhile. What worked? What didn't work? What is worth spending money on this year? What can be cut back or dropped so resources can be used more effectively?

A written budget can place ministry spending decisions in the hands of those doing the actual ministry

Most of us have experienced the frustration of having some other person, who is not directly involved with what we are doing, telling us how to do it. Churches are not immune to this. If every expenditure has to be approved by the church board, ministry can get bogged down in bureaucracy. On the other hand, if a ministry team knows they are free to spend a certain amount of money to accomplish their ministry, that can be very empowering.

A written budget provides transparency and increases confidence

People are more likely to entrust the Lord's money to you if they can see where it goes. This may be especially true of business people and others who are used to working with budgets.

A written budget can encourage creativity

Often people won't even consider new ideas because they think there is no money available to implement them. If people know your budget includes a line item for new ministries, they may be more likely to exercise their God-given creativity and pay attention to the dreams the Holy Spirit inspires.

A written budget can aid in fund raising

For some people, just knowing that the church is in danger of not meeting its budget can be a powerful motivation to give. For those who need more details, a written budget can allow you to use year-to-date income to project whether you may have to cut back on some ministries. That can encourage people to increase their giving to save those ministries, or to find other ways of funding them.

Presenting Your Budget

The way you present your budget can make a big difference in how enthusiastic your people will be about supporting it. When you set your budget, certainly include as much detail as will be helpful to your leadership team as you go through the year – and have a clear policy as to who can see those details, and under what conditions. But when you present your budget to the congregation, remember that for most church members, a summary into several broad categories is all they really need, and it's much easier for them to follow.

Keep in mind that **people are motivated to give when they can see why their gifts are needed and what they will be used for.** Quite frankly, it's hard to get people excited about paying an insurance bill. Here's an idea I saw that worked well for me: don't present your budget as a list of the bills you pay, such as rent and electricity and cleaning supplies. Instead, present it in terms of what the money accomplishes. You want to be able to say, for example, "60% of our money supports our Sunday worship services, 25% goes to discipleship and education ministries, and 15% goes to evangelism and outreach." It's clear and easy to grasp; it doesn't bring up details that might be misunderstood (some people love to question the details!); and most important, it highlights the good things the money is doing, which is what most people really want to know.

Here's how it works. Start by listing your ministries. Let's say you have a building, which you use for worship services, discipleship classes, fellowship meals, and an evangelistic outreach into the community.

Next, figure out how much time the building is used for each purpose. Keeping the numbers simple, we'll say that your worship service takes five hours per week. Wow, that's a long service! Well, not actually. For budgeting purposes, this includes the worship service itself (let's say two hours including gathering and leaving), but it also includes everything else that happens in the building that goes into preparing for the worship service, such as music rehearsals (two hours) and preparing the space (one hour). Using the same reasoning, we'll give the discipleship classes two hours a week, fellowship meals two hours, and the evangelistic outreach one hour – it actually takes two hours, but it only happens every other week. This adds up to an average building use of ten hours a week. Of that ten hours, 50% is used for worship, 20% each for discipleship and fellowship, and 10% for evangelism.

Now add up all your expenses associated with the building: rent or loan payment, utilities, insurance, cleaning, maintenance, and so on. Let's say it all adds up to $2,000 dollars a month. Applying the percentages we just calculated, 50% of that, or $1,000 a month, supports our worship ministry, $400 per month supports discipleship, another $400 is spent on fellowship, and $200 goes into evangelism.

Now, pastor, let's say the church pays you a part time salary of $1,000 per month. Go through the same process. What percentage of your church time do you spend on each ministry? Let's say you average ten hours a week on church work. Of that, you spend five hours on worship, including all preparation and actually conducting services. That's half of your church time, so that means half of your salary is assigned to worship. Of course, you may decide that your sermon is more of a discipling tool than an expression of worship. If so, allocate your sermon preparation time to discipleship. Do the same with the time you spend on pastoral care, evangelism, and so on. The exception is time you spend on administration. As best you can, divide that up among ministries as well.

For the sake of simplicity, we'll assume that building expenses and your salary are all the expenses you have that are not directly related to specific ministries. If you do have others, such as office supplies or payments to a denomination or association, divide them up the same way.

The last step is to add up all the expenses associated with each of your ministries. Let's say your old budget allotted $50 per month for worship expenses, such as candles or flowers or guitar strings or piano tuning. That doesn't sound like much for an organization that claims it's number one purpose is to worship God! But we just calculated that $1,000 per month of building expenses and $500 per month of salary are also used to support your worship ministry. Looked at this way, you are actually spending over half of your budget on worship. That sounds a lot more in line, doesn't it? And you do the same for all your other ministries.

Your goal is to wind up with all your expected expenditures allocated to some aspect of ministry. This can take some work, at least the first time around, but it can make a big difference in how people see the church's use of money – and it can be a real eye opener for you.

For instance, using the example above, you are only actually using your building ten hours a week, but you are bearing the costs of owning and maintaining and heating or cooling it 168 hours a week. Is that the best use of God's money? It may turn out that it is, but it never hurts to re-evaluate.

Perhaps your church claims evangelism as its most important priority. What does this analysis say about how you are actually prioritizing your resources?

To my mind, the best reason to go through this exercise is to show people that their gifts are actually accomplishing ministry. A pie chart is a great way to present this. Your people can see at a glance that you're not just paying rent, you're enabling worship and fellowship and evangelism. You're not just paying salaries, you're providing pastoral care and teaching.

Ministry Funding

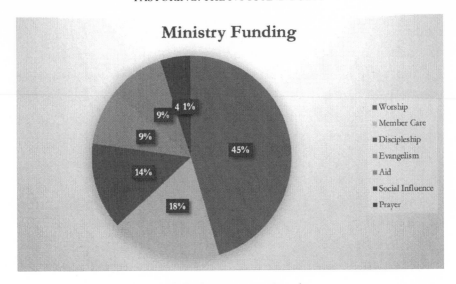

Sample budget presentation chart

Giving Money

From the very beginning of the church, one of its identifying marks has been giving money away. As far as we can tell from Luke's description at the end of Acts 2, it may have started as early as Pentecost afternoon.

Many of the 3,000 new believers were pilgrims from around the Roman Empire (Acts 2:9-11). The normal practice for this once in a lifetime trip was to arrive in Jerusalem for Passover and stay through Pentecost, reserving just enough money to get home. Now, having experienced more of God than they ever dreamed when they started their pilgrimage, they wanted to stay on, but they were out of funds. To enable their new brothers and sisters to continue in Christian growth and discipleship, it became the practice for believers of means to sell property and give the proceeds to the church, to help those in need (Acts 4:32-35).

Within a short time an organized food ministry had sprung up. This ministry especially targeted widows, for whom finding honest jobs was difficult in that culture and who had no one else to support them (Acts 6:1).

Thirty years later, Paul wrote a letter to Timothy, who was leading the church in Ephesus. His advice in 1 Timothy 5:3-16 sounds as if supporting needy widows had become a standard part of every church.

Most church members expect that part of the money they give to the church will be given away to someone or something else. In fact, they would question what was happening if it wasn't. But how much should the church give? To whom? For what purposes?

As with so many questions about doing church, the Bible does not give clear guidance about how much of its income a local church should give away. Giving to others can do God's work; funding your ministries can do God's work; investing in a building can do God's work. This is another instance where God wants us seeking him instead of consulting a rule book.

The Bible does give examples of at least four causes for which churches gave money.

1. **The needy** – *Pure and genuine religion in the sight of God the Father means caring for orphans and widows in their distress and refusing to let the world corrupt you* (James 1:27). When a brother or sister was in need, the church stepped up if no one else could.

2. **Disaster victims** – Acts 11:27-30 describes a gift sent from one local church to another to help with famine relief. Paul refers to similar gifts in several of his letters. When disasters happen to fellow Christians, the church should be there to help.

3. **Evangelists and missionaries** – In his letter to the Philippian church, Paul thanked them for supporting him on his mission trip. 1 Corinthians 9 implies that such support was common for the apostles and others who ministered from church to church.

4. **Cooperative ministries** – In Romans 15:26 Paul writes about a joint effort among the churches of Macedonia and Greece to raise relief funds for the Jerusalem Christians. He clearly encourages churches to band together when something is too big for one church alone. In

our day this may take the form of denominational support, association dues, or gifts to a parachurch organization.

Note that in every Biblical example, those the church helped were fellow Christians. Certainly God may lead an individual or a church to minister to non-believers. Sometimes this can have a wonderful evangelistic effect. But the church does not have a blanket responsibility to meet every physical need of every person who comes to them. In the first few hundred years of the church, many people came to faith because they saw how the Christians took care of their own (John 13:35).

Church Buildings

The minimum requirement for a church is not a building or a music program or even a pastor; it is two or more Christians meeting together. Of course, it's usually a lot easier and more comfortable in a building. A dedicated church building provides a place for classes and ministry activities as well as worship. You can leave chairs and other equipment set up for ministry. You may even be able to rent out space during the week to bring in a little extra income. But you can certainly be a church and have church without a church building.

For the first few hundred years of the church's existence there were no church buildings. People met in private homes. And the church didn't just survive, it thrived.

In many countries today, especially where the church is outlawed or persecuted, this is still the case. Even in America, with its Christian heritage and religious freedoms, the fastest growing part of Christianity is the house church movement.

Acts 2:42 describes the activities of the first Christians: *All the believers devoted themselves to the apostles' teaching, and to fellowship, and to sharing in meals (including the Lord's Supper), and to prayer.* All these things happened in private homes, with occasional larger gatherings outdoors or in other public places.

If you need a space bigger than a private home, often the cheapest way is to rent a space part-time. You might rent a theater for a few hours on Sunday mornings. If you meet on Sundays and another church meets on Saturdays, or even a synagogue, perhaps you could share the building, and the cost.

If your church is at the place where you need a building full-time, the easiest way to start is usually to rent. It takes much less money up front. Usually the landlord is responsible for maintenance and repairs. And if you find you need a bigger space, or a different kind of space, or a different location, it's a lot easier to change rentals than to sell a building you own and buy a new one.

Just be careful. People can begin to think church activities have to take place in the building. In fact, they can begin to think the church can't do anything that doesn't take place in the building. **Eventually they can forget that they are the church, and begin to think the building is the church.**

And don't over-commit yourself. Jesus said, *"But don't begin until you count the cost. For who would begin construction of a building without first calculating the cost to see if there is enough money to finish it?"* (Luke 14:28). I've seen more than one sad instance where this verse was apparently ignored. It came to seem as if the only reason the church existed was to pay off the loan on the building.

Owning your building can be a very good thing. It may convey a certain legitimacy in the eyes of the community and local government, which can cut down on petty harassments. It removes the restrictions of having a landlord who may not agree with your church's vision and mission. And if you are able to own a building free and clear instead of paying a mortgage, money that would otherwise go for rent is released for missions, salaries, new equipment and capital improvements.

If your church meets in its own building, here are some things you should consider. If you are planning to build or renovate, or if you are looking for a space to rent, these thoughts are even more important.

First impressions

"You only get one chance to make a first impression." Some people may decide whether or not to visit your church based strictly on the way your worship place looks from the outside. Is it well kept and inviting, or does it look like you don't care? Is the main entrance obvious?

Once they get in, is it clear where to go? If the place where you worship contains more than two rooms, visitors will feel lost. Invest in some nice-looking signs to tell people where to go. If you only use the space a few hours a week, you can put the signs on stands or tape them to the wall each week.

Cleanliness

Do you know the one thing that will almost always guarantee that a visiting family will not return? As a male pastor, this never occurred to me until I read it. Then it seemed obvious. You could have the truest doctrine, the best music, and the most inspiring preaching, but if this one area is overlooked, none of the rest makes any difference. This one most important factor is the condition of the women's restroom. A dirty or, worse, smelly ladies' room can undo all your other good work. If visitors have young children the same goes for the nursery, if you have one. If mothers don't feel confident that their children will be safe and well cared for, they are not likely to return.

Access

You want to make it as easy as possible for people to get to where you worship. Are you convenient to public transportation? If people drive, is there parking? If they ride, is there a safe place to leave their bikes or scooters? Are there stairs or other things that could make it difficult for elderly people or those in wheelchairs?

Safety and liability

When my wife was a child she attended a special Christmas Eve midnight service where everyone in the congregation was given a candle. Paula was looking around, entranced by all the little flames, when she suddenly noticed a bigger flame right in front of her. Her candle had caught her sister's hair on fire! They were able to put it out without mishap, but it could easily have been otherwise.

Keep fire extinguishers and first aid supplies handy. Clearly mark emergency exits and keep them unobstructed. If your local government has safety laws that apply to your gatherings, be sure you are in compliance.

I've met some Christians who feel that carrying insurance implies weak faith. I disagree. In our fallen world, bad things can happen to anyone – just like good things (Matthew 5:45; Luke 13:4). What if Paula's candle had caught a book or drapery on fire instead of her sister's hair? The church building could have burned down. Even safety-conscious people can have accidents. Jesus commended the five wise virgins who carried extra lamp oil as insurance against the bridal party being late. I think insurance comes under the category of being wise as serpents (Matthew 10:16). If you are in a litigious place like America, you should consider clergy malpractice insurance. Incorporating the church can also be an important way of protecting yourself and your leaders in case of a lawsuit.

Security

It's an unfortunate fact in many parts of today's world that churches can be targets for terrorist activity. If terrorists can make your people afraid to come to church or in other ways curtail your activities, they win. That's what they are aiming for. On the other hand, you don't want to needlessly expose your people to danger. If your local police are supportive, by all means consult with them and seriously consider their advice.

At the very least, you and your church leaders should have a prayerful and informed conversation about church security. What kind of thing is most likely to happen – vandalism, harassment, maybe even an attack? When might you expect an incident to happen? Are there any places that might be particularly vulnerable? What specific actions might you consider, such as stationing men at each entrance during church services, or installing an alarm system or cameras?

A church building can be a powerful ministry tool, but it won't take care of itself. Fortunately, most congregations have at least one or two people who love to maintain and care for the building. Encourage them to see that as the important ministry that it is, and celebrate them for it.

Points to Remember

- The money and property is not yours or your church's; it's God's.
- Mishandling money can destroy your witness, your ministry, your church, even your life.
- Guilt, fear and greed can motivate giving, but they are not fitting tactics for servants of the God of love who created and sustains the universe.
- Failing to spend money when necessary can be as harmful as spending it foolishly.
- The building is not the church, it's a tool for the church's ministry.

18

PROBLEMS

For we are not fighting against flesh-and-blood enemies, but against evil rulers and authorities of the unseen world, against mighty powers in this dark world, and against evil spirits in the heavenly places. – Ephesians 6:12

One of Jesus' least popular promises is John 16:33, *"Here on earth you will have many trials and sorrows."* True, he went on to say, *"But take heart, because I have overcome the world."* But you have to have problems before you can overcome them.

As pastor, most problems will wind up in your lap. Don't try to deal with them all by yourself. Where possible and appropriate, enlist the aid of your leadership team or other mature Christians. In some cases it may be helpful, or even necessary, to call for support from other local pastors or denominational leaders.

Most pastors want to believe the best of everyone. This is good, but don't be naïve. The devil would love to bring down your church and your ministry. Protect yourself and your church from his attacks.

Problem People

People are fallen. That means people have problems. When they come to church, they bring their problems with them.

This should not be a surprise. Jesus said he came, not for the righteous, but for sinners (Mark 2:17). Even after they come to Jesus, new Christians (and some not-so-new Christians) tend to do things in church the same way they've been used to doing them in the world. Ideally, as they grow under your ministry, they will learn more Christ-like ways of behaving. But you still have to deal with them until they do – and some never do.

Here are some of the common ways people create problems in the church.

Try to control the church through money

Every church has some people who donate more money than others. Sometimes those large givers can feel that their donations should entitle them to a commensurate amount of control. This is usually expressed subtly, but it can easily spill over into an explicit threat: "If you don't do things the way I want, I'm going to stop giving my money to this church!"

You need to remember, and teach your leaders and congregation, that the church belongs to Jesus Christ, not any person. **No one should be allowed to hold hostage the body of Christ.** Our God owns the cattle on a thousand hills (Psalms 50:10). Our God will supply all our needs according to his riches in glory (Philippians 4:19). If we bow to the demands of those who would use their money to control the church, we demonstrate that we don't really believe that God can or will provide what his church needs. But if we lovingly but firmly point out to the big giver the spiritual implications of what they are doing, God will honor our faith and provide what we need.

Try to control the church through influence

Some people have a lot of influence over other people in the church. They may be elders of large families, people of importance in the community, or just persuasive talkers. These people use influence the same way big givers use money. The message, implicit or explicit, is this: "If you don't do things the way I want, I'm going to another church, and I'll take all my family and friends with me."

Answer influence-controllers the same way you answer money-controllers. Remind yourself and them that the church belongs to God, and God will provide, if you stay with him and his calling.

Complainers

Constructive criticism and new ideas can be a blessing. Chronic complaining is entirely different. Paul said we should focus our thoughts on the positive (Philippians 4:8). Complaining focuses on the negative. Often, the complainer winds up doing the work of the Accuser, Satan.

Identify chronic complainers. Learn not to take their complaints personally. And never put chronic complainers in leadership. But don't label people as complainers just because they disagree with you!

No group of human beings will all be happy with everything all the time. The church is no different. But chronic complainers can damage your entire congregation. They are especially dangerous if they are influential in the church or community, or if they gain the ear of people new to the church.

Teach your people to focus on positives, not negatives – in the church as well as in their marriages and families and businesses. Teach them to refuse to listen to complaints. That's not rude, it's good spiritual discipline. And it's about the only way to help complainers break their bad habit of complaining so they can grow more like Jesus, who never complained.

Gossips

Gossips are similar to complainers, and can do as much damage. Romans 1:29 puts gossip in the same list as hatred, lying, and even murder. Never put a gossip in leadership, regardless of other qualifications. Especially be careful that gossips are not put in a place where they can gain access to confidential information, such as helping the pastor schedule counseling appointments, or counting the offerings.

Sometimes gossip comes disguised as a prayer request. "Oh, we have to pray for Sister A and Brother B, because I heard that somebody saw them doing such-and-such…" That is nothing more than malicious gossip, not matter how it is worded. Make sure your congregation understands that. Like complaining, gossip is a dangerous addiction that must be broken and replaced with healthy and positive habits of speech, for the sake of the person and the church.

Drainers

All pastors like to help people, or they wouldn't be pastors. It's a great joy to help someone over a rough spot and see them go on and achieve success and happiness. But some people never seem to run out of rough spots, no matter how much you help them. Whether their need is financial help or emotional support, they never seem to get enough. If you don't watch out, they can completely drain you of all your resources, and you will find that you have no time, energy or strength left for anyone else, including your family and yourself.

Guilt is a favorite tool of drainers. They are gifted at making you feel guilty if you don't meet their every need. They can do the same with your church leaders and members. And then, when they have sucked you dry, they'll move on to another church and do the same thing.

Drainers want you to take care of them, but they don't really want to change. They'll accept your money and sympathy and time, but they won't take your advice and do the things they need to do to put themselves into a better situation.

Pastors need to be able to identify such people. You need to protect yourself against their unreasonable demands, and you need to protect your congregation. And the pastors in a city should warn each other against such people.

Con artists

The main difference between con artists and drainers is sincerity. Drainers genuinely believe their stories, and they are looking for help. Con artists tell whatever story they think will get you to give them the most money.

Pastors like to think the best of people. This often makes them easy targets for con artists. Then either you give away too much of the church's money, or you become hardened and distrustful of people in general. Neither is a good situation.

Personally, I would rather give money to a con artist than refuse to help someone who is genuinely in need. And I like to believe people. So if it's left to me, I wind up giving away a lot of the church's money to con artists. I find it very helpful to have someone else in the church handle those requests, someone who is not as gullible as I am.

Con artists often go from church to church and charity to charity telling the same story over and over. The pastors in a city, and perhaps even the leaders of other charities and social agencies, should consider developing a way to identify these people and warn each other against them.

Self-appointed prophets and teachers

Paul, Peter and John all faced problems from people who came into their churches claiming to be teachers or prophets. It's important to show hospitality to traveling pastors and Christian workers, as well as Christian brothers and sisters visiting from other places. But it's also important to prayerfully discern the source of their message (1 John 4:1-6). Sometimes the reason they are visiting your church is because they have made themselves unwelcome in theirs!

Conflicting Beliefs and Practices

Most church conflict is caused by problem people. But there are many issues on which good, sincere, Bible-believing, educated Christians disagree. What are we to make of these differences?

John Wesley, founder of Methodism, said, "In whatever does not strike at the heart of Christian faith, we think and let think." The same idea was expressed hundreds of years earlier by the African theologian, St. Augustine: "In essentials, unity; in non-essentials, liberty; in all things, love."

This is a wonderful philosophy, in keeping with the biblical spirit of Romans 14. As long as the issue is confined to the realm of thinking, most of us have little trouble with it. However, once we move to application, problems arise.

It's one thing to have a polite disagreement about when a person is old enough to be baptized. It's another thing to decide whether or not, in a given congregation, you will baptize babies.

Some churches teach that the use of instrumental music in worship is against scripture. Some teach that pastors should be hired or fired based on a vote of the congregation. Some teach that women should not be allowed to do certain things in a church setting because of their gender. Other churches believe these positions misinterpret the Bible. Both sides can line up scores of impressively credentialed expert witnesses to support their views. So how is a local congregation to discern God's will for its practice in these areas?

In many churches, the preferred biblical understanding is predetermined by denominational affiliation or local church history. But what if someone from a different background comes in and raises a heretofore silent issue, and the members and even the leadership suddenly discover that they are split down the middle about what the Bible says and means?

In such a case, certain principles must rule.

Understand unity

Christian unity does not require that we all be alike or think alike. Beyond the non-negotiable truths that define what it means to be a Christian, church members disagree about all kinds of things. Unity does require that we agree about how we will approach our differences, and what differences we will tolerate even if we can't change each other's opinions. Each of us must have settled in our mind, what is worth fighting about? And what will we do if we lose the fight?

Use the Bible responsibly

The Bible is the infallible, inerrant, inspired written word of God. Yet each part of it was inspired and written by a certain person, addressed to certain people, for a certain purpose, at a particular time and place in history and culture that is foreign to every person living today. Naturally, as with any other book, we read the Bible through the lens of our own culture, our own subconscious assumptions, and our own history and experiences. Furthermore, the vast majority of Christians know the Bible only in translation, so what we are looking at through our lens is already one step removed from the original meaning. The wonder is not that Christians differ about what the Bible means; the wonder is that those differences are so small!

How can you be sure you are using the Bible responsibly? I went over this in more detail in the chapter on preaching. Let me repeat some points here in the context of resolving conflicts.

Prayerfully examine your motives

Are you really trying to find out what God is saying, or are you looking for support in the Bible for your own preconceived views?

261

Don't be dogmatic where the Bible is not dogmatic

God knew people would be reading the Bible in hundreds of languages and cultures for thousands of years, so he made sure the really important things are very clear. The Biblical standard for establishing a fact is *"two or three witnesses"* (Matthew 18:16; 1 Timothy 5:19; Hebrews 10:28). Where the Bible does not provide us with a minimum of two or three clear statements, we cannot be rigid in our interpretations.

Avoid the temptation to take passages out of context

Let the Bible interpret the Bible. If we don't look at all the different places where God addresses a certain issue, we may miss important clues to understanding. In seeking relevant passages, we must remember that the Bible is not a theology textbook, and it is not primarily written in propositional statements. Most of the Bible is narrative. The stories of how God used and dealt with people must be given much weight in our discernment of God's will.

If the Bible is not clear, consider tradition, reason, and experience

These three elements are great for framing a discussion. Unfortunately, they can also be highly subjective.

Disagree agreeably

What do we do if we've sincerely sought to apply all the above principles, but still find ourselves differing? If we have to take action one way or another, how do we agree to disagree?

The first step is for the proponents of the two views to **acknowledge each other's sincerity, love for God, and desire to do the right thing.** This includes admitting that, while each believes they are right, it's barely possible that they might be wrong, and we won't find out for sure this side of heaven.

Next, agree to focus on areas of agreement. Whether we focus on our differences or our unity is a matter of choice. **Division is a tool of the enemy**; carried far enough, every person can find "reasons of principle" to separate and divide from every other person. Emphasizing our agreement, while not minimizing our differences, results in unity with integrity.

Finally, I had a colleague who used to say, "always err on the side of grace." When it comes to rules and regulations, there are two basic philosophical positions. The first says, "Everything that is not expressly allowed is prohibited." That view can easily result in legalism. The second position says, "Everything that is not expressly prohibited is allowed." That view tends toward grace, and grace is a sign of God.

Sin in the Church

For those who have become new creatures in Jesus Christ, sin is no longer a part of their nature. Unfortunately, it may still be a habit. Temptation can still be strong. Weakness can still strike. The sad fact is, church membership is not a vaccination against sin.

As a pastor, **your job is not to seek out sinfulness.** Ideally, the sinner will come to you personally to confess and ask for help. If that doesn't happen, you might witness sinful behavior, or somebody might tell you of it. However it happens, odds are that the time will come when you need to apply church discipline to deal with a situation of sin in the congregation.

This is definitely one of those areas where you want to make your church policies ahead of time. If you wait until a situation arises, your response, and that of your leaders and congregation, is much more likely to be based on personalities, friendships and church politics than on clear biblical thinking.

Making sin difficult

If people want to sin, there is nothing that you can do as a pastor to stop them. But most of the time, church members don't set out to sin. They get tripped up by a combination of temptation and opportunity.

Sometimes it's possible to put policies in place that will greatly reduce these temptations, or the opportunity to act on them. For instance, you can create a policy that whenever church money is being counted and handled, at least two people from different families must be involved. You can require that a man and a woman not married to each other should not be alone together in the church building, or that an adult is never allowed to be alone with an unrelated child. These policies not only reduce temptation and opportunity for wrong behavior, but they also provide protection against false accusations.

Of course, **the best protection against sin is a strong desire to please Jesus,** combined with a growing knowledge of what does and does not please him. Your people will learn this through your preaching and teaching ministry, and through your example. But just in case not every person in your church has grown to that level of Christian maturity, the steps I've just described are a wise precaution.

What really happened, and does it require your response?

So something allegedly happened in your church. How do you move from "allegedly" to "definitely?"

Start by asking, is this charge serious enough to require an official pastoral or church response? Ideally, your church policy will define that for you. Perhaps the situation is best handled by privately talking to the person. Perhaps you should consult with a trusted leader in the church whom you know will keep it confidential. Perhaps you don't have to say anything, just pay special attention for a while to see if it recurs or gets worse. Or maybe it's one of those subtle sins, like gossip or pride, that may be best handled by preaching. If that's what you decide, be careful not to point out any identifiable current person or situation in your sermons.

If you decide the situation warrants further inquiry, the next step is to make sure that whatever is claimed actually happened. If the person confesses to you, then you know it happened. If you saw it yourself, you probably know what happened, but it is best to check with the person to make sure it really was what you thought it was. If a third party comes and tells you about it, ask yourself these questions before taking any action.

- Are there other witnesses (1 Timothy 5:19)?
- What do you know about the alleged wrong-doer?
- What do you know about the person who is telling you?
- How mature in the Lord are each of them?
- What is their character?
- Is this the first time the one has been accused?
- Is this the first time the other has brought accusations?
- Would the first have a motive for doing the thing?
- Would the second have a motive for wanting to believe they did?

If you are unable to just dismiss the accusation – your pre-written church policy should describe how that decision is to be made – and if the person accused is in a position in the church that would provide them opportunity to do it again, they should be removed from that position while you carry out your process. For instance, if the accusation has to do with stealing money, don't let the accused handle any more money until the situation is cleared up. If, God forbid, it has to do with mistreating a child, don't let them work with children until it is cleared up. Try to help them understand that this is for their protection as well as for the protection of the church. Again, a pre-written policy requiring these steps should help remove any sense that you are picking on them personally.

Through all of this, **keep the situation as confidential as possible**. After all, the accused may turn out to be entirely innocent. Or they may confess, repent, and be restored to the Lord.

Confronting sin

Let's say you've decided that something did happen that requires some kind of follow-up. How do you do that in a Biblical and Christ-honoring way?

Confronting sin is one of the few places where Jesus laid out a specific course of action. It's also one of two places where he used the word "church." Since we are talking about confronting sin in the church, he's speaking right to us.

> *"If another believer sins against you, go privately and point out the offense. If the other person listens and confesses it, you have won that person back.* [16] *But if you are unsuccessful, take one or two others with you and go back again, so that everything you say may be confirmed by two or three witnesses.* [17] *If the person still refuses to listen, take your case to the church. Then if he or she won't accept the church's decision, treat that person as a pagan or a corrupt tax collector."* – Matthew 18:15-17

Any sin within the church degrades the purity of the church and is therefore a sin against the church. Use Jesus' method of dealing with it.

The words of Jesus are clear. Let me just add three important points.

1. At any point when the sinner confesses and repents, the process of investigation and confrontation stops, and the process of restoration begins (see below). In most cases, the matter should not need to become any more public.

2. "Take your case to the church" does not mean naming names and details in a public setting such as a worship service, where people who are not church member may be present. Rather, it means a prayerful discussion with whatever body has the authority to impose church discipline in your congregation.

3. The goal of the process is always confession, repentance, and restoration. "Treat that person as a pagan or a corrupt tax collector" does not mean punish them or shun them. It means start over with them, seeking

to draw them back to the Lord.

Restoring the sinner

The first and greatest goal of church discipline is to protect the other church members. But a second and equal goal is to restore the sinner. Paul encouraged the Galatians,

> *"Dear brothers and sisters, if another believer is overcome by some sin, you who are godly should gently and humbly help that person back onto the right path. And be careful not to fall into the same temptation yourself." - Galatians 6:1*

He gives us an example in his two letters to the church in Corinth. In 1 Corinthians 5 he demands discipline for a case of open sin in the church. But in 2 Corinthians 2, having apparently heard that the sinner had repented, Paul instructed the church to welcome him back with forgiveness and comfort.

Part of your discipline policy should deal with processes of restoration. Of course, simply following a policy will not guarantee that wrong-doers change their ways, but it will help protect you and the church if they don't. In particular, think and pray ahead of time about what you will require before accepting the person back into full fellowship. Are words of sorrow enough? What if they cry? Will you require a minimum waiting period? A course of counseling or supervised study? Some other indication of sincerity and change? What you require may depend on what the offense was. And of course, all of this assumes that the person wants to come back to your church, and is willing to accept your terms. Remember, this is not punishment. **It should be offered as a loving corrective, aimed at helping the person become more like Jesus, and the church become more like the Kingdom of God.**

One last thought: receiving wrong-doers back into fellowship does not necessarily mean receiving them back into leadership, or allowing them to return to a place where they may be tempted to fall again. If they demand that, it may be a sign that their repentance was not completely genuine. In fact, any kind of demanding attitude indicates a lack of humility, which almost always means a lack of true repentance.

Ambushes

A favorite tactic of guerilla warfare is the ambush. It's a beautiful day. You're peacefully moving along a smooth road, minding your own business. You come upon an innocent-looking outcropping of rocks or copse of trees, or you turn a corner around a building. And all of a sudden you're under fire.

Ambushes can be effective even when they are expected. When they catch you off guard, they can be deadly. Here are a few phrases church people will say that I've learned can be cover for an ambush. Be on guard for them. I'm sure you'll add your own to the list.

"I'll be happy to take that on"

We pastors love volunteers. It seems like there's always more work than workers. Even Jesus had that problem. He told his disciples, *"The harvest is great, but the workers are few. So pray to the Lord who is in charge of the harvest; ask him to send more workers into his fields"* (Luke 10:2). So when somebody volunteers for a job in the church, we want to say, "Hallelujah! Thank you, Lord, for sending more workers!"

Experience has taught me this is not always the appropriate response. Usually volunteers are quite sincere and just want to help. Sometimes, though, they have an ulterior motive. If the job they want will put them in a position to make or influence important decisions in the church, be careful. Are they hoping to gain power or prestige? Are they hoping to steer things in their own direction? One person tried to gain a seat on the finance committee because he thought the church was paying me too much. Others have sought official positions because they wanted to replace me as pastor.

Be careful about anything having to do with church leadership, church vision and direction, church discipline, and how church money is spent.

When somebody says, "I'll be happy to take that on," thank them profusely. But if "that" is something that will allow them to pursue their own agenda instead of the way God is leading you, don't accept their gracious offer too quickly.

"People are saying"

This has happened to me more than once. I'm in a church board meeting. One says, "Several people have told me they're not happy about such and so." Another person says, "I've heard that, too." A third says, "A number of people have told me the same thing."

Wow! It sounds like there's a groundswell of sentiment among the congregation. A major movement is happening! We better do something!

Not so fast. Almost every time, on digging a little more deeply it turns out that the same three or four people talked to every board member. What sounded like a strong consensus in the congregation proved to actually be just a lobbying effort by a small minority. And once you figure that out, you know to be careful about those who were doing the lobbying.

"The whole church agrees with me"

Sometimes a person comes presenting themselves as spokesperson for the congregation. The issue is usually a change they don't like, but it can be anything. And very often, what they present as the unanimous feeling of the congregation is actually just their own opinion, perhaps with a few others. Yet they aren't lying. They actually believe they represent the whole church.

After many years of trying to understand this phenomenon, I think I've figured out the psychology. Note that these are not intentional or even conscious ways of thinking, but I believe for many they are true nonetheless.

They come to you, express an opinion, and add, "the whole church agrees with me." When pastors hear "the whole church," we think of everybody associated with the church: leaders, active members, occasional attenders, even those we are hoping to attract. Most people don't think that way. When they say "the church," in their minds they are picturing the people they normally see and talk to and do things with at church. There are other people there on Sunday morning, but they're kind of vague and peripheral and they don't really count.

So when these people say "the whole church agrees with me," what they really mean is, "all my church friends agree with me." And this is to be expected, because most people find it hard to be friends with those who disagree with them on issues they feel strongly about.

But it goes further than that. Some people have no problem forcefully expressing their opinions. A friend used to say, "It's my opinion, and you're entitled to it!" People who take it on themselves to tell pastors what the congregation thinks are likely to be that kind of person. But most people, especially people who are trying to be nice Christians, are not like that. In fact, most people like to avoid confrontations, especially in church. When somebody says something they disagree with, they don't want to start an argument or offend a friend, so they say something noncommittal and try to change the subject. The problem is, opinionated people are not often very adept at reading such social subtleties. In their minds, if you don't argue with me it means you agree with me.

So sometimes – not always, but more often than you might think – "the whole church agrees with me" actually means, "all my church friends agree with me." That actually means, "nobody argued with me." And some people carry it even further, because if someone did have the temerity to argue they are removed from the category of friends and placed with "those other people," who don't count. So the person can still say, and fully believe, "the whole church agrees with me."

All this is not to say that you should ignore people who come to tell you what the church is thinking. In fact, you need people who can reliably report the thoughts and feelings of various groups within the church. Just prayerfully follow up and verify what people tell you, especially when their thoughts are unsolicited.

"I can't tell you"

Confidentiality is a crucial value in our dealings with people in the church. If someone fears that you will tell others their secrets, they will most likely not share them with you, even in a counseling situation. Once that trust is broken, it is difficult to regain. I personally make it a policy never to use a story about anyone in the church as a sermon illustration, or in any other public way, unless I have first received permission from the person involved.

That said, one of the devil's favorite ways to keep his evil doings hidden is to raise concerns about confidentiality or fears of embarrassing someone. This is particularly true when people are reporting concerns or criticisms to the pastor. I once had a church member who repeatedly told me, "Pastor, people aren't happy. They don't like what you're doing, and if you don't change they're going to leave the church." But she wouldn't tell me who was unhappy. And she wouldn't tell me what I was doing that they didn't like. It was "confidential." Not knowing who it was, I couldn't talk to them about it. And not knowing what it was, I couldn't do anything about it. The only result was to add stress to what was already a very stressful time in that church, and distract me from using my time more constructively.

I try not to pay attention to anonymous notes or reports. If a person will talk to me directly, or write me a letter, or even give someone else permission to share their concerns with me by name, then I'll prayerfully consider them. If they are not willing to own up to their opinions, I am not willing to be concerned with them. The end result of anonymous communications is almost always trouble.

Unholy Spirits

Some churches just seem to exude a wonderful spirit. It seems like when you walk in, you can "feel" hospitality, or evangelism, or a love of Bible study or worship. Unfortunately, the same can be true on the negative side.

Some understand a negative atmosphere as a natural consequence of certain personalities. I believe there is often a spiritual influence as well. Casting out demons was a major part of Jesus' ministry. Paul warns that we wrestle not against flesh and blood, but against evil spiritual powers. We are not to be unaware of the devil's tactics, but resist him with appropriate spiritual warfare. Paul tells us how in Ephesians 6:10-18 and 2 Corinthians 10:3-5.

One of the less-appreciated gifts of the Holy Spirit is discerning of spirits (1 Corinthians 12:10). If your church seems to be experiencing more than your share of trouble and conflict, earnestly desire this gift (1 Corinthians 14:1). Some spirits, like criticism, deception, and greed, are common in many areas of life. Here are some unholy spirits that seem to focus on churches.

Religion

A spirit of religion tries to focus people on the religious acts they do, rather than on their relationship with God. These acts may be very good in themselves, such as tithing, daily Bible reading, and reciting certain prayers. But when the acts become the focus of the people's hope of eternity, rather than the grace of God, people's faith grows cold and their hearts grow hard. That is the goal of the religious spirit.

The Pharisees are the great Biblical example. They were so focused on properly practicing and protecting their religion that when the one they claimed to be doing it all for appeared among them, they completely failed to recognize him.

Legalism

A spirit of legalism focuses on the letter of the law rather than the spirit of it. When a legalistic person looks at himself, he asks, "How far can I go before I get in trouble?" When he looks at others, he focuses on their failure to observe every detail of the law. Legalism results in justifying self and judging others.

Suspicion

A spirit of suspicion often masquerades as the Biblical gift of discernment of spirits (1 Corinthians 12:10). If this spirit gains influence in your church, people will suspect each other, and especially you, of lying, using the church for personal gain, and having ulterior motives for everything you try to do. Suspicion suggests the worst possible interpretation for everything that happens.

Division

The devil loves "divide and conquer," especially since God loves unity. Sometimes it seems that division occurs more easily in the church than outside it.

Let's say it's time to paint the church kitchen. What color should it be? The pastor could decide. But let's say the pastor is trying to train the leaders to make godly decisions, and it seems this is a good case to practice on. After discussion and prayer, one group wants to paint the kitchen green, and the other wants to paint it yellow. Not a major decision, right? But because they prayed about it, each group feels that they heard from God. Suddenly, the issue is no longer what color somebody likes, it's who hears God best. A spirit of division will grab that and run with it. People will begin to feel, "I prayed about the kitchen and God told me it's supposed to be yellow, and if you want to paint it green, you are rebelling against God's will!" Of course, the green faction feels the same way about their color. The next step is, "It's my duty to God to do everything I can to make sure the kitchen is painted yellow, even if I have to drive you out of the church to do it!"

A spirit of division doesn't care what the issue is, and it really doesn't care who wins. If your church seems to be constantly in conflict, rather than settling back into unity once a particular issue is settled, the problem may be a spirit of division.

Poverty

Our God is a God of abundance (John 10:10). He created all the sand on the seashore and all the stars in the sky. The Bible says God owns the cattle on a thousand hills (Psalm 50:10). God has all the resources in the universe, plenty for every church and every Christian to have all they need to carry out God's plan to reach the world for Jesus.

The task of a spirit of poverty is to blind our eyes to that truth. It works to keep Christians and churches poor, or at least acting as if they are poor. It is wonderful to have support from brothers and sisters around the world, but I don't believe it is God's plan for any local church to have to depend on that for more than just its beginning stages. Every Christian and every church must learn to look to God as our source.

Control

A controlling spirit seeks to usurp the proper authority in the church. Often this manifests as people attempting to undermine the authority of the pastor, usually through various threats. "If you don't do things my way, I'll leave, and I'll take my tithes and my friends with me!" This can expand to a small group that tries to run the church. However, a pastor can also exhibit a controlling spirit, often by trying to tell church members what to do in every detail of church and even personal issues, rather than teaching the leaders and members to be led by the Holy Spirit to make godly decisions for themselves.

Combinations of spirits

Often problem spirits work together and reinforce each other. For instance, in a church beset by a spirit of poverty, a person who tries to exercise control by threatening to withhold giving will have more influence than in a church that trusts in God's abundance. A spirit of suspicion can turn up the fire under divisions.

Origins of unholy spirits

Where do these troublesome spirits come from? Probably most are brought in with troublesome people. Sometimes, though, they come with the church itself, from something that happened in its history, maybe even in how it was founded. Of the seven churches I have served, this was true of two that I know of.

When I first went to one church, I was told it was started as a daughter church by a congregation in a town nearby. After a few years I started hearing another version of the story. It turned out this church actually started as the result of a church split. A spirit of division had done its dirty work. Some involved in the split were still influential in the church I was now serving. At that time, I didn't know what that might mean, but I found out. The church was growing, attracting new people with new ideas, even talking to an architect about building a larger sanctuary. The old guard suddenly found themselves being outvoted in church meetings. The divisive spirit that was part of this church's birth raised its ugly head once again. Most of the new people left, the building project was canceled, I was moved to another congregation, and that church has never again reached that level of potential.

Another church I served also had an instructive history. I was told the original church was built on land donated by a faithful member. Sounds wonderful, right? But when we started digging into the records, some details emerged that shed a different light. It turned out the land was originally intended for the donor's daughter. But she fell in love with a poor man whom her father felt was beneath her. The father threatened that if his daughter married this man, he wouldn't give her the land, and she would be poor her whole life. She did marry him, and the father gave the land to the church instead. I don't know if the curse came true for the girl and her husband. I do know a perception of poverty stayed with that church for many generations. A generally healthy congregation was less effective than it could have been, because it saw itself as poor.

The Bible says, *"The Son of God came to destroy the works of the devil"* (1

John 3:8). Jesus did this first through his own life and death. Now he does it through his body, the church. Of course, the devil fights back. Jesus promised that the gates of hell will not prevail against the church (Matthew 16:18), but there are still battles to be won.

Dealing with unholy spirits

Here are three steps I have found to be helpful in dealing with problem spirits.

Expose them to light

The devil loves to work in the darkness. Perhaps that's because John 1 tells us Jesus is light, and the devil can't stand Jesus. The devil also can't stand the light of exposure. It's been said that the devil's greatest trick is to make people believe he doesn't exist. Don't let him get away with it. Peter wrote, *"Stay alert! Watch out for your great enemy, the devil. He prowls around like a roaring lion, looking for someone to devour"* (1 Peter 5:8). In your preaching and teaching, shine a light on that lion. Illuminate his hiding places. Teach your people to recognize his schemes, so they won't be outwitted by him (2 Corinthians 2:11).

If you discern that an individual has a problem, go to that individual privately. But if the problem is with the whole congregation, if you discern that a spirit of gossip or criticism or control or whatever is becoming entrenched, you need to publicly shine a light on it.

The way to do this is not to announce, "This brother has a spirit of gossip," or, "That sister has a spirit of control." That kind of accusation is the work of Satan, the Accuser. Instead, teach your people. Preach about evil spirits and how they can infect a congregation, how to identify them and what to do about them. Be sure that as you teach, you always speak the truth in love (Ephesians 4:15). In this way, no one should be embarrassed, and the whole congregation will learn to recognize this behavior and avoid it. Your goal is not just to refute a particular piece of gossip. You want to create a church culture where everybody knows that gossip, criticism, arrogance and so on are "not the way we do things around here."

Emphasize the opposite virtues

Luke 11:24-26 tells us that it's not just enough to evict evil spirits. We must replace them. If we don't fill the spiritual void, we'll wind up worse off than we were before.

Start by inviting the Holy Spirit to come and fill your church. Of course, you should always be doing that. In dealing with evil spirits, though, it's important to specifically invite the Holy Spirit to produce and manifest the graces and virtues that will counteract the effects of the spirit that caused the problems. If you're dealing with a spirit of division, pray for the Holy Spirit to produce unity. If the issue was a religious spirit, pray for the Holy Spirit to release grace.

Then act on your prayers. Encourage your people to focus on practicing the virtues and spiritual fruits (Galatians 5:22-23) that are opposite to the problem spirit. Combat a spirit of poverty by encouraging faith and generosity. Fight a spirit of legalism by encouraging freedom. It's not always wise to name the evil spirits to the whole congregation, but it's always appropriate to preach on the good things of God.

Binding and loosing

Jesus gave his followers the power to evict evil spirits (Luke 10:17; Mark 16:17; John 14:12; Acts 1:8). That power was never revoked. Unfortunately, the Bible does not give us step by step instructions for every situation. My goal here is just to make you aware of these issues. If God leads you to explore further, or if you ever find yourself in a situation where you need to know more, there is a lot of good information available. Of course, given the topic, there is also a lot of bad information. Remember Paul's advice: *Test everything; hold fast what is good* (1 Thessalonians 5:21 ESV).

Points to Remember

- Learn to recognize and deal with the problem people in your church.
- You can't help people who don't want to be helped.
- Handling conflict is a skill you can learn.
- When you need to confront sin in the church, don't do it by yourself.
- Your real enemy is not people; learn to recognize and deal with problem spirits.

19

WORKING WITH OTHER CHURCHES

I pray that they will all be one, just as you and I are one—as you are in me, Father, and I am in you. And may they be in us so that the world will believe you sent me. – John 17:21

One of the greatest ways churches can witness to the love and power of Jesus Christ is to work together. On a large scale this is often done by joining together in denominations or associations. Within a city or town this cooperation often takes the form of pastors meeting together, to pray for one another and plan cooperative ministries.

Denominations and Associations

Denominations are large formal groups of many churches. The pastors and churches share a common theological viewpoint and a common understanding of how churches should operate. There is usually a commitment to follow certain rules, and a means for disciplining those who break the rules. Sometimes the denomination plays a role in assigning pastors to local churches.

Associations are similar to denominations in many ways. The main difference is that an association usually has less authority over local churches, because membership is voluntary.

You or your church may already be part of a denomination or association. If you are not, most such groups would be happy to have you join them if you feel so led.

On the other hand, many pastors and congregations prefer to remain independent. They may object to what they see, often with good reason, as wasteful bureaucracy and interference from afar.

In many people's minds, independence is always a good thing. Why would anyone choose to come under the authority of some national or international group of churches? But let me suggest three reasons why banding together with an established group of other churches may make your church even better. I'm not trying to push you one way or another, just give you something to think and pray about.

Resourcing

One advantage to families of churches is the opportunity to pool resources. Such things as missions and relief work, pastoral training, curriculum development, pensions and benefits for pastors, and even purchasing of common supplies, can often be done more efficiently and less expensively by a large group of churches than by an individual congregation. A given church may only be able to offer a few dollars to a particular cause, but when that few dollars is multiplied by hundreds or thousands of churches, a lot can be done.

Voice

Jesus taught us to pray, *"Thy will be done on earth as it is in heaven"* (Matthew 6:10, traditional Lord's Prayer wording). Often the conditions that make earth different from heaven are systemic issues that are too big for one congregation to tackle. Whether it's advocating for religious freedom or seeking justice for an oppressed minority, government and the press pay attention to numbers. A pastor who can say, "I represent a denomination of a million people," is likely to receive a better hearing than one who says, "I represent a congregation of forty-three."

Oversight

How do you and your people know you're preaching and teaching orthodox gospel truth, instead of just your own understanding (or misunderstanding) of the Bible? How do you know you or your church are not accidentally violating some new law? Where do you go when you have a question about the appropriate way to perform some church function?

We already looked at the value of ordination: somebody is willing to stand behind you and say, "We've examined these pastors, and we're ready to testify that they're solid, they're trained, they're ready, and you can trust them with your church and your eternal salvation." Often an established denomination may have better resources than an independent local congregation, and perhaps higher standards, for selecting and preparing people for that statement of confidence. And they probably have a tested process for investigating allegations of heresy or ecclesial wrong-doing, and meting out appropriate discipline and rehabilitation.

Submitting to oversight is not an admission that somebody with a more impressive title has a better line to God than you do. It's a confession that it's just possible that you might not know everything, you might not always hear from God 100% clearly, you might not always do everything right. In the New Testament, the words of the prophets are subject to the other prophets (1 Corinthians 14:29). Even Paul submitted his preaching to the oversight of the other apostles (Galatians 2:2; Acts 15).

Other Churches in Your Area

There are things about being a pastor that only other pastors can understand. There are things about ministering in a particular community that a pastor or denominational official who has never worked there can never appreciate. And Jesus said the way Christians show love for each other will be a powerful witness (John 13:35). For all these reasons, one of the most important things you can do as a pastor, for yourself and for your ministry, is come together with other pastors in your area.

When the Bible refers to the church in a given city, it's not usually talking about a single congregation, but a collection of what we today would call house churches. Meeting in different homes, they inevitably developed slightly different ways of doing things. Still, all were part of the same body of Christ (Acts 2:46; 1 Corinthians 16:19).

In the same way, all the local Christian congregations near you, even with differences in the details of belief and practice, make up the church of your city.

What I'm saying is this: those **other pastors and churches aren't your competition. Your competition is the world, the flesh and the devil. The other churches are on your side.**

> John said to Jesus, "Teacher, we saw someone using your name to cast out demons, but we told him to stop because he wasn't in our group." "Don't stop him!" Jesus said. . . . "Anyone who is not against us is for us." - Mark 9:38-40

Local ministerial associations can have some of the same advantages in their area as a denomination has on a larger scale. As you identify needs in your community, your churches can work together to meet them. As you speak with one voice, you can influence local laws and policies. And as you get to know and trust each other, you can hold each other accountable

Prayer support

I have been part of a number of ministerial associations in different places over the years. Some were very effective; others were little more than social clubs. In my experience, those that were most helpful to me and effective for the community were those where we really prayed for each other.

Nobody understands the challenges of being a pastor like another pastor. That means nobody can pray as specifically and effectively for a pastor as another pastor. You may disagree about the sequence of events at Jesus' second coming, or whether communion bread should be cut or broken. But as long as you are all preaching Jesus Christ according to the Bible, you are all on the same side. As much as you can, you need to be working together. And that starts with praying together.

Pray for each other personally. Pray for each other's families. Pray for each other's ministries. Pray for each other's churches. And don't just do this once a month when the ministerial association meets. Take time during your church service to pray for the other churches in your community. It will help them, as prayer always helps, and it will send a powerful message of unity to your people and anyone who visits.

Cooperative ministries

Are there any homeless people in your city? Are there children who need after-school care while their parents work? Are there any children who can't go to school at all? Are there refugees? Are there adults who don't know how to read or write? Every town has problems like this. And probably every church has Christians who say, "Something should be done to help these people. But what can one church do?"

One church may not be able to do a lot. But what if all the churches in an area work together? What if you and the other pastors choose one project, and all cooperate? You can make a difference in your community. And your community will notice.

Joint worship services

There are reasons why all the Christians in a given place don't worship together all the time. It may be too far to travel. It may be details of doctrine or church governance or worship. It may just be that your members prefer your style of preaching, and others prefer someone else's style. For whatever reason, most of the time we worship in our own congregations.

Every now and then, however, it can be a wonderful thing if the different churches in an area can come together in a joint worship service. Imagine all the local churches in your city joined together to sing and pray and proclaim your mutual commitment to the lordship of Jesus Christ. It probably wouldn't work on a Sunday morning, but it might on Good Friday or Christmas Eve, or on a national holiday, or even just a random evening. Your members could be greatly encouraged to see that there are more believers in their city than just your own group. And it's a great testimony for non-believers to see the unity of the church.

Mutual accountability

One of the mysteries of God is that he uses fallible human beings to do his work. That includes us pastors. We are subject to weakness and temptation just like everyone else.

One of the great advantages to praying and working with other pastors is that you can hold each other accountable. The more you pray together, the more you talk together, the more you laugh together, then the more you will trust each other, and the more you will turn to each other for help when you are faced with these things. It's amazing how just knowing that someone else is watching out for you can help you resist when temptations come.

But what if that isn't enough? What happens if a pastor is accused of misusing church money, or behaving inappropriately with a church member, or some other sin? I think you'll agree it's best if you can resolve the issue without bringing some kind of criminal charges. And what if the accusation is doctrinal instead of moral? You don't want the government making rules about how you run your church or what you believe. Yet **the members of a congregation should never have to sit in judgment on their own pastor.**

Ideally, the denomination or group that ordained the pastor should have a process for investigating and handling such issues. But if they don't, or if the church members are the ones who ordained their pastor, then the other pastors of the area may be best suited to handle the situation. But this can only really work if the pastors have already built up a relationship of mutual trust by praying, fellowshipping and working together. Otherwise, there can be a strong temptation to try to take advantage of the unfortunate situation by luring away the members of the affected church.

Church hoppers and con artists

I heard a story about a man who was marooned on a desert island for several years. Among other things, he occupied his time in building. When he was finally found, before he left he wanted to show his rescuers the various structures he had made. They recognized his sleeping area and his kitchen and the hut where he stored coconuts, but there were two buildings they couldn't figure out. One, he told them, was his church. And the other? "Oh, that's the church I used to go to."

Wherever you find two or more churches, you are likely to find people who left one to attend another – often several times. Some of these people are genuinely looking for the place God wants them to worship and serve. Some may be upset about something that is actually a misunderstanding, that could easily be cleared up if the pastor only knew. And some are chronically unhappy people who leave a trail of conflict behind them.

When the pastors of an area talk to each other and trust each other, they can help each other with all these people. If someone visits my church but is clearly looking for something more like what you offer, I can recommend your church, and vice versa. If someone comes to my church because of something they think you said or did, I can let you know so you can clear up the misunderstanding. And if someone leaves my church after spreading conflict and discontent, I can warn you about them.

The same is true of con artists. Some people have genuine needs, and meeting those needs can be a fruitful area for local churches to cooperate in ministry. But some people just tell sob stories in hopes that the church will give them some money, and they tend to tell the same story to every pastor in town. When pastors work together they can identify these people, so they can use the Lord's money to help those who are truly deserving.

Multiplying Your Church

When God is sending revival, there may be so many people coming to Christ so fast that existing churches are overwhelmed. It happened at Pentecost, when three thousand people came to Jesus in one afternoon. Thousands more were added when God healed a lame beggar (Acts 4:4). Throughout church history there have been times and places in the world where evangelistic meetings and movements resulted in hundreds, if not thousands, of new believers.

Just in the last 250 years, for instance, America has experienced the First and Second Great Awakenings, the camp-meeting movement, the Pentecostal Revival, and the "Jesus Movement," as well as the mass crusades of preachers like Billy Sunday and Billy Graham. In recent decades the ministry of Reinhard Bonnke in Africa has had huge effects.

We praise God for such preachers, but God doesn't always use a big name. Often he uses people you and I will never hear of until we meet them in heaven. In parts of South America today, churches are multiplying so fast that you aren't even considered a pastor if you haven't planted five or ten congregations. In these situations, the problem is not drawing people to the Lord, but conserving the fruits of revival.

When I was a young pastor, I read stories of those revivals as if they were what God expected from me and my church. Over time I came to realize that these are the exception, not the rule. Absolutely we should study revival. Absolutely we should pray for a revival. Absolutely we should be prepared to minister if God sends a revival. **If you aren't preparing for what you are praying for, are you really praying in faith?** (See Acts 12:5 and 15.)

But the fact is, for whatever reasons, most of the time, in most of the world, church growth doesn't happen like that. And I think that's alright. After all, when Jesus taught about the growth of the Kingdom, he didn't describe an explosion. He said it would be like a seed growing, or a batch of dough being leavened – slow, often not very obvious, but happening nonetheless, in God's own good time.

I don't know if God wants you to be a famous evangelist preaching to thousands of people in sports stadiums. If he does, praise the Lord! What I do know is that God wants you to be faithful in whatever he calls you to do.

That's why you should **prepare now for a great harvest in the future.** What will you do if God chooses your city for the next big wave of revival? You may only have thirty people in your church right now, but in the next five years each of those thirty could be needed to care for a group of new believers, and train them to care for the next wave. Who knows? It may well be that God is just waiting to send revival until there are workers trained to care for the baby Christians (Luke 10:2). It's your job to prepare those workers. Then, whether the growth is explosive or slow and steady, you will be ready. The harvest will not be lost.

Addition or multiplication

In America, churches of over one thousand people are called "mega-churches." Around the world, some churches are much larger than that. These churches can do wonderful ministry, and I praise God for them.

At the same time, I don't believe God wants every church to become a mega-church. Some studies have shown that five churches of two hundred can be more effective in reaching people and advancing the Kingdom of God than one church of a thousand. And there may be situations in which twenty churches of fifty people can be even more effective.

Does God want you to keep adding people to one congregation? Or is he calling you to form them into new congregations, perhaps in different places or with different styles or targeting different people? There is no one right answer for every pastor and congregation. Even for the same church, God's strategy may change over time.

If God is calling you to continue growing one congregation, there's not a lot I can add to what you already know. Questions of staffing, building use, and congregational care will arise, but by the time they do, you will be able to afford the kind of specialized training that will help you answer those questions. What I can do here is suggest a few possible scenarios if God is calling you to grow by multiplying congregations instead of adding new people to your existing group.

What does multiplication look like? You could start a satellite location. You could plant a daughter church. You could start home groups, with the goal that they will grow into congregations. If you are in a place where there are few churches or Christians, you could be called on to provide support and oversight at a distance for someone who came to Christ under your ministry, but lives in an area without a local church.

Whether these new groups are the result of a carefully executed strategy or they just seem to happen, you need a plan to train the people in your church to take on the responsibility of discipling and caring for these new groups. You need a plan for how the resulting groups will relate to each other. And you need a plan for how you will exercise oversight over these groups.

Satellite locations

A satellite location is your church holding services in two or more places. Depending on distance, available people, and technological resources, you could preach at both locations at different times, or you could designate a pastor to preach at the new location. You could even use video of you preaching in one place to be seen and heard in the other. Satellite locations are clearly one church in two or more places. They use the same church name, the same general style, and major decision are made by the same leadership group under the same lead pastor.

Daughter churches

Daughter churches are churches planted by your church with the hope that they will become self-sustaining, autonomous congregations. Most daughter churches start when a group that has been traveling some distance to worship grows large enough to start meeting on their own, closer to where they live. Others are started as intentional missional outreaches to an under-served area or people group. In either case, as with a satellite location, you may consider asking a certain number of your people to volunteer to form the core of the new congregation for a period of time, until it's established.

House church networks

Throughout history and around the world, probably more Christians have worshipped together in small groups in homes than in designated church buildings. Certainly this was the case in Bible times and for the first few hundred years of the church. It's also true wherever Christians have been unable to build or rent buildings dedicated for church use, whether because of persecution or economics. Even in places where church buildings are free and plentiful, many Christians prefer the unique dynamics of a small group meeting in a home. One of the best ways to multiply your church may be by establishing a network of house churches affiliated with your church.

Most churches have small groups of people who meet together for Bible study, prayer, fellowship, some kind of service or mission, or a combination of these. Often these groups meet in homes. What is the difference between one of these groups and a house church?

Small groups, sometimes called cell groups, usually have one main function, such as Bible study. Fellowship, and sometimes prayer, is a by-product of getting together for the main purpose. In many cases they have a limited span of existence – a certain number of weeks, or until a certain study book or task is finished. The usually meet on weekdays. They are clearly a ministry of a particular church.

House churches, on the other hand, are intended as **fully functioning local churches**. They often meet on Sunday morning. They include worship, preaching, prayer, children's ministries, Bibles studies, and mission or service projects. Depending on the size of the house, they may run from four or five up to perhaps thirty people. Usually they include a group meal after the service. The close fellowship that develops through this is one of the major draws. Another is the fact that there is almost no "overhead cost" to operating a house church; the leaders are all volunteers and the meeting space is donated.

When house churches stand alone, they can be limited by their small numbers and lack of resources. Also, the person doing the preaching may have limited Bible knowledge or training, and there may be limited oversight, if any. This can sometimes lead to unorthodox interpretations or dangerous practices. But if your church intentionally starts a network of house churches, these problems are alleviated. They can band together for projects, pool their resources for missions, and you as the establishing pastor can provide doctrinal and practical training and oversight.

I already mentioned that the New Testament church met in this way. Let me give you one other historical example.

The English church in the 1700s was by and large very formal, very much about appearances. The idea of a personal, loving, two-way relationship with God was a foreign concept to most English church members. Then a young Anglican priest named John Wesley was invited to a Bible study. His journal describes his experience this way: "In the evening I went very unwillingly to a society in Aldersgate Street, where one was reading Luther's preface to the Epistle to the Romans. About a quarter before nine, while he was describing the change which God works in the heart through faith in Christ, I felt my heart strangely warmed. I felt I did trust in Christ, Christ alone, for salvation; and an assurance was given me that He had taken away my sins, even mine, and saved me from the law of sin and death."

Wesley immediately started preaching about his experience. Many who heard him had the same experience of true faith. The numbers soon grew too many for Wesley, and the few pastors who joined him, to adequately care for the new believers, especially as the movement spread to other towns and villages. So Wesley turned to the Biblical model. He had them meet together once a week in somebody's house. Sometimes an experienced layperson from Wesley's group would feel led by God to move to where the new group was and take leadership. Sometimes a person from within the new group would show leadership skills, and Wesley would recognize this and appoint them as leader. Wesley or one of the other actual pastors would travel around to visit these new churches. Since they rode their horses to visit a circuit of house churches, they were called "circuit riders." Once a year they all got together to pray and discuss ministry matters.

Where there were no churches, the circuit riders started them. Where churches had been planted, they visited when they could, to preach and teach, deal with matters of church administration and discipline, and perform weddings and funerals. When the circuit rider wasn't there, the laypeople went ahead and had church without them.

They were, in effect, a network of house churches. The fruit of this network can still be seen in the Methodists and other Wesleyan denominations.

This model worked well in the civilized environs of England. It was even better on the American frontier in the 1800s. With modern transportation and communication technologies, it could work still better today.

House churches are great for identifying and raising up potential leaders. A small group of people in a living room feels like a safe environment for a first-time preacher or worship leader. But **every church or home group does need oversight** by someone trained in theology and church history, as well as the practical points of running a church. This kind of knowledge can help leaders recognize mistakes or wrong directions before they become too big to easily correct. If local leaders don't have this training, they should be clearly accountable to someone who does.

Points to Remember

- Joining together with other churches can provide resourcing, voice and oversight.
- Nearby pastors should be supporters, not competitors.
- Cooperating in ministry with other churches can strengthen all of you.
- You can multiply your ministry with satellite locations, daughter churches and networks of house churches.

AFTERWORD

Pastor, church leader, your assignment is to equip your people to do God's work until they become like Jesus. Your task is to train them to create a welcoming, loving home for God their Father, imitate their big brother Jesus through the grace and power of the Holy Spirit, and invite everyone they meet to join God's family. In other words, teach them to be the church and be ready to have church any time, any place, with anybody.

That's a huge task. The words of Jesus apply: *Humanly speaking, it is impossible. But with God everything is possible* (Matthew 19:26). Thank you for taking it on.

Allow me to close with this prayer for you:

> Lord God, Father, Son and Holy Spirit, everyone and everything is yours. You created the world out of nothing. You created humans from the dust of the earth. Then you redeemed us by the blood of your only begotten Son, Jesus Christ. By creation and redemption, we are doubly yours.
>
> I thank you for those who read this. Thank you for the call on their lives. Thank you for the churches they serve, or will serve. I pray that you richly bless them with an overflowing sense of your love. Give them peace, joy, wisdom, favor, provision, protection, and every blessing. Give them skills in prayer, Bible reading, preaching, teaching, administration, and everything you call them to do. Give them friends, mentors, confidants, intercessors, and encouragers. Give them health, strength and energy. Give them an overwhelming desire to seek your will and your way, and let them know it with clarity, accuracy, confidence, and timely obedience.

Through their ministry, may many be drawn into your kingdom, and grow into the full and complete standard of Christ. And give them grace to persevere to the end, that when their race is over they may receive the crown of righteousness and hear you say, "Well done, good and faithful servant. Enter into the joy of your Lord."

Amen.

About the Author

Thirty-seven years as a pastor, and counting, have honed David's passion for helping people connect with God and make a difference. Add a varied church background, a first career in engineering, and graduate degrees from three seminaries (mainstream, Wesleyan-evangelical and charismatic), and you can see why he expresses God's truth in ways everyone can appreciate.

Raised in the Episcopal church, David has also been part of Nazarene, Pentecostal Holiness, and non-denominational congregations. As a United Methodist pastor he has served small, large, and multi-cultural churches in rural, small town, suburban and urban settings. David served as a regional church consultant in the Maryland – D.C. area and has led workshops for pastors in Turkey.

In 1974 David married his college sweetheart, Paula. Their five children are actively serving God in the US and around the world.

David earned a B.S. in Systems Engineering from the University of Virginia; two Masters of Divinity, from Melodyland School of Theology and Wesley Theological Seminary, and a Doctor of Ministry in Christian Leadership from Asbury Theological Seminary. He enjoys the outdoors, writing worship songs with his guitar, and playing sax and flute in jazz and blues jams. His heroes are John Wesley, Abraham Lincoln, and Martin Luther King, Jr.

An outline of Ezekiel describes David's calling: to equip God's people by teaching God's words and proclaiming the Holy Spirit, who revives dry bones and forms them into a dwelling for God and a source of the living water that heals nations.

You can connect with me on:

- https://www.pastordavidwentz.com
- https://twitter.com/pastordwentz
- https://www.facebook.com/Pastor-David-Wentz

Also by David Wentz

As a thank you gift for reading this book, I'd like to send you my favorite Christmas Eve sermon. Just request it by email at *pneumagape@yahoo.com.*

Doing Christianity is my website and blog. New resources are added regularly. Visit www.pastordavidwentz.com to check them out. While you're there, sign up to receive the Doing Christianity blog in your email inbox.

Like and follow my Facebook page for inspirational quotes and updates. Just type "Pastor David Wentz" in the Facebook search bar.

I'd love to hear your questions, comments or ideas. You can email, leave a comment on a blog or Facebook post, contact me from my website, or message me from the Facebook page.

Each day our decisions either
invite heaven down or pull hell up
into our lives. Life or death, Light or darkness
Your Kingdom Come, your will be done
On earth as it is in heaven

Made in the USA
Coppell, TX
07 February 2020